Modern Poetry in Translation
New Series / No.20

Russian Women Poets

Edited by Daniel Weissbort
Guest Editor Valentina Polukhina

Published by
KING'S COLLEGE LONDON
University of London
Strand, London WC2R 2LS

Modern Poetry in Translation
No. 20, New Series
© Modern Poetry in Translation 2002
ISBN 0-9533824-8-6
ISSN 0969-3572
Typeset by WM Pank
Printed and bound in Great Britain by Short Run Press, Exeter

Editor:
Daniel Weissbort

Manuscripts, with copies of the original texts, should be sent to the Editor
and cannot be returned unless accompanied by a self-addressed and
stamped envelope or by international reply coupons. Wherever possible,
translators should obtain copyright clearance. Submission on 3.5" disk
(preferably Macintosh formatted, in MSWord or RTF) is welcomed.

Advisory Editors:
Michael Hamburger, Tomislav Longinović, Arvind Krishna Mehrotra,
Norma Rinsler, Anthony Rudolf
Managing Editor: Norma Rinsler

Subscription Rates: (two issues, surface mail)
UK and Europe   £22.00   post free
Overseas   £26.00 / US$40.00 post free

Sterling or US dollars *payable to King's College London*
Send to:
MPT, The School of Humanities,
King's College London,
Strand,
London WC2R 2LS

Represented in UK by Central Books, 99 Wallis Road, London E9 5LN
tel +44 (0)2 0845 458 9925 fax +44 (0)2 0845 458 9912
email magazines@centralbooks.com

Contents

To The Reader

With *Perestroika*, under Gorbachev, in the late 80s, there was a burgeoning of poetry in Russia. Suddenly, it seemed, the whole of world literature, including the work of Russian poets living abroad, became accessible. Nobel prizewinner Joseph Brodsky's influence grew enormously and was assimilated, profoundly enriching the scope of poetic language. Arguably, *Perestroika* had no less dramatic an effect on the cultural life of the country than the so-called Thaw (late 50s, early 60s), and Khrushchev's revelations of Stalinist excesses. This period witnessed, among other things, the startling popularity of performance poets, notably Yevtushenko and Voznesensky. Bella Akhmadulina, also included in the present issue of *MPT*, is associated with the latter two but, as Catriona Kelly comments, "[H]er work has little in common with theirs; she writes for a small circle of readers, rather than an auditorium and does not pose as a political commentator." The alarming prospect of a disintegration of Soviet power, with the Hungarian uprising in 1956, led to a re-imposition of controls by the Party and the stagnation of the Brezhnev years, many of Russia's best poets eventually being forced to leave the country, most notably Brodsky in 1972, and later, Gorbanevskaya, Loseff, Kublanovsky and many others.

Originally, our intention was to represent the whole of contemporary Russian poetry, but we quickly realised that this was far too ambitious. We then decided to focus on women poets, not least because we had noticed that the anthologies still appeared not to be giving equal or adequate representation to women writers.

There have been a number of anthologies attempting to represent recent literary developments in the former Soviet Union, but none, to our knowledge, based on a comprehensive survey of the scene nation-wide. Of course, in the past the difficulties and dangers of *samizdat*, not to speak of censorship, which sometimes yielded surprising or unpredictable results, made for a certain selectivity. Technological advances as well as the Internet have hugely increased the availability of writing, from Moscow to Vladivostok. This greatly complicates the task of anthologists, particularly when the net is cast as wide as it is in the case of the present issue of *MPT*. An interesting recent anthology, for instance, *Crossing Centuries* (Talisman House, 2000) focuses on conceptualism, polystylistics, the elimination or demise of the so-called lyrical hero, retreat from ego-based poetry, the apparent apoliticism of post-Thaw poetry (even if the subversive nature of this was arguably no less real than that of the dissident writing of the 60s). However, the emphasis on language as such, harking back to the avantgardism of the early twentieth century, renders translation into other languages problematical. In any case, we do not accept that the lyric hero is as dead as has been claimed. Consequently we have tried, in our selection of contemporary women poets, to be somewhat more eclectic. In a recent article in *Novy Mir*, the poet and critic Dmitry Polishchuk writes: "The 25-35 year old generation is now experiencing an efflorescence – a new type of poetic vision, with a distinct poetic language, a new kind of baroque; with novel structures, combining the far-fetched, the heterogeneous, the incompatible, in a poetics of contrast." This is particularly true of women's writing, which transcends post-modernist or even feminist (Western style) tendencies, otherwise so much in vogue now in Russia.

It was our aim from the start to concentrate on more recent work, on writers who achieved prominence or at least visibility in and after the mid-80s when Gorbachev and his team took over. Our focus, therefore, was on what is now the middle-generation, writers who have lived through the changes as adults. But we have also sought to represent the most recent generations. Furthermore, we have done our best to look further afield than Moscow or Petersburg, and to examine what was being produced in provincial centres like Voronezh, Saratov, Samara, in the Urals, Siberia and the Far East of Russia. Poets from outside the two traditional capitals, Moscow and St Petersburg, were featured at the Second International Festival of Poets in Moscow, in October 2001, converging on the capital from Novosibirsk and Ekaterinburg, from the Krasnodar region and the farming community of Vesyolyi in the Rostov region. Also represented in our collection are Russian-language poets in former Soviet Republics, like Ukraine and Georgia. Finally, we have included a handful of poets residing outside Russia (e.g. USA, England, Italy), although not as many as we might have wished, a primary concern being to represent those who had remained in the country.

Even so, our limited generational focus would not allow us fairly to represent Russian women's poetry at this time. We have therefore extended the range somewhat to include a few prominent poets of older or founding-mother generations, such as Bella Akhmadulina, Yunna Morits, Inna Lisnianskaya, and abroad, Natalya Gorbanevskaya.

Although, as has been noted, there was a practical reason for making gender the basis for this selection, it soon became clear that the very notion of an anthology of women's poetry, or of poetry by women, was a problematical one. Strangely, from a Western European or American perspective, "women's poetry, as such, seems hardly to exist in Russia". Dmitry Kuzmin, in an exhaustive account of types of anthologies ("Present Day Russian Poetry in the Mirror of Anthologies") does not even mention the possibility of an anthology of women's poetry. Nevertheless, I should like briefly to address this issue, since it seems to me a real one.

We put the question to several Russian women poets and received some quite equivocal responses. Naturally, many were pleased at an initiative which presumably would encourage the translation of a number of admired and hitherto untranslated female poets into English. On the other hand, familiar and sometimes rather unfamiliar objections to the notion of such a collection were also raised. Some poets, not so surprisingly, felt that this enterprise was dated and even demeaning. As Tatyana Voltskaya points out in her essay, it inevitably puts one in mind of the question, formulated by mediaeval theologians, as to whether women were even human! Russians, male or female, were more critical, less ambivalent, in their responses to our initiative than, I suspect, West European or American writers might have been at this time. (This may in part be due to the fact that Russians – if I may be pardoned the stereotype – are more adamant in expressing their opinions. But in any case I'm not sure what it signifies and wouldn't wish to speculate here.) In the event, rather than abandon the enterprise, we stubbornly pressed on, but decided also to print two or three of the responses we had received, even if they were implicitly or openly negative.

Valentina Polukhina has read or scanned work by nearly 800 poets. Still, she does not feel that the task she set herself of comprehensively surveying the scene is by any means complete. Indeed, it would have required a team of readers to complete it, and then the collection would have lost whatever unity a single sensibility can give it, although she insists that she has been relatively objective, applying critical standards acquired in a lifetime of scholarly and artistic activity devoted mainly to poetry and poetics. It remains for me to pass on her caveats! Firstly, that there are many other poets, even as we go to press, of whose existence she is becoming aware and whose absence from this collection she regrets. As noted, we have attempted to represent poets from non-metropolitan Russia. Again, while to some extent we may have succeeded, it would have required a team of researchers and a good deal more time comprehensively to survey the regions. Indeed, it would have been hard to do so from abroad, since many of the publications that should be consulted, are unobtainable outside Russia.

Some 70 poets have been selected. This is a very large number for the magazine, but under the circumstances it was felt that inclusiveness was necessary, to give a sense of the range of poetry being produced by women in Russia. We tried to match authors with translators and we were, as always, limited by what we could accomplish in this respect. It is no use asking someone to translate a poet for whose work he or she has little liking. Furthermore, there is such a thing as *translatability* (or, more accurately, translatability *at this time*).

A personal note. Since we wanted to represent so large a number of poets, I have myself translated more than I might have done otherwise, though I have no regrets about the time spent with these poets. In one or two cases, I simply failed and as a result the poet is not represented.

Often I was able to benefit – and benefit immensely – from direct (or e-mail) contact with the authors themselves. If I wasn't entirely sure before, this has convinced me of the use of e-mail in this context – it is certainly the next best thing to direct communication, and somewhat better, I think, than the telephone; one is not conscious all the time of the expensive minutes slipping by, particularly since translation (as any visitor to a translation workshop can confirm) requires an inordinate amount of silent thought.

So much for excuses! We hope, nevertheless, that the present issue of *MPT* will do something to complicate, as it were, the rather simplistic – and depressing – picture of post-Soviet reality that is generally propagated. To that end, we have also included a handful of essays and short interviews, some of the latter conducted especially for this issue, others excerpted and translated from other publications. Poetry has always been particularly significant in Russia and even though poetry sales there are now more like those to be expected in the West – and greatly reduced from the huge print-runs of the Soviet period – its influence is still formidable. The provinces in that vast country are beginning to assert themselves and poetry again is one of the principal cultural means of doing so. With so much poetry being produced and published, in one form or another, the need for anthologies is, of course, greater (as Dmitry Kuzmin points out also in the essay alluded to above).

Now, some thanks! Besides reading as much as we could lay our hands on for over a year, we have followed many leads. Small volumes of poetry have been arriving from all over Russia and from Russian poets based abroad. Advice was forthcoming from Russian poets (both in the country and abroad). All those we approached responded with extraordinary generosity and enthusiasm. Thanks are due also to scholars, critics, editors, in particular Dmitry Kuzmin, editor of the Internet journal for younger poets, *Vavilon*/Babylon [see his article in this issue], Aleksei Alekhin, editor of the only magazine in Russia dedicated solely to poetry: *Arion* [see his article], and Gleb Shulpiakov, poet and critic, poetry editor of *Ex Libris*, a *TLS*-type supplement of the mass circulation *Nezavisimaya Gazeta*) who also interviewed some of the poets for us. We have surveyed leading Russian journals, like *Zvezda, Oktiabr, Znamia, Novy mir* and *Novaya Yunnost*, as well as many of the principal non-metropolitan literary journals.

Heartfelt thanks are due to the poets who, despite sometimes questioning the validity of an anthology devoted to women's poetry, allowed us to translate and publish their work and, in many cases, collaborated in the translation thereof, answering questions put by their translators. As noted, e-mail has immeasurably facilitated this kind of collaborative work, permitting an immediacy obtainable hitherto only when translator and translated were in the same room together. I suspect that these electronically generated translation "papers", drafts and comments, as they begin to proliferate, will be of considerable value to would-be translation theorists and critics, and the translation theorist in me cannot help but urge translators, if they can bear it, to preserve them, not consigning them to the ether. So, equal thanks are due to the translators who have contributed to this collection: scholars and Russianist poetry translators, like Peter France, Gerald Janecek, Catriona Kelly, Angela Livingstone, Robert Reid, Stephanie Sandler; poet-translators of Russian poetry like Richard McKane; and poets like Maura Dooley, Ruth Fainlight, Elaine Feinstein, and Carol Rumens and Yuri Drobyshev, who worked, in most cases, from drafts and who interacted directly with the Russian poets they were translating.

In particular I should like to thank my co-editor, Valentina Polukhina, who has given herself entirely to this work. It had been my original intention to present a dozen or so contemporary Russian women poets, most of whose names were already familiar to me. I knew what I liked and was not interested in looking much further. For practical reasons and also because it was magazine policy to represent poets by a fair number of poems each, rather than to present a large number of poets with only one, two or three poems, *MPT* has tended to limit the number of poets presented. I took some convincing that in the present case it was well worth being more inclusive, which, in practical terms, meant considering as much as Valentina Polukhina was physically able to take on. The result is a collection which at least aspires to comprehensiveness, even if it cannot of course include every noteworthy poet. The further we looked, the more we found, but in quite a few cases, it was simply impossible, in the time available, to match poets with translators. There is of course room for other anthologies, reflecting other tastes and receptive to other schools or tendencies, even though we have, as indicated, aimed at a certain catholicity.

It is our hope that others will draw from the present collection – focusing on the work of individual poets and / or groups of poets that we have been able to sample. To render this further work a bit more manageable, we have appended Valentina Polukhina's bibliography. The reader will note the large number of magazines cited. The proliferation of journals publishing poetry is a feature of the contemporary scene in Russia and Valentina Polukhina has asked me to mention that she has by no means consulted all of them. Nevertheless, publication of this bibliography is some kind of tribute to her dedication and extraordinary industry.

Daniel Weissbort

Rhyme is Female

by Tatyana Voltskaya

In the Middle Ages venerable scholastics would often consider the question as to whether women were human and whether they possessed a soul. Since then, as this question with a few reservations has been decided in the affirmative, women have acquired a large number of useful rights – to study, to vote and be elected, to become astronauts, to have abortions, to wear trousers, to get divorced, to apply themselves in all spheres of human activity. Still, I cannot escape the feeling that the shadow of that accursed question, formulated by pedantic theologians, still hangs over us, like the smile of the Cheshire Cat.

Otherwise, why should one publish an anthology of women's poetry?

The expressions "women's cinematography" or "women's painting" do not exist, but "women's poetry" figures at least in the imagination of critics. So, no smoke without fire?

Yes, there is something about poetry that obliges one to consider the question. The most apposite comment on the subject, in my opinion, is by the Petersburg writer Samuil Lur'e: Poetry has a female voice. The voice of prose is male, but that of poetry is female – or not so much female as high-pitched.

It seems to me that this conjecture about voice, intonation is of the utmost significance. It touches on the very essence of poetry, its celestial dimension, if you like. Not, of course, that it follows that poetry is an exclusively female concern; among the voices is the soprano, but there is also the tenor. It is in the gap between tenor and soprano that we can justifiably talk about male and female poetry (if such exists).

A single preface or a single anthology cannot, I think, decide whether female poetry exists. But that there is poetry written by women is undeniable. Moreover, in my view, if one ignores the very summit (Brodsky, in particular), women-poets in Russia, in recent decades, have been better writers. There are many reasons for this, one of the main ones being that the machine of Soviet ideology (and of any other) damaged women less, not because they are superior to men, but because they are more concerned with the private sphere, family, feelings – those areas that it is harder for any political entity to penetrate. The male tendency is to try to grasp the world as a whole, from the outside; women, on the other hand, try to grasp it from within. And in daily life as well as in art women resort to detail – nappies, love-letters, clothes, flowers. For bloodthirsty ideologists all this seems petty and inessential; however, it is precisely such matters that enable a human being to remain human even in inhuman circumstances.

Let's you and I sit down, two elderly sprites.
In the kitchenette drinking coffee.
Wherever you look – magical trophies:
A white coffee pot, blue plastic mugs,
A decorative board for bread.
And on the finger, a little ring with amber,
And the storm clouds of a newly constructed sky
Over this peopled wasteland.

writes Nonna Slepakova. She is not just drawing up a chaotic list of trivial objects, but creating out of this chaos a defence against external forces, hostile to human beings. With that defence in place, it becomes possible to look down at the ground, as well as up at the sky. And one may even move in the latter direction, which is what almost predictably happens at the end of the poem:

Your features lost their wise helplessness
You unfolded your swelling wings
More and more and with greater boldness
In your six metres of kitchen.

By the way, this last detail, "six metres of kitchen" saves the poem from the abstract, unearthly coldness, which was already setting in but which has now, in the nick of time, been warmed by a living breath, a sad smile. It seems to me that in Soviet times female poets wrote far fewer poems composed to order than did men; more often their domain was "the quiet lyric", which was mocked, and sometimes noisily condemned by leading party literary hacks. Even in those times that secret linguistic business, which always manifests itself in poetry, did not cease to be conducted in their notebooks. The significance of this process can hardly be exaggerated. As Natalya Gorbanevskaya said – "History is the sister of poetry / and nothing else".

Or, from another angle:

Into the skin it writhed, also the pores,
like coal, the Russian language
penetrated into all conversations too worn out.
The soul asks to be released from the body,
preferring angelic speech.
In the end what is to be done with it –
bite it, grind it, set it on fire?

Elena Shvarts asks this question – a light breath, lines like tongues of fire. Although "angelic speech" suggests temptation, from which one wants to shield oneself like the Apostle Paul, who differentiated between human and angelic speech, the question has been put.

It is put to poetry in general, so we must for a while distance ourselves from the question of women's poetry as such. In my view, we have reached a point when poetry, having attained a zenith at this given stage in its development, has grown weary, bored, and is casting around – how else can I entertain myself? – taking upon itself functions not germane to it, the essay, articles, scientific (or rather pseudo-scientific) treatises, diaries, notebooks, porno-postcards, sermons, social sketches, feuilletons. Poetic substance is less and less visible, hidden behind the external details, which never become events of the inner life. Irresponsible metaphors abound – things are not entirely blameless; one recalls Brodsky's comment that aesthetics is the mother of ethics. What is ugly and meaningless is immoral. All that remains is the hum of a wind-up motor, the grinding of the gears of verse, the shuffling of obstacles, which muffle the voice, turning poetry more and more into a game, a convention. But the Muse is a goddess, and, like all divine beings, she demands sacrifice. It seems to me that women writers are more conscious of this than male ones.

Poems can be remarkable, virtuoso performances, but if the author hasn't trembled before writing itself, hasn't been inspired by more than the desire to write something, the reader too will not tremble, will not be inspired, will not be tempted to place the book under her pillow. I remember arguing with some Italian female academics, at a conference, about what constitutes good poetry. They insisted that if a text meets their intellectual requirements, formed by Derrida and Lacan, then it is worth considering. Still, we were able to agree on this ultra-simple, even comical proposition: that good poems are those which we place under our pillow.

> Amid our hopes and ruins,
> Amid trees with foam on their lips, –
> How night passed, bed remembered,
> How day passed, notebook remembered,
> How life passed, snow and fluff will remember,
> How death passes, dust and ashes will remember.

This poem by Inna Lisnianskaya is from her book *Muzyka i bereg* (Music and Shore). Like a naked wire, alive with electricity, it doesn't even let you put the question: "Why?" This phenomenon is rare in our time: direct speech, in its directness and nakedness has unprecedented effects. The same device (if one can talk about devices) is employed by

Lisnianskaya in her poem "Letter", a penitential address to her daughter, before whom the lyrical heroine of these poems feels guilty:

> By the sea where you grew up,
> We were not often together,
> I did not read you stories,
> I gulped down poems with wine.

Probably, this is more a tragic human document than poetry, the creation of which, however, requires not only skill, but also courage. Awareness of personal parental guilt is no pleasant matter, not susceptible to the romantic treatment. But Lisnianskaya is unafraid. The occasion is a real one. Music calling speech to life. The word becomes flesh.

> And by remembering you increase your tears.
> And I increase the salt in my bones . . .
> Forgive me, if you can,
> And if you cannot, forgive.

The flesh of these words is not just real, lucid, having already achieved that "unprecedented simplicity", that tension-free atmosphere, where even the absolute need for metaphor passes. You cannot say whether this is a quatrain or an actual lump in the throat. How this can be, I'll not presume to say, but the mystery of poetry is manifest.

Adjacent to this lofty simplicity in women's poetry there is another, earthbound, perhaps, even deliberately everyday, as for example that of Zoya Ezrokhi. All her poems are, as it were, lit by a simultaneously wise and mischievous smile. Of course, what she writes may be incomprehensible to anyone unfamiliar with the specifics of Soviet life. (But that's another matter.) Here is a tiny poem "On Luciferisation":

> When I walk around with an empty can,
> And there's no sour cream to be found anywhere,
> In my soul the light of heaven fades.
> I turn into a Luciferite.

Someone who has not walked around in the empty spaces of Soviet shops can hardly be expected to understand what she is on about. But poetry shouldn't get bogged down in daily life: grim or humorous descriptions of communal squabbles, daily cares, divorces, illnesses, transformed all at once through some inscrutable image into a deep philosophical meditation on the fact that women have the power to bring the unborn to life, those who hitherto were "beyond suffering". Do they have the right? Zoya Ezrokhi is horrified that she did not spare her son, that by giving birth to him, she condemned him to the human lot:

> How did I dare to summon him,
> Wrapped in my mind, my skin,
> From a safe non-existence
> To this white divine bloody world!

A certain human boldness is required to formulate such questions directly, and no less boldness to use these three adjectives, "white divine bloody", without commas. This, too, may be called *direct speech*, but of course women's poetry is not so confined.

These days it contains all: a noble simplicity, as well as the fig leaf of postmodernism, and the Alexandrian splendour of an over-mature literature. Polina Barskova's poetry, for example, is refined, complex, and distinctly virtuoso, insofar as it demonstratively shoulders the burden of culture:

> On the one hand, The New World, Ancient Rome,
> Chechnya.
> On the other, dyr-bul-shchir, ulyalyum, fignya, *
> And I say: "Guys, it's a draw, it's a draw!
> Seems to me you're managing without me."

* David Burlyuk's famous pure-sound Futurist formula.

Ancient Rome un-selfconsciously rubs shoulders with well-known quotations from Kruchenykh and Khlebnikov; the lyrical hero (heroine?) jokingly waves from the hypothetical hill, inviting herself (or the reader?) to go further, "limping like the hands of a clock": "While someone in your breast with a verb/ Has still not scorched out a little hole for a whistle?"

But Svetlana Kekova does not deploy this burgeoning irony; instead, there's clairvoyance, sorcery, music and – odd though it may be to speak of this in a secularised culture – faith. It can be seen at once, with the naked eye, as in the old frescoes: "Yes, in everyone you meet God is concealed, / as in the sound of waves, a sonata". The best confirmation of the existence of faith is to be found in god-doubting poems: "You are God. But are we in your power? / And is anyone's will Yours?" But the religious theme in contemporary poetry is another matter, too complex to be dealt with here.

There is poetry, as it were suffused with sunlight, filled with admiration for the endless metamorphoses of matter, the changing patterns of life. An example of this is Nina Gabrielian's work: "There the grass is greedy and thick / Filled with animal vigour . . . / And the ancient temple, alarmingly red, / Still awaits the pagan god". And there is poetry transparent like water-colour, somewhat remote, like a landscape after the first snow; some of Olga Sedakova's poetry seems to me of that ilk: "The sun shines on the just and unjust, / and the earth is no worse here than anywhere else. / If you wish, go east, west, / go where they tell you, / if you wish, stay at home." From the classical lines of Nonna Slepokova to the vacillating metres of Olesia Nikolaeva; from the verbal exuberance of Bella Akhmadulina to the asceticism of Inna Lisnianskaya; from the inspired visions of Svetlana Kekova to the not so much avant-garde, as already in practice non-verbal experiments of Rea Nikonova; from the truly realistic poetry, characteristic of the 60s of the twentieth century, to existential obscurities; from prophetic cadenzas to eastern meditations; from passionless simulations to the passionate love lyric, the pendulum swings so violently that it seems it might break through the hard cover!

So many schools, generations, temperaments, psychological conditions, cities (a serious matter where Russian geography is concerned), different degrees of talent, fates! Where so many names are included, the result, willy-nilly, is a maelstrom, a Persian rug, whose elaborate design can be studied endlessly. Is there any sense in such a motley collection? If it's a matter of acquiring a good understanding of each poet in detail, no. If of getting a sense of contemporary poetic trends and schools (Petersburg versus Moscow etc), then also no, because you cannot do that if you limit yourself to female poets. But if of shedding some light, however partial, on the mysterious question as to whether there is such a thing as women's poetry – is it myth or reality? – then certainly, yes.

It seems to me that the metaphor of a rug is apposite. On the one hand, following closely the elaborate coloured patterning; on the other, positioning oneself at some distance and seeing what is not otherwise visible. Rug apart, these are such distinct images. You can gaze at them for hours, and nothing appears, but at a distance, finding a focus, suddenly in place of the vague patches, you see a recumbent lion, or a flower, or a ship under full sail. That's what an anthology is like – things held in focus so that out of the patchwork chaos, an image of what might be called women's poetry is precipitated.

It is not up to me to determine whether such an image actually exists, particularly since I prefer to divide poetry not into male and female, but into good and bad. On the other hand, I do recall once writing a poem which contained the following lines: "Rhyme is female, changing clothes, / plaiting a rose into its hair . . . " I still believe that rhyme is female.

[Translated by Daniel Weissbort]

A City of Women

by Aleksei Alekhin

I must confess that the very notion of assembling and translating into English an anthology of Russian "women's" poetry surprised me.

It has always seemed to me that divisions according to gender should apply only to changing-rooms and public toilets – because of natural bashfulness. In poetry, there is nothing to be ashamed of.

At least, in Russian poetry, particularly of the twentieth century, women have always had a place – and often in the front rank: Zinaida Gippius, Marina Tsvetaeva, Anna Akhmatova, Bella Akhmadulina; the list can be extended, of course. And from the point of view of readers' predilections there is no boundary – one can't, for instance, say that female readers are more drawn to female poets or male to male. As regards the work of our young contemporary Vera Pavlova, clearly men value her work more highly than do women. So what!

On the other hand, it is precisely in the last century that women's voices in poetry changed from isolated instances into a powerful lyrical chorus, so that it has become possible to talk of a *phenomenon*. Still the same has happened in almost every other sphere of life. It probably wouldn't occur to anyone to assemble a collection of the work of women mathematicians, for example.

Russian poetry today really is, in the full sense, the product of a heterogeneous marriage. Women poets are not just represented, but are, to a great extent, defining its character, temperament, development. It is no accident that in the poetry journal I edit, *Arion* (the only professional, large-scale, all-Russian poetry journal, a quarterly which has been appearing since 1994), there are as many female as male names: not because we aim at political correctness, but simply because we print the best available to us.

Russian poetry of the end of the twentieth and beginning of the twenty-first centuries is unimaginable without the poetry of Inna Lisnianskaya, Olesia Nikolaeva, Tatyana Bek, Elena Ushakova, Elena Shvarts, Svetlana Kekova, Irina Ermakova. In the last decade, Vera Pavlova, Elena Fanailova, Olga Khvostova, the very young Mariya Kildibekova have added their powerful and quite distinct voices to this chorus. Nevertheless, to isolate them from the general text and context and to assemble a separate "women's" issue of *Arion*, or an anthology, is something I simply wouldn't be prepared to do.

Firstly, because poetry is a *whole*. Imagine an opera being staged without the male parts. Secondly . . .

A little over ten years ago, when I was living in China, I got to know two American women. The younger one was taken up with feminism and was writing a book about the position of women in the PRC. The older one was a serious journalist, who had worked, as far as I can recall, for the BBC in Panama and had even been imprisoned there by the regime. Now she was collecting material for a book on China's reforms. In a café, one day, over a cup of coffee, our young friend told us enthusiastically about the opening somewhere of a museum of "women's fine arts". At which the other one rather coolly remarked: "I don't think I need a museum like that. I do not consider myself less talented than men . . . "

Need I say that I sympathised with her?

I am very happy for the contributors to this collection, that finally English readers will get to know their work a little. They deserve it. As for myself, I would be bored without women – on a desert island, in paradise, and even in books . . .

Moscow, 10.03.02
[Translated by Daniel Weissbort]

How we built the tower – "The Vavilon project" (www.vavilon.ru)

by Dmitry Kuzmin

The project, in different forms, existed for over a decade. Only very few such projects in contemporary Russian artistic life can boast of such a span. What is the reason for this? I think it's because Vavilon is open to everybody. It is constantly striving to expand, to seek out new participants. Therefore, at different stages, the leading positions are occupied by different authors. Besides aesthetic pluralism, the desire to gather under one "roof" the heirs to different aesthetic traditions has fostered a considerable potential development and mutual enrichment. This has given Vavilon an enormous advantage in respect to other groups, which from the start focused on participants of a similar poetics.

Vavilon was begun in early 1989 by five writers: the poets Vyacheslav Gavrilov, Vadim Kalinin, Stanislav L'vovsky, Dmitry Kuzmin, and the prose writer Artem Kuftin. The oldest of them, myself, was twenty years old and the youngest, Gavrilov and Kalinin, were not yet sixteen. I'd often dreamt of such a group, most of all as a setting for creative communication and all through 1988 I'd been drifting from one literary locus to another, looking for like spirits.

The name "Vavilon" [Babylon] was chosen by secret ballot from three proposals (mine being "Escape") . . . There is no direct allusion to the Scriptures, even less so to the then-unread Borges, but rather to Boris Grebenshchikov (a Russian pop star) for whom Vavilon was a potent image.

> Babylon is a city like any other
> No need to be sad about it:
> If you walk, we walk in the same direction –
> Because there is no other direction.

This was our formula for aesthetic pluralism.

I produced the magazine on a typewriter and Vadim Kalinin, poet, artist and rock-musician and now a prose-writer, designed the cover. Apart from poetry and prose, we had two main sections: In "From the well-forgotten past" we published items from poetry collections of the first two decades of the twentieth century (Komarosky, Shkapskaya, Piast, Bobrov). In "The Peak" ("a corner for graphomania") we published the best of Soviet poetry.

In spring 1999, we announced no more nor less than an All-Soviet

Competition for young poets, placed an ad in several newspapers, received, apart from the usual rubbish, works by some sixty writers. This material was passed on to our jury. We invited Kushner, Levitansky, Krivulin, Bunimovich, Zhdanov and Aronov to be the judges. That's how we conceived of the poetry spectrum. Polina Barskova from St Petersburg topped the list. Eight years later she also won the TENETA Internet literary prize.

The crowning event of this Festival was a reading by all the finalists, which took place 1-3 November, 1991. This was a miraculous happening in the post-Soviet context. I simply approached the Cultural Committee of the Supreme Soviet and the Minister Mikhail Seslavinsky issued instructions for the necessary funds to be made available to us. Everybody remembers this Festival for its celebratory atmosphere.

During the Festival the establishment of a Union of Young Writers, Vavilon, was announced. This organization potentially united all of literary youth; we even registered it with the Ministry of Justice.

The next important event in the history of Vavilon is the transition from samizdat to typographical publication. In 1992, the first publication of the magazine *Vavilon* took place, drawing largely on material gathered for the Festival. In samizdat we published sixteen issues and more than forty young writers and poets . . . The problem was the subsidy. Help as usual came from abroad. A few years earlier, at a conference dedicated to Brodsky in St Petersburg, I had met the well known scholar Valentina Polukhina, who lives in England. I complained about the lack of funds and she simply sent me $30 with which we were able to publish two collections of poetry: by Zviagintsev and by Barskova. The publishing house we established was called ARGO-RISK. In the six years of its existence it published some twelve books by young poets, seven issues of *Vavilon* (140 writers). Since 1994, ARGO-RISK has published books by well-known authors of the older generation: Sapgir, Aizenberg, Prigov, Rubinshtein, Krivulin, Kekova . . .

In 1994, a second festival of young poetry took place with seventy participants. But we didn't have any new stars. This forced us to consider other channels of information. In September 1997, Vavilon opened its own site on the Internet (www.vavilon.ru). By February 2001, Vavilon had 98 pages dedicated to contemporary writers, beginning with the oldest: Satunovsky, Sapgir, Sergeev, Blazhenny, and Rein.

Another important part of Vavilon's activities today is the literary club Avtornik, which opened in the autumn of 1997. This is not exclusively a club for young authors, but an attempt to represent the whole of contemporary Russian literature, as seen through the eyes of the younger generation.

What awaits Vavilon in the future? Hard to say. It depends on the new generation of eighteen-year-old writers: their literary interests and opinions etc. From the heights of my thirty years, it is impossible for me to be aware of all the shades. So, in March 1999, when we celebrated Vavilon's tenth anniversary, I handed the direction over to the twenty-two-year-old poet and prose writer, Danil Davydov.

Excerpted from Novoe Literaturnoe Obozrenie, *No. 48, (2), 2001*

[Translated by Daniel Weissbort]

Bella Akhmadulina

Translated by Catriona Kelly

In the Botkin Hospital

As though good Doctor Botkin in his wisdom
had turned his mind to me well in advance,
giving his knife, in time, to Soldatyonkov,
I opened life's door again and stumbled out.

My brain sped off into receding twilight –
an ark sealed snug and tightly, hooped and braced,
it was restored by Soldatyonkov's genius
into its proper, from the other, place.

He's still the same: no time for shows of honour,
for bowing and for scraping, even praise –
in any case, concern for us poor sufferers
is quite enough to keep a soul sustained.

But can you tell? I was in mines of nothing –
for seven days the doctors sank me deep:
there's no-one there. Bulát, I didn't see you,
or maybe was forced to silence by decree.

Placid machines performed a clerkly function –
the pulses leapt and twittered on the screen
transcribing the twin hillocks, the two humplets
of my rearing, bucking, dromedary brain.

This crown of flesh, this mystery of juncture,
lives close beside, but sealed off from my life:
like sharing a vestibule, perhaps, with some shy scholar,
who greets you as you pass, but with dropped eyes.

So how to read its thrust inside my temples?
A survey? an attempt to make its peace?
Grounding in inner space is quite unwelcome:
only the higher places bring release.

We're not well-matched. Its job, I think, is torture:
teaching one's skull to list among the waves
of thought. That's right. The outer coasts of knowledge
are banned to knowledge – why, we cannot say.

The brain's not good at contemplating brain-power,
and leaving the bed one's made and where one lies
is far too much. I'd rather walk on point-shoes
or fish for pike in the canals on Mars.

One's lips spend all their time yawning or eating
but cannot speak – they seem to wear a gag.
The moment of transcendence can't be uttered
or compassed: it must simply be endured.

The ward – my world – is wide and bleached to whiteness:
My head is dark and barren as a moor.
To set down ' . . . doesn't seem so bright' in writing
requires a miracle of one's brain-power.

My brain's not there. Some maleficent witches
have withered all cognition on the stem.
But now I hear: just try and write more simply,
and let your mind begin to come to terms.

To Await Arrival

in memory of Galina Starovoitova

That's how it was: I turned my sickroom gazes
on the yard outside the ward, as though on groves
or open fields. I tried to write 'quite simply':
as it turned out, the impediment was this:

my mind was racked, tortured by constant fretting
about my mind, a tic I couldn't curb:
my neck was weighed down with the convolutions,
the empty effort made me more disturbed,

my feeble gift – the speck I'm proud of sharing
with prophets – flagged; the inner sight was lost.
When you edge along a shelf above a sheer drop
you gasp and do not grasp. That's not enough.

But I *did* feel a quick flash of foreboding –
a bubble from the deep rushed up and burst.
A dog's instinctive knowledge gripped my body,
though consciously I tried to brush it off.

I brushed it off – it didn't cloud that evening
when the motif long trapped inside my head
beat at my skull, but didn't jolt me forward
in the pose you use when praying for the dead.

Then suddenly, the exiled television
opened its eye, into the world beyond.
St Petersburg, some stairs, a silenced bullet.
A death that made a splash, but not a sound.

The desert of the dark and of my pupils:
no tears could make this drought-struck landscape drink.
This child, this Joan of Arc, was my blood-brother.
An ellipsis of affection was our link.

Meetings were dotted. In June, was it, the last one?
Hiding from empty smalltalk and the rest,
like schoolgirls playing truant from our classes,
risking the ire of prefects, we embraced.

A handclasp, an embrace, puts one in contact
with good and bad. An answer not provoked
by any question raises skin in gooseflesh –
words know our lives are fragile, though we don't.

How near what we desire in fact lies to us:
easy to grasp a shoulder, touch a palm:
(how often, too, we let affection blind us:
no rogue, we think, could offer us his hand.)

Spurning the sly-faced bankers and the banquet,
in that hall with its spread feast in time of plague,
she blurted, gauche as any girl of twenty,
'You know I'm married!' 'Goodness! I'm so glad!'

Having choked the air with mindless social babble,
I sipped my glass of government champagne.
I should have yelled, 'St George, leave fighting dragons,
take care of *her*!' – for nearby hung his flag.

She let it out; aghast at her own frankness,
she bit her lip to hold in further words.
She had a young girl's tense and radiant shyness.
A face like that suits flowerbeds, bandstands, parks.

The moment swelled. I felt a rising panic.
My mind gave way to nursery dreams of flight.
Give me a veil, four horses, and a carriage,
And let me gallop into a velvet night.

Was it just then a chink of foresight opened?
Seeing a soul stripped bare is ominous.
But there's more horror in the revelation
that joy and sainthood very rarely fuse.

In any case, to stammer a faint suspicion
ahead of time won't baulk the march of fate.
A hand wearing a wedding-ring is fragile
and cannot force a viper's jaws apart.

Long in advance the count of years is reckoned:
The furies need fresh blood to slake their thirst.
Moths do not flee, but rather seek out, candles,
The target calls, the rifle cannot miss.

The calls for vengeance are no more than foolish:
talk of 'reprisals' leaves me feeling sad.
A life like this imposes its own duties.
In the face of it, revenge should be abjured.

So now I sit in iron and stone December
and think of June to warm my memory.
I wonder if she'll hear me if I call her.
I miss her more with every passing day.

Death is the twin of triumph, its blood-brother.
A martyr's fate can break the hold of time.
Even in draft, her life was virtuoso:
It reached perfection with its final line.

Liana Alaverdova

Translated by Lydia Stone

Inventory of Things Left Behind

Things left behind: one casserole, enormous,
Ideal for pilav; Great-grandma's samovar
In brass, antique (or nearly); with medallions
Assorted works of art, still life with melon,
My portrait (in batik), some child-sized chairs
And table (made by Papa for my daughters)
Fat dictionaries (dog-eared); school books, texts
In like condition; reproductions, one
(My grandpa's favourite) depicts Columbus
Disputing with professors (God knows what for);
Striped mattresses, large-sized handmade by old Elmira
Next door (who washed and dried the wool then beat
It with a stick), who'd sit on our verandah
And talk incessantly about her grandsons
(Who cared nothing for us nor we for them
And yet somehow we always listened, even
Responded); thus we'll list: one neighbour, also
Verandah, one, glassed-in, but needing repair
(The money for repair required elsewhere),
Whence we had: view of yard with parched acacias
And stunted pine (which clearly could not thrive
In Baku's heat). We left behind as well:
Bazaar, one, rich in languages and smells
With vendors, brazen and devoid of scruples
Alike as brothers, each one black of moustache
And white of smile (not toothpaste, but genetics):
Let's add: one boulevard, discreet eyewitness
To adolescent gropings, one cinema
To which we flocked, athirst for spectacle,
And sat in stuffy dark for hours on end
Not knowing then the value of those hours.

Put on our list as well: one childhood friend,
The house she lived in too, though old and damp,
With courtyard like a well and well-worn steps
Predating even Great October, clearly.

Let us complete the list with family graves.
The wind alone now strokes the granite stones
And only rainfall washes them with tears.

What then do we regret?

Vera Anserova

Translated by Daniel Weissbort

Short Poems

I long for the silence of the yet unhatched butterfly.

*

The closer the gaze gets to the ceiling
the more it entangle itself
in webs.

*

You are woven out of endless love
it will burst from your lips
your eyes
from your body so impetuously
at the prospect of meeting anyone
that all thoughts of advance notice are forgotten.

And your memory is on fire
with endless loving relationships
that involve just one woman.

Mariya Avvakumova

Translated by Daniel Weissbort

From Baltic Meditations

Minuscule bouquets in minuscule earthenware vases –
they tell you so much about the Latvian soul.

*

Even a dog waits for a smile before closing in.

*

By the edge of the sea and the shore live white gulls,
by the edge of the grave and eternity, radiant folk.

*

Autumn. Observe the foliage.
Be alone in your silence . . .
Perhaps you'll hear steps . . .

*

The church will pencil its request on the sky.
You have only to enter.

*

Over the sea, magnetised by its own passion,
clots of primary material:
gulls.

The Gift of Speech

You have overcome so many trials . . .
The lot of muteness was so great
that now,
when there's a chink of light,
there's no longer any desire to speak –
besides the tongue is leaden.

No words to speak with.
No air to hover in.

Polina Barskova

Translated by Peter France and
by Vladimir Bolotnikov and Eric Crawford

Evening At Tsarskoe Selo

Akhmatova and Nedobrovo
strolling at twilight in the park,
it calls for a stage direction, say:
'A park. September.' He is stirred
by tittle-tattle, news from the front,
and his last article, while she
is stirred by the horizon's slant,
the bench, grown into the ailing oak,
and an unfinished line of verse.
He says: 'Tomorrow I shall be
at the Stray Dog. And you?' And while
he waits for her to answer, Anna
watches her shadow glazing over,
and her clear voice utters these words:
'This has been an unnecessary day.'
His heart beats faster. Will she? Won't she?
But she knows all too well she won't.
The sky casts down on everything
fragments of heavy mist, like ballast
thrown from a sly earth-bound balloon
deaf to the orders of the pilot.
Nedobrovo rips off a scarf,
it's stifling, scratchy, out of place.
He wants to know! She doesn't want.
Already she has the solution,
half-muttered, to that comic line,
and then, dear God, she bursts out laughing,
and night steals up and licks their shoes.

The poet has passed away

The poet has passed away. Or rather, snuffed
it. How did the world taste at his last gasp?
We don't know, and we are ashamed to guess.
Like cranberry jelly, maybe, or perhaps

like peas boiled to a mush. But he himself,
he neither wished for life nor termination,
nor children, nor a father. Everything
is repetition, mass, continuation.
And we, his hashish smokers, what are we?
Just nothingness, some kind of super-nil,
plastic sneaked in to take the place of gold.
They'll ship him to the Island of the Dead,
the waves gleaming with sperm and diesel oil,
between palazzos crumbling to death.
Shivering in silks and lace, the youthful widow
sits in the gondola, and the gondolier
will understand: it's not the words, the slush,
nor the ambassadors of his indifferent homeland,
but above all the metrical hysterics . . .
His wishes
– what are they to us? And we,
when our time comes to quit the sandy shore,
when our hour strikes, we'll have our wishes too.

And yet he also wished . . . And how he wished!
As long as our high wishes still are cased
within the leather binding of our bodies,
he is alive – is life – is fuss and trash,
and therefore he is humbleness, a shrine
flowering among the universe's ruin.
What does death mean for him? Another flight.
Who do they sing for now, what do they sing,
his guttural speaking voice, his raucous laugh?
No, people of his kind do not die. No,
they leave, and as they go, turn out the light, –
but the grain cannot flourish in the dark.
It lies there unavailing, white and blind,
crushed by an unintelligible fate,
plunged into silence till the moment comes.
What can they mean for it, the empty words?
What can she mean, the captivating widow?
And what the prophet's immortality?

[PF]

Prayer II

Oh, Lord, look down yonder and bestow upon me your sorrow
On this glittering noon, on this transparent night,
For I have already forgotten how it happens,
How I and my beloved girl friend, descending into silence,
Would scrape the inside of the can of sweet condensed milk with an
      ancient teaspoon, a family heirloom,
While at the Liteinyi Avenue the street car's thunder would
      grow out of bounds.
How we'd put on warmer things and would walk to the Garden
Shouting from time to time at that crazy smiling dog,
Which would waylay the duck and her caravan of ducklings.
How, having had gotten to the canal, we would skirt the fence.
How we'd move forward, groping in the autumnal murk.
How my life seemed to me then
Copied from yours, written for you.
How did we joke, without remorse, about our lovers,
Almost not remembering their faces, mixing up their names.
We would joke in the same way about our deceased
Who had abandoned us here, having left us to . . .
Then we'd take our time putting the kettle on the stove,
      cutting the cheese and the loaf of bread,
Opening Poplavski on the page with the longest poem.
The dog would close her eyes, happy, remembering the walk
And the waves on the river feverishly tossing because of the flood

The 51M

I was riding on a bus in which
everyone was crazy.
Lunatics, wholly, every one. I'm not
indulging in facile hyperbole, shameful
to discover in the language of a poet
so
thoroughly dedicated to the mining of ontology
as I. But all of them were, quite frankly,
not firing on all cylinders.
Prudently lighting upon their perches,
their eyes turned toward nothingness.
They talked as one, each separately
to someone conjured, ghosted
and they reeked of neglect.

One guy, a ponytail and rings on every finger
was bending the driver's ear.
A genteel yet toothless mouth
transmuted a buoyant stream
of curious, opaque witticisms
into a juicy jumble. The orator,
mind you, had no idea.

Aligned on the corner cusp
sat his neighbour, swinging a shoe.
He directed his gaze out the window,
struck a stately pose, and proclaimed
to someone out there: "It's all too simple
to merit deep reflection. Fellow Americans,
you catch my drift? There's no point
thinking things all the way through.
It's clear as day. The blind
have no words of wisdom for the deaf.
They don't lack insight. Everything's
as plain as the nose on your face.
It's all known, understood,
and contains the seeds of the end."

I sat spellbound by the ravings
of the sad philosopher, when an old man,
dozing on the next seat over,
flung open his fly with a handy flourish,
bounded for the door and started to piss
into the night.
We rode on past a park where people stood shouting.
The passengers sat silently.

The next guy over, once black,
was now a moist bouquet of scabs.
Squeaks escaped his swollen face,
and like an idiot, he
scraped it with clumsy stumps,
trying to soothe a febrile itch.
(Thus the resigned wrestler taps out,
blood and tears streaming
into snot from a mangled nose.
But I digress.)

A fifth nut
plagued me with his unrelenting query:
"What's the time?" "Seven to twelve."
"Five to twelve." "Twelve o'clock."
A banal transaction.
The fool tried to get off the bus,
but was too loaded to find his feet.

That's how it went down. You won't squeeze
Anything more from my tale,
No sorry cliché, like,
"The whole world's a nuthouse."
No learned words on man's subordination to nature.
In the end, like pups at the teat
Of a none-too-Roman bitch.   No, my two-bit scripto
Was guided by something else entirely:
The aesthete's inherent desire
To pull the emergency cord and break out the glass.

[VB and EC]

Tatyana Bek

Translated by Robert Reid

Beneath the flakes of Russian snow

Beneath the flakes of Russian snow,
Where logos demands caution like a ford,
The cruel bliss of separation lurks,
Resists and dies away.

Beneath a fierce torrential cloudburst,
Brief as blessing,
Controlling fate's a droll endeavour,
Droller than an ancient tooth.

But to continue: under a western wind
Both style and character erode . . .
Does this not constitute (yes, this perhaps)
The hidden source of the soul?

We've all got history on our hands . . .

To Zoya

We've all got history on our hands . . .
But through debauchery and plague
'I will survive' (as Gloria sang)
Survive with ease, survive with rage.

Reducing love to touch once more,
Preserving safe within the head
The subconscious and its niggling sore,
All tightly bracketed away.

Within me Europe's felled by Asia
And freedom weeps for loss of rights
And my untamed imagination
Goes pale at what's before our eyes.

But I swear by what is best to swear by,
Through long nights of prophetic vision,
That I'll survive (oh, yes) survive,
Strong
as the moss that thrives

Larisa Berezovchuk

Translated by Richard McKane

Calm rocks to sleep in your usual place

Calm rocks to sleep in your usual place.
Sooner or later
you will have to believe in the reality
of tales about the Leviathan.
How caressing is the music of inertia. We swim on,
swim on, blessing the darkness . . .
Further. Only occasionally
alongside us it suddenly becomes empty –
that's some submarine creature
disappearing too early: the outer casing
could not stand the friction. The tension
becomes ash
in the materialised length of the womb.
Well? For those left behind
the loss is not noticeable.

But sensing the inevitable,
the adrenaline starts to scream, although
nothing is happening yet. What can happen
in an identical situation? If you do not know
the beginning and end;
for a stream, the middle is everywhere.
When you are alone you get out of the habit of fearing. The
place is the source of gravity. Fate –
and it is the same for all of us –
of the centrifuge, a somersault which is not noticed.
If you are not ill with schizophrenia, you begin to feel
gravity – the balance
between the poles: to know that the womb is shaken
in the surf by the arrhythmic waves. In it
the specks of submarines
spark with the potential of another's energies.
The switch of tension is switched on,
interfering with the reading of the monster's pulse.

Marina Boroditskaya

Translated by Ruth Fainlight

Now I am a fan of silence

Now I am a fan of silence
a watcher of snow-covered roofs.
Cupid landed on my window-sill,
but I told him to bugger off.

Christmas Eve

If Christians threaten to start a pogrom
    I'll paint a cross on the door.
If Muslims suddenly arrive
    I'll draw a crescent.
Buddhists are peaceful people,
    though a bit spoilt by progress.
I'd better put some sort of hieroglyph there.

I would draw all this
    on my children's foreheads –
but how could I explain
    that such funny signs are better
than ordinary-looking numbers
    branded on pallid forearms:
as if stamped by the devil?

Sound Letter

Hullo, Lord!
A minor poet
is writing to You,
a voice from the choir,
a little pine tree from the forest,
a clarinet in the school orchestra.

Do You think it is so
easy, Lord,
to be a voice in the choir,
a fish in water,
and not disturb Your order?
Yet worse is the icy fate
of those appointed
first violin, or the highest
pine on the mountain.

No hardship for us,
year in year out, day after day,
to sink our roots in deeper
and practise our scales,
waiting for the conductor
spot-lit on the rostrum
to point his baton –
and a noble solo rings out
making even the mountains weep.

So much gentleness from unknown men

So much gentleness from unknown men
for no particular reason.
Once in Paris a waiter turned to me: "Chérie!
Don't forget your cigarettes."

And in a London market, when
I wanted to buy a Beatles record,
the stall-holder sighed: "What can I do, love,
if the price goes up again?"

In New York airport, an old black man
took me to the right gate, saying:
"Don't panic, baby, just follow me!"
And I followed in his footsteps.

So much kindness from strange men!
Why the hell should I need more?
Lie peaceful in your oyster, pearl.
Stay calm, Moon, in the heavens.

Poor composer

Poor composer,
useless without a piano,
poor prose writer,
hopeless without a desk.
And poor artist,
who needs his easel, brushes
little tubes of paint.
I couldn't manage it.

Poor poor sculptor.
Poor film director.
In this world, only
the poet is fortunate.
He walks in the park,
a stanza in his head.
(As long as you don't shoot him
– like Pushkin – in the gut.)

Ekaterina Boyarskikh

Translated by Richard McKane

A person is reflected by the whirlpool, not the face

A person is reflected by the whirlpool, not the face
in the intelligent Angar, crazy January water.
Silver foil speaks in all human languages
and those of the angels. It makes the New Year
secrets ring out.
The mirror in the town-house is covered by
the white of the royal mourning.
Beyond the sheet – steam, beyond the snow – desert.
A person is reflected by the cold, winter spectacle
and blood flows
into the liquidity of the shaky door.
What can one ask for from the deaf and dumb almighty,
using a fish, a toy animal with a knocked-out eye,
primitive silence,
a torn eyelid,
the youngest child in the family?

I plunge a ladder for myself through each prison spy-hole,
into the quaking sands
at the bottom of the eyes.
Go away, reflection, quickly,
or else I'll think again.
Silver foil, silver foil.

[2001]

Vera Chizhevskaya

Translated by Daniel Weissbort

*

Take my heart, proffered
as if on the palm of the hand.
A clever horse
takes titbits that way,
gently,
so as not to frighten
the giver.

*

It seems to me
that the first Song
was one of Joy
Birds sang it
delighting in flight.
The Song of Sorrow
was invented by Man
yearning for flight.

A Free Man

He chose flowers
and it was noticeable
how rarely he offered them to anyone.

He deceived a woman
and it was evident
how often he
told untruths.

He forgot to soothe
the child . . .

He owes nothing to anybody.

A free man . . .

Moon Bathing

The whiteness of fog
approaches a river.

"What does it want?"
asks the grass.

"What's it looking for?"
marvels the sand.

"Why doesn't it clear?"
wonder the stars.

But the fog waits
for the moon to emerge from the stream,
shaking the water off.

Svetlana Chulkova

Translated by Daniel Weissbort

The Repetition of What Has Been Experienced

How swiftly two walkers distance themselves from one
      another:
he in the direction of point A, her mother-in-law, she in the
      direction of point B, his mother-in-law.
How much water has been used in the five years of bathing
      their mutual child.
What decree has turned them simply into foreign language
      lessons.
(Divorce is the equivalent of a diploma in "termination".)
But they are determined to exploit all the colours of the
      rainbow . . .

Svetlana Den'gina

Translated by Daniel Weissbort

Autumnal Equinox

I am sick of
the rustle of paper and rattle of umbrellas opening.
In the dark room,
among slumbering carp
and scattered beads,
again I want to be
a willow twig in a jug of water.
Again I'll forget how to listen to people
and I'll see my time off,
gazing into the depths of the huge dish.
Hops and haricot beans,
a wild vine and the evening breeze
will stay outside.
I'll forget about bread, milk, coffee.
But for several days
the wax-like yellow star
signifies for me
the most extravagant day of the year
and the most pellucid night.

Russia

If I never again saw your eyes . . .
Moistness . . .
If I didn't hear your barking cough . . .
The light's been used . . .
If I asked you for happy songs . . .
Gaps in the stairs . . .
If there were no reddish-green skull,
smashed against the snowy bank,
no eyes, drowned in the snows,
if in the frames there were no darkness
of effervescing ice . . .
Then I would pity you.

Regina Derieva

Translated by Kevin Carey

Beyond Siberia again Siberia

Beyond Siberia again Siberia,
beyond impenetrable forest again forest.
And beyond it waste ground,
where a blizzard of snow breaks loose.

The blizzard has handcuffs, and the snow-
storm has a knife which kills at once . . .
I will die, pay a debt
for others who live somewhere,

out of spite, out of fear and terror,
out of pain, out of a nameless grave . . .
Beyond the wall another wall,
on the wall stopped dead one sentinel.

On the sea-shore, smell of iodine

To Graziano Motta

On the sea-shore, smell of iodine,
and square as in Sicily, and dancing.

An intellectual that came from the common people,
preparing himself to be Rosencrantz.
He decides to serve Claudius and therefore
spy on Prince Hamlet from the fountain.

All over the world – the prison. At the world's
end a certain John plays the piano.

Already darkness, and the end is in sight :
Ophelia crying in an empty hut.
And Hamlet walks to and fro with a white headband,
in order to be recognized by the Ghost in the gloom.

Theory of Recruiting

Sons of bitches
were born
with hearts of stone,
cherishing this stone
all their life.
Children of
sons of bitches
were born
with hearts of grenade,
in order to
blow to pieces
everything,
and to leave as a message for their descendants –
entrails
(still smoking entrails)
of sons of bitches.

If Hamlet

If Hamlet
had not made up
Shakespeare,
if Werther
had not made up
Goethe,
if Raskolnikov
had not made up
Dostoevsky,
if J Alfred Prufrock
had not made up
Eliot,
if Gorbunov and Gorchakov
had not made up
Brodsky,
what would we know
about disenfranchised
persons?

Marina Dolia

Translated by Daniel Weissbort

from **Silence**

II

A white iris sprang up
by the dark stone,
a yellow-beaked nestling, shy.
I see no end to its early happiness,
as I don't see the glow above it.

For miles around saturated torment spreads
in the scum upon stagnant water.
One so wants to stretch out a greedy hand
and pluck it,
remove it from danger.

Beauty – too loud for these environs,
a sound painful to the ears. Nothing.
A wasteland, ideal, arose from ambiguous
secrets and stares at it.

Evidently, someone called it to this hopeless place
where there's no love without damage done.
A white iris sprang up like a wise child,
and silently gazes at itself.

IV

Even the longest day
contains the inevitable moment
when the soul
burns
with desire to give away treasures.
Your
concealed double emerges from
himself,
stretches

towards the fire, and demands his reward.

For this lunar day. The brace scrapes,
takes away
a minute and doesn't add happiness.
Your cast-off wreath my double will braid.
My candle will not go out by distant shores.

A hundred flaming wheels of raging silence,
and, following
this, smoke and burning, evil shades crawl.
My bonfire, hard but just that, don't be in such a hurry to weep,
while there's still the smell of grass, and stars, like a sign.

Irina Ermakova

Translated by Daniel Weissbort

. . . towards morning around seven
when a strip of light under the doors
was redder than The Petersburg
Arrow *
maybe you will read me
at a glance –
snow
acrid clover
dark grapes
idly you think you lived
like a butterfly which
the admiralty spire reached burned through
that it's the eighth hour and there's no sense
in going to bed
it's late and thank god
life has passed
that everything will happen after
that wings wither under glass
although they're far more visible because of it
that I was the amusing specimen
in your collection
that I was . . .

* famous express train between Moscow and Petersburg

Author's note: It perhaps goes without saying that
fanciers should not ignore the less striking species, especially
smaller butterflies, the study of which lags behind that of
large squamous winged creatures.

Gethsemane

The moon swims to the fore in the pale heavens
all god's shrubbery illuminates
grows and blankly stares like a blind woman
at everything knowing it all by heart

Crazed of countenance
blood drained
on the dark side the other side her eyes
unsleeping shameless she is attuned
to every sound we make at the
end of time

Hearing is split and the age
like an echo
in which the clash of swords offends the ears
By feel the moon rips open
the river with finger-like rays
and dims the glare

In the sub-lunar world not a glimmer
the Kedron gushes
through sombre hills
A detachment walks by fours
A branch snaps and a different darkness tells

No time
footsteps in the garden steps
fire-flies sport above upturned faces
they cannot wake – tiredness overtook them
unseen free and easy
we sleep
– fists outstretched cruciform
side by side beneath the burning bushes
like Your first disciples

Crucified by Lunaria's dream Gethsemenian
in Sardinia Samara in Virginia
on a motionless globe
in the second millennium
and a hollow moon
the silver coin spent
is larger than the very heavens

Lullaby for Odysseus

He speaks: My poor Penelope, my little lass,
you've grown so old, while I played the ass,
America is covered in ice, Europe in broken glass,
here, only here, at your feet do the living ages splash.

Dear, while you loafed about,
all got buried in clover,
with its acrid heartlike leaf, pink sticky clover,
free time's a weave, sewn with finest clover,
I'll make you a bitter deathless infusion of clover.

Drink, wind nails the prodigal vessels to the shore,
drink, the suitors are extinct, at sea fateful doldrums,
drink, the sons have grown, are about to undiscover America,
drink, the heavens have paled, drink, Odysseus!

Sleepy waves fawn, petals cling together like a fan,
the ends of your surfacing motherland join in a clover bowl,
enticing as the myth of fidelity, the clover spirit spreads,
drink, do not grieve, drink, my joy, my former joy.

Galina Ermoshina

Translated by Gerald Janecek

And also – the Minotaur, farmer, owner, respondent

And also – the Minotaur, farmer, owner, respondent,
on the sleepless page he is the same age, a petitioner and a weaver.
To the dedicated he is light, to the detained – reaping and stoves
in the last Tauride, where the ship's acrobat still lives.

And a marked sign is a lodger and a stepchild of the word,
right when a floorboard creaks – the first step or gesture.
This is an ovary and a backwater, returned, left again,
his best tower – for foam, for veins, for a cross.

And it depicts as melted – thinner than the cracks in a ledge,
the cursed lightness and audacity of fragile chimney swifts.
But the writing pads and grains are a doggedly learned list
on window conciseness and the stinginess of pass-through declensions.

Autumn your bellringing, the apple of bright weeping

Autumn your bellringing, the apple of bright weeping.
It does not hurt – the boatman, pendulum and carousel.
If you had been here – all would have been decided differently,
but who can search for you on the gypsum bottom, Odysseus.

Or follow the traces left of the black road,
only an end of yarn will knit consent into speech.
Let Penelope wait – thus spoke the gods,
and a circle of milk in a bowl, and the oven of a potter's wheel.

If the cup is glued too, and the halves fit together
of an apple, of damp earth, of a page read,
and the trace of yesterday's snow, and the ice of Christmas clay,
then all the same the shore and a seashell of sand will remain.

Zoya Ezrokhi

Translated by Daniel Weissbort

A Day at Home

Today I stayed home,
Fearing a pogrom against the Jews,
In the name of Russian Christianity.
The dog pointed its muzzle at the door
"Don't ask", I snapped.

Since morning I'd felt depressed,
The way you feel on a narrow little island,
At the hopeless hour of the flood tide.
Clasping an anti-Semitic pamphlet,
Brandished
Its fist.

I'd long been weakened
In the bitter struggle with dust, moths,
With spiritual and bodily sickness.
Now *Pamiat'** is affecting my nerves,
With the connivance of Minerva,
Who evidently doesn't give a damn.

Maybe we're getting too cocky?
After all, look at the blessings bestowed on us Jews,
As for me, iambic and trochaic verse do my bidding.
Jews are everywhere – in every argument,
And a Jewish acquaintance of mine
Even sings in the church choir.

But, after all, I didn't crucify Christ!
I never ever approved
Of such a finale.
I took a lot on my shoulders,
And, when I die, I won't quit the Russian language
Without leaving my mark.

Today I stayed home,
Fearing a pogrom against the Jews.
It was hot outside.

I went nowhere,
But stayed very snugly just where I was,
And I even wrote something –
Every cloud has its silver lining.

[1988]
* *Pamiat'*: an anti-Semitic organisation

My Wishes

Do not rendez-vous with me, fairy,
Where I strayed among pines.
And even if I rescue you, o golden fish
Thank me some other time!

Into my desperate hands,
Magic wand, do not fall.
Swim with god, past my fatal tub,
You pike from a fairytale.

And don't crawl out, you jinns and afreets
cast up on the shore,
For millennia unshaved, unfed
From capacities, by me uncorked!

Better for you that for all those thousands,
You saw neither palace nor tower,
Than that you fulfil those delirious wishes,
Which make even me cower!

Repetition

Poet, do not fear tautologies,
Do not blaze roundabout trails.
Even if the stern critic is displeased,
Say it again and again:

"How buttery is butter!
How light's the light I saw!"
And you'll see how much good sense there is
Where there seemed to be none before.

Let the chemist find fluorine and strontium,
The truth is visible to you:
How sunny, sunny is the sun!
How moony is the moon!

Amid the glades, automobiles, towers,
Wend your way enthusiastically,
Murmuring: "How homely's home!
How rainy the rain! How bestial beasts!

How mindful is the mind, how businesslike is
business, fear fearful, gloomy gloom!
How deathly is death! How lively is life!
How youthful youthful youth."

Elena Fanailova

Translated by Stephanie Sandler

*

Better this way: it's you with nothing to hold on to,
Only you (in a taxicab, in darkness), only you.
Quick, like poison running through water, distorting out of tenderness
The undefined features of a face.

O don't wait there clotted up over my soul or behind my back,
Order up some oblivion, some sleepwalking paradise.
I'll launch the little ship and the tiny gold fish through my veins,
In search of sweet daydreams, of manmade heaven, of *the seven seas*.

Like it or not, my heart will stay in one piece.
Vodka shines its dry light like a gypsy.
How blinding it all is: the winter solstice,
These unimaginable, inhuman words,
This other fate, the triumph of verse.

Frida's Album *(Frida Kahlo's Album)*

Frida sits coiffed (in whiteface), sits next to the canvas,
A lacy underskirt, apron, earrings, braids in a wreath,
Death at her left hand, headless Diego on her right,
An umbilical cord links them, the vessels, the threads like wiring,
A crystal globe hangs on a thread before her,
Showing skies, room, people, ocean,
Her heart stops, her heart beats in her throat,
Grass has overgrown her bed,
Frida sits there like a stone idol.
In the air hovers a Mother of God, a crucified Frida lies in a cradle,
Crucified Frida lies there
Diego is with Paulette Godard

Frida sits there like a queen, shawls, brooches, flowers in her hair,
    Look at her tears, lockets, bracelets, beads, embroidery, ribbons,
            pendants, fringe,
Dead dolls lie next to her, portraits *(retratos)* of leaders hang at
           the bed-head,

Frida sits there corseted in staves, covered in scabs,
Grass is overgrowing her bed
Grass grows from her head
Diego is with María Félix
Frida is dressed as a little boy, look at her cigarettes, stones, crystals,
                    bits of mica,
Her monkey hugging her, her parrots, women drowning in hair,
Stars in her ears, mirrors in the garden, lace,
Corpses, deer, weird breeds of dog,
The deceased Prince Dimas
Angels cradled by a heart,
                                        pierced through her breast
Frida is with Lucienne Bloch
Frida is with *Eva Frederick*
Frida is at home with his wife Lupe Marín
Frida is in a cradle, Diego is in mourning,
                                        look at the cards, marriage,
                                mariage
There are two Fridas, two Fridas are there.

Nina Gabrielian

Translated by Peter France

A Phoenician Statuette

Your hair is tied back in a puritan bunch,
but an animal heat flows out of your eyes.
You are just as the god created you once
from the red meridional clay.

An archaeologist dug you out of your bed
among primitive tools and bones of the dead.
Millennia had passed, and no-one had caressed
your strong thighs and your young girl's breasts.

For centuries lust for your torrified land
will rage in you, hopelessly seeking a vent.
And your half-open mouth is cracked by a thirst
that can never be quenched.

Tortoise

Where the scorched quietness is swathed
in the sun's violet rays,
it lies, unmoving, like a trace
of neolithic days.
And on its broad armour plates
the sun scatters its hot dust.
Like someone's lonely breath appears
black, in white sands, one bush.
In this place once children played,
here once existence flowered . . .
And the vertebrae of centuries crunch
beneath its heavy tread.

from the cycle **Erebuni**

1

I hood my eyes against the savage light . . .
Why am I here, and what do I want here?
Why do these ruins drag me to this place
with the mortal grief of blackened stone?
Am I the keeper of the dead?
I mutter
Cain-like:
'Am I their keeper?'
Graveyard grass crawls over stone,
strong in its underground knowledge.

2

The fortress is immobile
in the haze of noon.
Dead emperors gaze at me
as if their underground labour
had built this world, this city.
Unbeing
longs so to be incarnate,
to raise altars to itself.
Sculptors of unbeing, emperors
and warriors,
whisper to me:
'Look, here it is,
the capital of our realm.'

3

Midday sleep, the veil of sleepy maya,
hides the black earth from my eyes.
Grasses whisper,
rustling, dry,
and it seems I am not I . . .
On the town of the dead
heaven rains its flame,
and immobile – straight in my eyes –

a grasshopper stares from a stone
with its fearful faceted gaze.
And pinned to the wall
by premature horror,
I cannot tear myself
from its bulging mica stare,
from the stare of alterity.

4

Above me hangs the dry firmament of the Urarts.
Immortal it floats,
the ancient city,
like a gigantic ark
with its weighty cargo
down the dry bed of underground rivers.

Marina Galina

Translated by Daniel Weissbort

Ghazal

> *I shall idolise a Turkish woman from Shiraz,*
> *return Samarkand, and Bukhara for*
> *the sake of her birthmark,*
>
> *(Hafez)*

For the sake of a Turkish woman from Shiraz, consumed in the
            deadly fumes,
I shall pull the post-modern infection out by the roots.
For the moon's face and the shapes of gazelles and tight curls,
I shall drop Jaspers, Derrida and Deleuze, and Jung too
Ah, no need of more in the garden of frantic delights.
There, weeps Mircea Eliade, no Iliad can match his plight.
What's so special about Jaspers – it's the jasper of her cheeks,
            the agate of eyes,
onto the grass her variegated, argus-eyed silks cascade . . .
You're no passion – you're a splinter that cannot be pulled out by force.
Towards you the native tongue creeps through snows from our kolkhoz
to the moony fields of the East, to its mine fields,
where the gentle palm of a prophet lifts up a sword with its
            crescent maw.

What, in July's honey heat, do you weep for, poor goy

What, in July's honey heat, do you weep for, poor goy,
unshaven, naked, what are the snares you flee?
Saturated in lime-tree scent, the boulevard recedes,
and to the acacias clings the hot groin of a cloud,
spray flickers, glimmering on the town clock,
the horny heat of turtledoves seethes in the heavens,
and a sail rummages, listing in a sunny négligé,
while you sit, like some prince, robed in golden mange.
I don't know what I'm weeping for, but I know at whom.
It's the lord, his beggar's bowl, and the entire town,
myself, poor goy, mischigener ascetic, I sorrow
that there's no other life, and this is no life either.
I loathe the morning and the glorious light –

no longer is it for me, or I for it,
and the burning wind flees the darkness of the steppes.
Take pity, Lord! What you're doing to me? Tell!
From the heavens seeping like resin, flows a pitchy dark,
and my youth has passed, and my life, too, has passed.
The pollen from the poplars has tumbled down, the evening light dies,
and towards night three hags are paraded by the lord of the flies.
Bags of bones, they file past, uncouth –
the one bringing up the rear my love . . .

I said to him – don't throw me into this prickly bush

> *"Do what you like, only don't throw me into this prickly bush."*
> *(Tales of Uncle Remus)*

I said to him – don't throw me into this prickly bush:
this is my dear home, blossoming behind me.
Where each leaf trembles, there's a rustling hush,
the berries are shot with black enamel and the colour blue.
I said to him – better to burn me in the bonfire,
blue-grey smoke has already floated overhead by morning,
and a shrike sings among the thorny branches
in the prickly bush, at the time of its dawning.
Better to throw me into the water, because the water tastes bitter,
like a prickly berry and down below it's the same coloration.
But in the prickly bush fixated on a needle is a star,
not needed for the time being by any of the neighbours.
Ah, Brer Fox, you're nobody's fool,
don't be won over by such notions or ideas.
I'll seek out whatever creatures make you drool,
I'll lead them out to your blackthorn lair.
I myself can't go home – too sharp is the thorn
that has lodged in my chest – my left paw aches.
Better pay attention to the fine bonfire behind you
and right there beside you, a splendid lake.

Anna Glazova

Translated by Max Nemtsov

solo

the wire. the ghetto. an eastern landscape.
over the sea the sedge rustles softly and in front of the pupil
the reeds resound
the city withers in the shackles of the night watch
the double body sinks to the meat straw
with a crinkle of dense grass.
zooming cicadas skewer slowly.
slowly the curtain goes down like a shroud
this is the first time i taste your life –
you wince but there is no tearing off –
the palms of your hands
your knees
your births
your departures into a hollow name
your touches
your
– drink
to drink of yours
– to drink
– to drink

the grant of death

job came to the rabbi
sei gesund job
hayweh willing rabbi
rabbi cabba
you're like golem job
you let me kill myself rabbi
bless you job god
be off rabbi to see
how i will kill myself rabbi
rabbi: yahweh son job – for the love of god
job: in peace
and in pain
rabbi: let's go

from **Cities**

venice

an enormous clock at the sandy mansion:
the cramped square's bugging out its fisheye
the ponderous sky is squeezed into a narrow frame
and crisscrossed with blue and white laundry over the channel
the laundry smells of fish
the water smells of the lagoon
which smells of the boat
a water taxi

st mark's square is interlaced with crabs
and the doges' palace windows with water and fish
and i've been squirming like a tapeworm all day long
in the recta, jejuna and colons
disgustingly white on the food
painted
red
white
and green

and in the end of the day
without a chance to blow my eggs
i tumble about in the lagoon effluvia
searching for the next fish

berlin

a bloated face. with the fust
of the humid jaundiced ash
of the bovey coal the mouth
of berlin will pant right into the face – mine still mine
still the face – how many times
the city you'll say the word alien.

like a smack off the berlin wall
with the physiopsycholechery
of berlin the dear hungry mouth
will ravage my alien lips:
how many times will i bite and lap up
the cruelly grey
palate over berlin

Natalya Gorbanevskaya

Translated by Daniel Weissbort

My Fortinbras, poor brother

My Fortinbras, poor brother,
behold this, my Denmark,
sprung from my side,
the very image of me.

And this, my game, behold,
now it is yours –
the path of virtue, obstacles without end,
the mystery of being.

Take all, all that was mine.
Or else, stop, wait,
and then change your mind.
You're not yet king.
Leave now, the drums silent,
let this part be.

[1962]

This moan of ours, this sob

This moan of ours, this sob,
this cry of a dactylic passage,
this howl of the begging mob
hungering for Lazarus

is called a song,
i.e. verse,
and feeds on mildew
and crushed glass.

from **Thirteen Eight-liners**

The rhymes picked me in a ditch,
shook me a little, bathed me,
clothed me appropriately for my age,
which means hand-me-downs from other kids,
rubbed oil into me, removed the scabs,
cleaned me, cleansed me of passions,
washed out my ears and my thoughts
and all but finished me off.

Someone phones, calls me at night

Someone phones, calls me at night.
Someone wants to hear my voice, but himself
has taken refuge in the receiver, not a sigh,
his soul compressed between shoulder and ear.

Leaves, something in my ear you twitter

Leaves, something in my ear you twitter
hardly audible, you whisper to my cheek, tickle,
you'll not cure my soul's deafness this way.
I'll not shed tears, remembering those nights

which existed, no more do, and behind which
there's no catching up, even at breakneck speed,
neither by express train nor direct,
to reach the bare-legged, dewy dawn.

I kept a keen knife, in case of love.
I warn the shower:
"Don't!"
Leaves, something in my ear you whispered,
rustled in under my ribs, tickled the larynx . . .

This, from the diagnosis

"The children's fate doesn't bother her."

This, from the diagnosis,
rings out like a silvery clarinet,
has lost the colour of danger,
but my memory's not been wiped clean of it.

It's good when the breathing in the next room
is my sons' and not a cell-mate's;
it's good to wake up, not groaning
at an envenomed reality.

It's good not to feel the brain's convolutions –
has there been a change? – is it yourself, isn't it? –
not settling down to breathe in, from underneath the rubble
the dust of what, please God, is irrecoverable.

Natalya Gorbanevskaya *
by Yury Kublanovsky

Legendary times – the Sixties! What now, in our tranquil cultural
climate, is commented upon in hardback books found on shelves, in
those days was passed from hand to hand in the form of blurry,
typewritten sheets. You would go to your history lecture, and these
items were handed on, row by row [...] Of contemporary poets the most
frequently circulated texts were by Brodsky and Gorbanevskaya. [...]
And a little later, Gorbanevskaya achieved another kind of prominence.
A dissident activist, with a babe in arms, she went out onto Red Square,
to protest against the occupation of Czechoslovakia. Her painful road
through the madhouse [psychiatric prison hospital] led finally to
emigration.

   In the West – in the USA, in Paris – she published several books, but
in post-totalitarian Russia her poetry is little known. [...]

   Gorbanevskaya's poetry had to solve a complex problem. On the one
hand, attentive to the needs of the country and her own social conscience,
she made no attempt to eliminate all pathos from her poetry; on the other
hand, she could not bring herself to write "simply", as several of her
older contemporaries did. In her work you find devices drawn from the
most experimental poetry, which rejected narrative and moralizing ...
At the time – a sign of the times – Poland seemed like a beacon of hope,
the freest of the countries of the socialist *lager*; Gorbanevskaya, like

Brodsky, learnt Polish, became an enthusiastic "Polonophile", doing as much for the Polish freedom movement as for the Russian one. In gratitude, Polish twentieth-century poetics helped our unofficial poetry – and in particular Gorbanevskaya's – to define itself in terms of new prosodic developments. [. . .]

In spite of the brevity of individual poems, which sometimes seem to be no more than snapshots of a spiritual reality picked out of the flow of time, Gorbaneskaya's poetry is always epic and in its way epochal; it is like a section of an old tree with a plethora of rings, allowing you to reconstruct in detail the past, where your life too is represented. Remarkable is the selflessness, the disinterestedness of her poetry; adaptation, conformism are utterly foreign to it. Her voice, with all its pathos, was from the start not intended for the Luzhniki Stadium, or even for the pages of Soviet journals, but for a circle of fellow thinkers, the very best of our people at that time.

Typewritten Samizdat texts, it seems, were so closely linked to their own production process that regular publication later was for them a test. Time was an even more rigorous test. [. . .]

[. . .] The originality of Gorbanevskaya's poetry – and with the years, in emigration, this tendency has increased – lies in the fact that most of her poems do not develop in a linear way: introduction; development; resolution. Economical, lapidary, her texts go straight to the heart of the matter, apparently devoid of a framework. Metaphorically speaking, one might say that she constructs not "houses", but "nests". In her lyrical heroine there is indeed something of the tireless builder of nests: ever busy . . . And the reader suddenly feels that it is a privilege to be a contemporary of this indefatigably intrepid worker, tough, at times even harsh. There's a certain phonetic, rhythmic, imagistic complexity that is more a sign of something organic than a defect. [. . .]

What an amazing phenomenon: from month to month, year to year, decade to decade – the survival of the lyric, the constant subordination to it of life and creativity, when writing is not a profession, but existence itself transcends any mercenary goal.

True, there's a danger of making the poetic event humdrum, everyday. There are many who reach a certain level and just stay there, never rising above it, forgetting that poetry has to do with revelation. But, the dramatic nature of Natalya Gorbanevskaya's lyric heroine does not allow her to write in clichés. She is never tedious or monotonous.

"[A]nd the same Slavic laments / we bequeath to the great-grandsons, / the way of penitence, like the path of sin, / is never-ending."

[Translated by Daniel Weissbort]

* from a review, published in *Novy Mir*, No. 7, 1997

Nina Gorlanova

Translated by Daniel Weissbort

from **Three-liners**

The children saved their money
For ice cream
And gave it to daddy for beer.

*

The middle daughter
Was keen on reading
Thanks to my prayers.

*

Nowadays it's only
In my dreams that I see
People who have made it.

*

Everything's gone up.
Even when we're mad at each other
We don't break plates . . .

*

My daughter brought me
A bunch of bird cherry from school –
I must take a look in my diary . . .

*

My younger children
Read like the ancient Romans
Aloud and recumbent.

*

Reading Brodsky's prose,
I discovered a spiritual kinship:
A consuming interest in dust . . .

Lydiya Grigoryeva

Translated by Richard McKane, by Ravil Bukharayev
and by Daniel Weissbort

Modigliani

In the attic, in the half-dark of cobwebs
a dead artist is drawing a picture.

A line to the right. Oblique.
Yellow paint. A white temple.

A naked woman wearing a red beret
is posing before him on a folding stool.

A line to the left. A line up.
There will be a picture – a success.

The painting will go on for years.
Children, neighbours, kindred have died.

The measured strokes of the dead hand:
"You see, only fools die."

A white body. And blue paint
obliquely. A red brush stroke.

The artist is dead – he can barely stand.
His distant descendants will be enraptured

by the feast of lines, the paleness of her shoulder,
the bravery of genius and executioner.

[RMcK]

To break the window glass

To break the window glass –
to jump into the dark,
for there is life and night –
trees spreading down under . . .

And to get smashed
in blood, indulge in pain,
but not in idleness or slumber.

There, in the waste, a paper bag will stick
to my face, wrapping sweat, absorbing tears,
oh, to lie calmly in the dark,
till aching disappears.

Or just to hang head down
from the branch,
composing a verse with no hurry,
what won't fit in those lines, I could
share out piecemeal, like bread,
to all and sundry, –

But they won't take it.

Oh, to plunge – to kill
The cause, the reason
For my silly tears . . .

All's possible,
But for those endless squeals,
and shrieks of cars,
down there changing gears.

[RB]

Even here it did not cease, the pain

Even here
it did not cease, the pain . . .
Where can one run? There's no dry land!
From the creation until time runs out
the world's
end was more visible from England.

[December 1999, London]

Under a heavy cloud now sprawled

Under a heavy cloud now sprawled
a raven, stern, combustible,
now
a spectre purplish blue,
now a literary image.

I stand there, waiting for a tram

I stand there, waiting for a tram,
hoping for
wealth and
fame.
How inhospitable is life!
As if it began just yesterday.

   [DW]

Faina Grimberg

Translated by Richard McKane

The reflection of a wet finger . . .

The reflection of a wet finger that slipped over the faded oil-cloth
like a watery speck of potato settled on the saucer,
rolled in a meandering stream, slow and slender.
This happened in never-never. It was completely before you . . .
To inhale the steam from the hot, yellow potatoes . . .
And having screwed up one's eyes to smile into the coloured darkness
hiding into grandma's round apron, veins throbbing at the brow.
This happened in never-never. It was completely before you . . .
And to take the towel rubbed to weak gauze:
Grandpa really could not have wiped his face with it – he must
        have spread it on the dew.
To feel Grandpa's soft: *"Haisl maine"*.
This happened in never-never. It was completely before you . . .

Elena Ignatova

Translated by Daniel Weissbort

Then there was the rose I fell in love with

Then there was the rose I fell in love with, –
a December rose.
                            When we say "Eden"
amid our snows we have in mind
the image of a rose garden in December.
I pluck a December rose,
similar to these.
Yes, when, amid our snows, we say "Eden"
we conceive of a vale
overgrown with olive trees and laurels
reaching to the flat heavens.
A deer, its antlers entangled in the roses,
a lamb, a lion . . .
                            No lamentation, no tears.
On the other side of the ravine, over the heads of the roses
the valley of Ajalon, rough like a sail,
from those times when the sun of Joshua
frizzled its edge. And the blazing little town
ran with blood beyond the sugar-lump walls.
Mountains of folks, donkeys, goats . . .
                            Quantities of blood let.
No, December rose, Eden's no magical garden.
On the ashy sole its hills, liner of blood –
just as amid our snows, but more ancient by far,
and the tops of the trees spattered with death's rust,
and the December rose, tight like God's scroll,
like the Lord's wrath, weighs on my heart.

To sob, pressing oneself against the officer's greatcoat

To sob, pressing oneself against the officer's greatcoat –
gives one a special colonial thrill.
West is West – but this is East.
Do you see where we've got, you and I?
The famous atmosphere of the Fifties
has staled here, back to front.

Preserve of childhood.
                    Again, again
the shoulder-straps on the uniforms of young fathers
smell of oranges and gold.
How many of us are at table, how crowded it's got!
Dream of childhood.
                    The family clan
closing ranks, like the crown over the head
of the eternal tree. Its scent is corporeal.

Don't wake. The lips of mothers
taste silver and mint.
How deathless, how rich
we were in their love . . .
We were born off into the dream, into the dark.
You will wake – the desert in full bloom,
soft sound of singing on the other side of the wall –
a coachman, who keels over towards the snow,
a spring, where the light is hot
over the icy waters of life.

Nina Iskrenko

Translated by Stephanie Sandler

Another Woman

When I cannot stand
to muster strength against misfortune
when I cannot sleep
and face an entire tank of dirty laundry
when I
mistake my children
for dinosaurs
but take the favorable disposition of luminaries in the sky
for a simple act of courtesy
when at a quarter to
eight I have to go
and at a quarter to nine I have to go
and at a quarter to eleven I
have to go
and the radio
is saying all manner of bad things
when the telephone finally tunes out
because it can't take this any more
and a piece of butter brought to mind
does not spread on an imaginary piece of bread
and what's more I stumble in the dark of night on
the bicycle in the hall

the sleepy and slightly irritated striking of a match is heard
and smoke reaches under the door
This is you
starting to talk on and on to me about another woman

    Another woman in your place
    Another woman in your position
    Another woman at our level of civilization would pay no attention
        to these regular monthly whims would not pay attention
        would not pay

My forehead tenses up with the effort to imagine the seductive
adaptability of a n o t h e r woman to o u r level of civilization and
when finally I succeed I smile the trustingly disdainful smile of the

Cheshire cat or of Julio Cortazar gladly giving up my place at the stove
to the other woman and in sleep and in all of my horizontal-vertical-
trigonometrical knee-eared cold-nosed spiral-eyed positions and while
she masters them paying me no attention whatsoever I steal up to the
front door feeling for my shoes and thinking only about how not to get
snagged by the bicycle in the hall

The doorbell rings
I open the door
Another woman with a plaintive voice jumping out of her dress asks me
to call the police her husband got drunk and she hit him with a skillet full
of cutlets you wouldn't have any valerian would you thank you what is
this disgusting stuff I've never taken anything like it good God some
people have proper lives, quiet and calm and happy

Coming back into the room for a handkerchief
I notice that another woman resiliently-weightily has collapsed onto
something brown-red and dirty-blue She has a splendid golden almost
masculine torso cut off by a frame and blind eyes smeared over in black
It seems in my position she is pretty satisfied although Modigliani does
not like being looked at

The television flickers
Another woman on the screen
whispers and wails into an invisible microphone
fatally shuts her eyes revelling in her
shrewish gait and animal longing
for another man
For you probably

In half an hour another woman in a crooked veil
and work boots
suddenly falls off the book shelf onto my head
and lies on the floor all open in a swoon
at that page where the enemy has just burned down a Russian village
where Catholics ceaselessly butcher Huguenots
and Turks do it to Armenians
and the bronze horseman wears down the bronze steed
riding from Petersburg to Moscow
trying to get there for the morning execution of the Streltsy

Bunchberry sauce for meat and chicken
is something we never have
Bunchberries do not grow at our market

probably another woman is in the kitchen looking through
the cookbook she turned to me with her
tasty bunchberry butt pasted on a card-
board wrapper of German-made stockings

Blue twilight is soaked
and its contours are lost in the little river and for hours and minutes the
suffering cello squeak of the doors
winds around the digital lock in the entryway

In the yard wheezing children work hard to carve from snow
another woman
Her head keeps falling apart
it's like some sort of punishment to make this stupid head
who ever thought it up
you could just cut the eyes in her stomach

Growing dark   Starting to drizzle   Growing light
   Stretching out
Peering through   It started to freeze

Another woman in my place looks in the mirror
turning her face so that
the circles under her eyes aren't seen

Another woman in my position sorts through the spoons
and climbs up to the top shelf to get washing powder

Another woman at our level of civilization
walks along the sidewalk in dirty tattered jeans
looks through magazines at the kiosks
gets bored talking with friends
figures out the story's ending after the third
paragraph although it only has two

and she comes out of the metro
walking toward the Pushkin monument at that very moment
when the poet with his stiff stone face
takes off his top hat
and turns toward Tver Boulevard
listening wearily to the noise of airplanes
to the light clatter of carriage wheels
and to the squeak of floorboards in Mikhailovskoe
He is watching with feigned indifference

another woman
who pays him absolutely no attention
as she melodically moves across the street
Her face turns pink in the shining warning light
of the traffic signal   Brakes squeal
She shrieks and runs
without looking back   choking on the frozen air
mechanically reading signs and being reflected in
every face until finally she falls
flat in the dark of night
accidentally tripping on a bicycle
in the hall

Translator's Note: This poem has also been translated by
Olga Livshin, and I have borrowed several of her locutions.
See *Slovo*, no. 28 (2000), pp. 98-100. Here, and in my translations of
Elena Shvarts and Elena Fanilova, I have also incorporated some
excellent suggestions from Catriona Kelly, for which I am grateful.

Olga Ivanova

Translated by Jenefer Coates

To Russian Women

She'll not nag if there's no bread for breakfast
But by nightfall is sure to provide,
A runaway Rolls Royce she'd stop in its tracks
And she'll always stump up some cash.

She's clever at handling money.
But, the fool, she'd not keep a penny.
This land over, poor Russian women
Will never give up, or give in.

Whatever life brings, she will shoulder:
Needs must, she'll just soldier on.
Yank in her belt by yet one more notch,
After scrimping for your hair of dog.

And once the last penny is gone –
Out will come her dregs of "Obsession".
With tough childhood now left behind,
Mad happiness fills her mind.

Note: This parodies the famous Nekrasov poem
"Russkie zhenshchiny" which praises Russian
women for their idealised virtues, here substituted
by a realistic stoicism needed to endure modern life.

Do I hold the past in my hands

Do I hold the past in my hands
Perhaps
A little too tightly?

Time turned inside out

Time turned inside out
Hangs down from me
Like empty sleeves

I meet myself each and every day

I meet myself each and every day
Never do I leave myself alone
Am out of sight not for a single second
And so I simply fail to understand
What can have happened to
That face
Which stares back at me
From old photographs

Svetlana Ivanova

Translated by Jenefer Coates and by Angela Livingstone

O caterpillar, daughter of the butterfly

O caterpillar, daughter of the butterfly
You too one day will soar past tower and roof,
Past boring little dachas in the suburbs.
Yet no mere louse are you fated to remain –
You'll outstrip yourself, slipping from your skin.

Wherever – over earth or leaf – you crawl
Your body has to work a little harder,
You're a real
Shakin' break-dancer,
And a hundred flowers all blaze bright for you.

[JC]

Note: Line 3 recalls a line from Blok's famous poem
"Neznakomka": "… nad skukoi zagorodnykh dach",
which refers to the famous boredom of Russian country life.

Bird, start up your moan, your whine

Bird, start up your moan, your whine,
whether like a gunner's star
or a ladder's upward climb . . .
fish, beast, gift of a tsar.

'Tails' each time, and this must mean
muteness – yet do throw the coin –
I forgive you in return
for a penultimate copper tone,

and for a penultimate number,
for the sunshine trees of sleep,
all turned inside out – and steep.
So a master forgives the monkey

in its fustian cap, pell-mell
pulled behind him on a string . . .
How to guess which hand it's in,
you, with you I cannot tell.

You're watching me with constant eye.
Do you prophesy or call?
Count it out one final time,
Re-count, re- . . . anything at all

with a teardrop graphomanic,
with a drop of heavenly grace
and with foliage gethsemanic
over a wept and chasmic place.

Subterranean River Poem

Either archival youths or Aegean men
looked through the blue of the sun
or was it through a March day's windows,
flying through a dance of dust
from the bottom of the reflected morning,
where among stones of a dusky pont,
new-born water
was wholly filled with movement
and, along the Acheron, Neva's ice
moves like sable ships
and voices float in light
in the library's Lethean sleep.
Shout – you get quietness for reply,
nothing but thawing light-blots.
O and turn round – there's only a palm
mutely flashing,
a wave of farewell, a speechless fire
through water.

[AL]

Inna Kabysh

Translated by Fay and Jay Marshall

Making Jam in July

A woman who's making jam in July
is resigned to living with her husband.
She won't escape with her lover, secretly.
Otherwise, why boil up fruit with sugar?
and observe, how willingly she does it,
as a labour of love,
even though space is at a premium
and there's nowhere to store the jars.

A woman who's making jam in July
is preparing to be around for a while.
She intends to soldier on, to hibernate
through the discomforts of winter.
Otherwise, for what reason, and notice,
not out of any feeling of duty,
should she be spending the short summer
skimming residue off jam?

A woman who's making jam in July
in all the chaos of a steamy kitchen,
isn't going to be absconding to the West
or buying a ticket to the States.
That woman will be scrambling out of snowdrifts,
buoyed up by the savour of the fruit.
Whoever's making jam in Russia
knows there isn't any way out.

Whenever the Prodigal Son returns Home

Whenever the prodigal son returns home
he arrives at the height of day;
whereas when the prodigal daughter comes back
she slinks in after dark.

A daughter may have learned her lesson too
but she'll arrive encumbered with children.

Katia Kapovich

Translated by Richard McKane

Something from an untidy Russian life

Something from an untidy Russian life,
from homegrown truth in the trough,
from a dried bunch of grapes:
I dream of these since there aren't enough events.

I dream simply of circles in front of the eyes,
the harsh chords of alleys in perspective,
so that my face is suddenly flooded
with tears. This cloudburst stands in my throat.

The doors open in the morning of their own accord
like a book at the required page.
Then I dream of some little square without
a subject and then simply of water.

So the sense of loss is growing dull,
memory gradually rusts like a knife.
Even when I am dead I will dream sometime
of these eyes, greener than the river by day.

Parting makes simple sense

Parting makes simple sense,
there's no special sense in it.
The air will be to blame,
the garden full of birds whistling.
The smoke and the strip of water
there by the mossy forest.
Even that the sunset cut
across the rows of pines.
It will turn everything into ashes
with the quiet oncoming of night,
so that in tormenting dreams
the eye should fall for
the thousandth time
to the keyhole of the world

not finding in the light
that which it sought in the dark,
aiming at the door with the little cross-key.

And you raise a pale blue
pupil in the summer sky.
You will not share life with me
and couldn't care less about freedom.
But there is a terrible truth
hidden in your madness.
As though you know everything
about everything. Even more than is necessary.

Svetlana Kekova

Translated by Ruth Fainlight

Space is arched like a sail

Space is arched like a sail
its laws the same everywhere,
and the broad faces of moths
compose its outer tier.

While we are balanced
on the chasm's meniscus,
we will not let our pointless sadness
misrepresent God's realm.

Life, that unresolved question,
we leave till later.
Both the crazed woodpecker
and the gaping fish

are like broken keys
jutting from rusty locks,
or an ignoramus
flaunting his ugliness.

With much effort, I glimpse in the darkness and rubbish

With much effort, I glimpse in the darkness and rubbish
unbaptised beings standing in every corner.

Above the bed, hiding its entreaty,
hangs a tarnished mirror with an ulcerated forehead.

Night has the mysterious gift of blindness:
you cannot be seen nor see anyone else –
only the square mouths of cut-glass vases
and the dim copper of a cold teapot,
only the devil's net and the airy cage
where space sits, like a song-bird,
where a candle starts to smoulder and
enclose you in a circle of pale light.

Your naked helplessness, the lord knows well! –
and that faint birthmark near the mouth.
The fallen angel, with an almost imperceptible
tremor of orange wings, opens his lifeless eyes.

Running water is cold, the river from Eden flows east

Running water is cold, the river from Eden flows east,
a lower-case letter appeared on a page of rough copy,
the flowers' pollen settled, fragile life seems exhausted,
slant rhyme craves to be used, but the hand refuses.

What kind of word, uttered, leaves salt in the mouth?
Soon your death is exhausted, sinks like a stone. There
is the source of false light: in the impossible world's centre
the fallen angel Lucifer distorts the music of the spheres.

Everything disappears in a motley flame, rising to heaven.
A host of angels inscribe the letter "S" on a banner.
Again the apple is bitten, flesh forbidden,
but that which God created cannot be destroyed.

Do you see in unhealed sores the dark foliage of apple trees,
exhausted woodland creatures in crippled forest giants?
'Theta' sleeps and 'ishitsa' dozes, 'yat' slithers from under your hand,
beetles move in brittle armour across the tree-trunks' bark.

I don't want to count my losses or hear the terrible roar of flesh.
The spirit betrayed us, but matter transforms to language.
The focus of a former life hides wherever it can,
and stuttering words sprout from the fertile earth.

The tsar sits on his throne as if he sat on bones

The tsar sits on his throne as if he sat on bones.
Around him, a world of deserving objects,
and the tsar's staff is strong, strong as Rakhmetov*
sleeping on his famous bed of nails
as an example to the young. A coffer stands
high as the throne which the tsar mounts –
he keeps his silver in an oak womb.
Some creature walks over the ruler's skull

and his staff will strike it a blow,
as at our first mother Eve.
The Old Testament serpent sits in a tree
and picks up our thoughts, like radar.
And a blind mole who lives in the worm-eaten earth
has scooped out a dark burrow in the space
between an apple and a plum tree, as in the rind
of the world, and insinuated itself there.

* Rakhmetov: a character in Cheryshevsky's famous novel,
What is to be Done? The revolutionary hero toughens himself
by sleeping of a bed of nails.

Look, a man is flying and

Look, a man is flying and
doesn't know where or why.
He remembers his past life,
glorifies it, curses it, and
watery tears gush from his eyes.

Seductions of this world,
like moments, run in sequence:
naked apples of summer
glistening red currants
basins of rain water.

At dawn, a threesome splits up:
flesh, soul, and restless spirit.
Needles of tender larch trees rake
the thickening air like a comb.
The last rooster sets the tune.

Louder than the instant before the walls collapse,
a white willow thrashes above the ravine.
In the filthy pit of Gehenna
our death burns to ash,

and whirls like a fiery squirrel.
Fine dust irritates the eyelids,
and your suitcase, human sinner,
is spotted by celestial whitewash.

You returned with all your old mistakes,
your previous pain and new misfortunes,
and clouds are heaped
in the blue sky above the white water.

Already, no more suffering, no

Already, no more suffering, no
more speech nor space nor time.
In the city of Bremen, only music
still survives, and light.
Over the bakery, a pretzel gleams,
summing up foolish life,
and in the dark of midnight
a repulsive white flower blooms.

Dusty brakes of yellow acacia
clustered around an empty platform
revealed the law of gravity,
but its effect on the spirit was slight.
Life should not slip away like dross.
Again you climb the hill, but
the faces ripped open like bellies
disclose only the viscera of clocks.

We die, we sleep and eat,
weep loudly, form words
and pursue certain ends,
with no idea of what it's all about.
The fir-tree branches flutter
in a dazzle of eyelashes,
and round-headed nurslings of death
materialise in the maternity wards.

No more honey, hops or malt,
no burning water, no fire.
The blasted gold cavorts across the sky,
in too much of a hurry.
You'll break the moon like crockery
and, approaching old age, learn how
to persecute those irrepressible Jews.
So your youthful days return.

How the winged horses clip-clopped
over the hot paving stones of the bridge.
We saw Mandelstam, or Blok,
head bowed, walking off
into inordinately deep air-pockets,
where words echo death's knell,
where your disobedient golden head
still seems to be alive.

Interview with Kekova

by Inga Kuznetsova

Grigory Kruzhkov recently wrote in Arion *about metaphysical poetry and he used your poetry as an example of this among contemporaries. Did John Donne play any part in the development of your poetic style?*

Well, poetry is in essence metaphysical. Even a very simple metaphor is metaphysical, disclosing a hidden relationship between things. Rhyme, in its essence, is also metaphysical. The correspondence between phenomena of the visible world is reflected in poetic language and shows that everything which exists has one source, one Creator.

For me, without metaphysics, poetry loses its value. But to what extent my own verse corresponds to the canons of metaphysical poetry, I can't judge. As for Donne, I was not influenced by his poetry at all.

The March 2001 issue of Novy mir *published a cycle of your poems, expressing a deep love for your parents. Can you say something about them?*

My father was a military man. He was an ordinary soldier in the war, he fought at Stalingrad, Kursk and on the Dnieper. He never told us anything about the war, but every year on May 9th he'd put on his medals and weep. He was a very kind man, loved children and people in general. He could talk to anyone; he had some kind of special gift.

My birth is a sort of miracle. My aunt, father's sister, told me that during the war my father suffered shell-shock and at one point was taken for dead and was about to be buried in a common grave. Only by accident did they discover that his heart was still beating and he was taken to hospital. After the war he graduated from military academy and stayed on in the army. The family moved from place to place. For several years we lived in Sakhalin where I was born. Afterwards we lived in Tashkent, in Tambov . . .

What did your mother do?

She was the wife of a military man with all that follows from that. In the most difficult circumstances she demonstrated truly Christian virtues: humility, patience, gentleness. She followed father everywhere and took us with her. For a long time she had no job – with all the moving around it was impossible. When I was older I left for Saratov University and mother found a job.

My parents were raised in the same village in Penza Region, attended the same school. They both came from large families – my mother had five sisters. One other interesting fact: father's birthday is the same date as mother's Saint's Day.

You were born in Sakhalin. That is pretty exotic. What do you remember of it?

Very little. We lived in the southern part. Our house had been occupied by a Japanese family before us. So, it was an old Japanese house. Rather miserable premises.

Is Japanese culture of any interest to you and did it influence you?

Yes, Japanese culture is something special. It has its own aesthetic of the home, and a particular attitude to objects. There's a mysterious connection between landscape and architecture and ceramics. A silence of rivers and lakes. Drawings on silk always stimulate and attract me. Artists and poets in Japanese culture don't cut themselves off from nature; they work in so-called parallel perspectives, where there is no far and near, past and future. Everything is happening here and now. As a result, experience of the moment is particularly intense, the equivalent of eternity. In my childhood I loved books on the art of China and Japan. The poetry of these countries embodies an experience which is close to me on a subconscious level.

At the beginning of the 80's I saw a film by Kurosawa, "The Shadow of a Warrior", every scene of which I found electrifying. I couldn't understand why. None of the European films, including those by my favourites, like Tarkovsky, has had such an effect on me. The impression was not just of something close; there was a veritable explosion in every cell of my body. It was such a powerful experience that I found it hard just to sit there, in the cinema. I thought about it a long time and realized that it had to do with my early Sakhalin experiences. I wasn't baptised until I was three years old and the spirit of those places seems to have got hold of me. My parents told me once that, as a child, I was carried off by a wave, but they scooped me out like a fish! Water, fish, the whole submarine world attract me almost unbearably.

When did you first write poetry?

I started writing very early, before school. Although I can't really say 'write' – it was oral, as with most children. At school, I wrote poetry – it was just a natural part of life. And then I suddenly noticed that what I wrote about quite often happened! And I saw that poetry doesn't coincide with life, doesn't describe what happens in life. It is about something else altogether.

Did you have any teachers who influenced you as a poet?

Not as such, but I was always interested in poetics, in the logic of the development of a poetic text. For instance, when you read Mandelshtam you always think: Why does he use such metaphors. Or early Zabolotsky. How would you explain a "square of wheels". I developed a whole analytical system in my dissertation: "The Poetic Language of Nikolay Zabolotsky. An attempt at a reconstruction." I came to the conclusion that a poet reveals his world view through a system of tropes which, like a net, he lays over the world.

When did you start exploring Biblical themes?

Biblical themes, as far as I can recall, were always there in my poetry. It's just a matter of to what extent. In the last few years, everything I write is related in some way to Biblical themes.

Was it difficult to get published?

I never contacted any editor and didn't think about publication. My first appearance was in *Literary Georgia*, in 1981. There's a whole story behind that, but . . .

And then in the magazine *Talinn* and in 1989 three poems appeared in *Yunost*. In 1990, a large selection was published in *Znamia*. Then two books were published, with the help of Tatyana Voltskaya and Gennady Komarov.

What is the impulse for a poem? Some event, something you've read, music?

Very often, just the first line appears or a musical image, some intonation without any words at all. And then the words emerge. And sometimes it takes a month or more and the whole line will lie dormant and then suddenly a poem grows out of it. And the combination of words falls into a rhythmic pattern; religious philosophy and spiritual writing help me a lot. I find some kind of seed or bud there. I love dictionaries, especially Dal's, and encyclopaedias, especially Biblical ones.

Is a poem a conversation with God or with people about God?

In one of the Psalms there's a line: "Every breath praises the Lord." This is the real task of poetry. The real conversation with God is a prayer and not every poem is a prayer. There are poems where you want to tell people about God and about your own soul. Sometimes you experience enormous joy and happiness but you write tragic poetry, and then you realize that it was a false joy and happiness. You begin to understand your own poetry.

So, what do you write poetry for?

I think a human being writes for himself, moving freely in time. A conversation with God or with the readers about God? A very good question. In Russia now they write a lot about God with a capital letter, and some readers are annoyed. Why be annoyed? It is a tradition and not just a Russian one. Why should we reject it? Poetry always thought about or meditated upon the relationship between God and Man. And where other than in poetry will modern man encounter this theme? Look at the life of a modern man or child. He walks down a street and what does he see about him?

You are very pessimistic about contemporary young people.

It comes from my extensive experience in teaching! I've worked with students for the last twenty-five years. I can see how these eternal questions are much further from the young now than they were from me when I was that age.

Could you name any twentieth-century poets who are close to you?

I can think of Arseny Tarkovsky, Akhmatova without doubt. Akhmatova's life is absolutely unique for an artist. I read a lot about her, but I don't know about her religious life. I very much like the poetry of Inna Lisnianskaya, Olga Sedakova and Olesia Nikolaeva. In my life, my encounter and correspondence with Sedakova was very important.

And what about the younger generation?

I'm very fond of Irina Ermakova and Polina Barskova. Barskova was very young when she published her first collection.

Your poems, even those which express an admiration for the world, always sound a tragic note. Is that how you conceive your personal fate or is it a feature of Christian consciousness?

You know, Inga, the essence of the Christian view of the world is expressed in the words of the Apostle Paul: "Always rejoice, pray endlessly, give thanks for all." But this ideal is a long way off! Man cannot help noticing that people around him, those close to him, are suffering. That he is mortal. This alone is enough for him to regard life as tragic. How does man overcome this and what does he do with himself? That's the big question and it's what his creativity is all about. Man lives and man writes.

Excerpted from Voprosy Literatury, *March-April 2002*

[Translated by Daniel Weissbort]

Olga Khvostova

Translated by Richard McKane

Migration

Either this is temporary, or, alas, it's just deserts.

I'm talking about exile, when you're forgotten, small, fearful,

where you get the wet rope
from every bitch and judgmental arsehole;

the migration of the soul from the seething cauldron
of Asia, which will burn to ash,

the flight of the body from the ancient
Arabian plane trees to the Russian birches.

Quo vadis? Yes, across,
tearing with a crackle rag after rag.

Feel horror, complain, burn, southern woman,
you poor one, tender one, convict woman.

Let them hiss about the vulgar opposition and falsity,
go on, go further,

to get lost, get old, dissolve,
to go out there where wrongs are done,

to sing Alleluia to another nation!
Search for that place, where the forgiving ones indulge their whims

where difference does not
appear, similarity crawls in,
ah, send your superiority home!

Gather up your belongings, leave shelter,
go further, though they'll hammer you.

Day

Why do you, arriving at the sea, sit by the river
of time, washing your feet in it, crushing your brains,
turning your hooked nose up to the sky?
On many days there's not even a miaow or a bark.
Like this river, this water,
silence grows on you like a peasant's beard
and while a sea urchin or star floats up from the bottom,
you think
'Yeeees',
how voracious time is, the herd of bodies
has gone for a moment, disappeared
among the rowboats and schooners,
the Sirens sob on their last journey.
the dolphins catapult.

Mariya Kildibekova

Translated by Roy Fisher

Pizza's a populous island

Pizza's a populous island
where mushrooms like sad Mexicans live.
Set among crimson pepper squares
an onion surrenders. In the oven
cheese gets above itself, clutches
tomatoes, spreads all across the green
its sweet yawn.

Everybody was going on talking the same talk

Everybody was going on talking the same talk –
ageing, breakdown, the sense of failure –
so I dreamt myself a Celebrities' Liner
loaded with Perrier and Beaujolais and crowded
with opulent riff-raff. Maybe
the *Titanic*. Maybe.

There was Kennedy, Marilyn and – odd –
a very young Arthur Miller. They'd not
met? Stalin, sadly
smoking a pipe and singing
words I can't make out, Georgian most likely.

Complacent, in a coat cadged
from a Greek café proprietor,
Osip Mandelstam sits writing, notebook on his knee,
cellphone on his belt. A ring.
"Who? From Koktebel? No,
I don't remember. I don't owe you
anything. Cheers, then."
No sign of Nadezhda. Not far off
Blyumkin of the KGB
goes past, grinding his teeth.

In the crowd, Oskar Schindler, drunk,
and Hitler run into each other. That perfunctory

salute. "Hi, Oskar! How's it going? How's trade?" "Well.
I've brought a few really good workers. You'll see."

Some very amusing
kids, I just can't remember whose – except
the one on the left's the daughter of the Kuwaiti
ambassador to Russia. And a whole brood of lovely
curly-haired madcaps from Palestine: cast
any one of them as Judas. Zhabotinsky
the Zionist poet keeps an eye on the fun.

Cast him as Christ.

Bankers, ponces, hackers, traders,
Egyptian sheikhs with harems in tow,
a soldier and a businessman at the bar –
"Vietnam?" "Oh no: Chechnia. Stone dead."
Nureyev, Freddie Mercury in purple, all
hot and bothered, both of them.

Hippies without tickets on the liner,
a ballerina from Chile, transvestites,
and somebody sweet and familiar
in a crumpled velvet jacket; also
his friend, the puny, bespectacled
expert in kitsch, his nose
eternally in a book, and uttering
never a word about the sick twentieth century.
Grimaces, giggles – two girls! Heading
they don't know where, looking for free
tangerines, as far as they can get
from their sad mothers.

And I wander bewildered for a while, then suddenly
this character charges up – "Just
how long do you think you can just hang around?"
– smacks me across the face and hauls me
into the kitchen. And now I'm holding
a heavy tray: fruit, chocolate,
champagne, drugs, books.
– "Serve the guests!" And I'm crying
in total terror of Hitler.

Nina Kossman

Translated by the poet

*

A bomb said to a city:
"I'm falling."

The city asked:
"Whose side are you on?"

The bomb said:
"I take no sides. I'm falling."

The city said:
"Look around you."

The bomb said:
"Too late."

The city did not say anything.

*

I evoke you but you're asleep.
I awaken you but you don't hear.
Your sleeping breath reaches from here to there
In a majestic arc thrown from shore to shore.
When I'm near you, I'm near an ocean:
Voices, wave-like, break their will to the ear
Of the mind that only seems asleep.
The intelligence of sleep you've given me,
the goodness of thought that comes from
                    a deeper peace,
from under the static rippling the surface.

To still the surface, I evoke you.

*

See your image
steeped in my shadow

change, yet resemble you,
tighten its fingers
around my soul
faltering, yet staying,
disguised, yet true.
Fingers unwrithing,
limp on my gown:
seeing is finding
but upside down.

Eros and Chaos

Eros's castle
of seven red stones

(seven on either side,
seven behind)

built for the Soul:
she lives in the ring

of flame. Four
trees shot up

after the stones fell.
Four blue flames

leapt up,
their heads touching.

The duplicity of love,
daimon,

you, who obscure the imagery,
both divine and human,

Babel of our minds,
Chaos of our loves,

– I will step into the fire myself –
Tell

Phanes, the light-bearer,
Hermes, the envoy;

when the fiery ring vanished,
it disclosed

Eros and Chaos, brothers.

Cassandra to Agamemnon

I've warned you of the bloodbath:
a bath, with your blood in it, literally.
But there you go, blundering right in,
no hand of fate can stop you,
the hand that wants you dead.
And I, who will be killed soon after you,
why should I care – when, or whose hand.
So don't stall – go on, go in,
step blindly into your matron's trap,
hero of the great war, great murderer yourself.
Before I die, I'll see you flounder,
like a fat carp, in the fishnet of your queen.
But what is this water in my eyes?
My eyes that have seen my brothers killed,
My city razed, before and after.
Nobody weeps for you, therefore I will,
I, Cassandra.

                *

See how nothing
keeps out of Pluto's gorge,
silently drifts
towards it, waits, sinks
into the thickening dark,
the unreflecting water,
grave made of mud and stones:
this way – to hide lizard shadows,
that way – to rob of flesh.
Although mercy's an unprofitable profession,
save me from too much death.

In Her Own Words

"And the seventh angel poured out his vial into the air . . .
And there fell upon men a great hail out of heaven . . .
and I saw a woman sit upon a scarlet-coloured beast . . ."
Revelation, 16::17, 17:3 (King James Version)

The kings from the world over
heard me speak with the seventh seraph
saw me pour out his bowl on the briar
I poured air over the earth

my kings have forgotten my sorceries
my grief I meted out as air
my city rose out of ashes
the famine fell on the day of a fast

the kings the kings met me in mind
with the ravishing of the grain
with the thousand-mouthed black flame of air
the fire inside my face

*

When life was for me an intoxication with air,
you came and set a match to it and it burned
I mixed its ashes with glue
and built a thin but durable house
it stood firm for 17 years
I slept in it for 17 years
unaware of the passage of time.
But you knocked on the door
and the house blazed up
and I walked out
into the light of a brand-new love

Layer by Layer

Melt into his joy,
like a fruit in his mouth,

bear his fame
not as a near-misfortune

but as the future
your own cautious name

has awaited.
Swaddled for worship,

become the promise
of wings that took

an oath of staying
affixed to a mummy;

your bone-cage,
supple enough for liberty,

will suffer idolatry
at his hands,

while his thought
is there to unpeel you,

like a rare fruit,
layer by layer,

until you wither into
a semblance of yourself,

a mere phantom.

Backward Sound

I'm a backward
sound of myself.
I twist, I turn

through sheer virulence
of habit sleep
that measures me in bursts

of agony, hoary and private.
I ask, I bless.
I speak the raw material of memory;

only flowers here still recall the dead.
I am a green begonia.
I am a red

petal on the stem of morning.
I am, I am . . .
Black sweetness,

save me from these shattered
words, repetitive illusions.
I am dark, uncountable.

I am the meaning of a syllable
the ancients said and dropped.
I am the one the clouds dream of

when their vapour eyes are shut.
The weeping wall, the nakedness of heart . . .
Disinterestedness, now let me go.

You said: it's guaranteed –
the backward glance, the exit,
the twisting back, back, back . . .

Now let me go, beauty grass.
Your kisses pain me
like all that dies pains that which doesn't.

I am the eye-nerve of your marriage,
grassy sky.
I bless, I bless.

I am a friend to all that breathes.
I beg you: do breathe me in;
and let me disappear in you:

Forever, earth.
Forever, sky.

Irina Kovaleva

Translated by Daniel Weissbort

I can still make you out

I can still make you out
through the glass fragment of days,
but as if the candle were being taken away
and the radiance dimming, dimming.

I still see the dazzle, as of wingbeat or eyelid,
and the motley dark.
I remember that gasping fright
at your name.

But there, behind the dream's heavy drapes,
behind the window's sash,
where earlier there'd been bustle, a running about,
a rustle and in general much commotion,
there was now silence

and a void. The drift
of clock hands stopped, ended.
Light snow falls indifferently
from void into void.

[1997]

And there was beauty

. . . And there was beauty –
A hem, flying up – above a slender foot,
Over the greyish timber of the bridge.

Morover there was love for apples. Each fruit
Was divided into two but he,
Recalling the story, with a tilt of the head, declined
The apple. The hand . . .

His wings are buoyant,
Dazzling, like flickering

tongues of flame – burning heat –
But when he goes – the heart,
Which was like a star,
Stays empty.

A word, uttered by your voice,
Became golden
And round, goldenly translucent, ripe
In the radiant air, golden and white,
And, immutable, it remains whole.

This, of course, is not the garden, but close enough.
And a branch, glancing out of the garden,
Is reflected in it
Like light, falling into a pool.

[1999]

Ella Krylova

Translated by Yuri Drobyshev and Carol Rumens

The Pilgrims

Over the earth they come,
alpha-rays scorching them,
beta-rays scorching them,
gamma-rays scorching them,
passing Mecca and Rome,
passing Jerusalem,
ruins in front of them, ruins
behind them: the pilgrims.

Over the mountains they come;
the sea's like dry land to them:
they suffer no harm, they succumb
to no plague, no famine.

They all have coins on their eyes,
and rockets in their hands,
and floppy discs in their minds.
They travel over the planet,
the round and empty planet,
though they're not on earth any more,
and there's no-one on earth any more,
and there isn't an earth, any way,
any more.

Cornflowers

Cornflowers, cornflowers,
little blue-eyed beacons,
little land-sailors,
they say you're only weeds,
my poor *vasil'ki*.

Uselessly lovely ones,
whose loss is the farmer's gain,
my poems, perhaps, are the same
– weeds like you, my cornflowers,

whose modest good looks do not suit
the teeming oatfields
that fill the masses: maybe, at harvest-time,
pitiless God will tear out every root
– mine and the cornflowers'.

Who, then, created me,
gave me a dress of sky,
brought turquoise water for my thirst,
fed me at sunshine's breast?
Who whispered lines of verse,
came to me in a trance,
and wrapped me against the cold
in swansdown whiteness?

I stand above the cornflower sea
of that island-basilisk
which sheltered but never housed me,
rooted into my flesh but never caressed me,
vasil'ki-blue Vasil'evskii:
I repeat – Who are You? Who am I?

Marina Kudimova

Translated by Catriona Kelly

*

Prison, *zona*, the camps, Taldái-Kustanái, and the low road,
Let sparks fly up as my soul squeals into a bend.
May my heart be smelted in patience's slow-burning furnace,
Snatch me and raise me – heave ho! – but gently, on high.
Let the low road batter me, dislocate me,
And catch up my free-floating angst in a long prison train
To Vologda. Howls lie thin on our mouths like tin-plate.
Shoot to kill if we try to escape, abuse us, and then release us:
These are a masochist's joys, the feathery whine
Of branches of birch in a steam-bath, coming down on your thigh.
What I see is the sapping of wills; but when pain's nearly stifling
Your wrist turns into a perch for a gold-finch, a cross-bill,
A kingfisher, even. If you fly, you don't have to sing.
See the one bird, silently moving her interlaced beak-halves
Or the second, giving his tinselly, gurgling laugh,
The other's a humble bird, won't cry out if you snare him:
He'll sing on and on, quite true, not jibbing at all,
A ballad of life in jail to excite and delight you.
As we ride the low road, the convict road to the *zona*,
The rails move closer, apart. They flank us, encircle like swordsmen
In a Roman legion: a stale old optical trick.
The light burns into our eyes like flares on the front line
And shadows fall on the windows like masking tape
To hold in the glass if it goes. So bring out the cards!
Let's get back the sum that we lost playing stoss with the century,
We were just one point to the bad, or a player was short.
Let's finish the round, and hey, for Vologda say I!

*

The pleated strata of air,
The fir-branches crimped like wheel tracks,
And October standing by
Saffron and bald, like a Buddhist;
A fancy foreign car
From nowhere, no-man's land,

Has stamped its designer soles
Over the slant stripes of grass.

How short the lease,
How quickly the russet speeds by,
If this crumbling tentative track
Will be whited out come All Saints.
Soon winter will hobble close,
Putting out its dreary dust-sheets.
So burn while you can, October,
Like puerperal fever, melting the brain.

Inna Kulishova

Translated by Daniel Weissbort

Till now

Till now
I've not been able to imagine
what it's like to long for water
in a desert,
and striving
to make flour out of the sands.
Evidently,
it's worth surviving
so as to experience something other than writing.

[October, 1991]

Total darkness

Total darkness.
The light's off in the kitchen,
and people will go into the room.
The window shut,
they turn on the tele, where a poet
(much loved) says we're all going to die
and yet
something will remain, just a trace.
Although it was not he, no way,
not he, who said this. Straight off,
all's forgotten. But
that doesn't matter. The main thing, a trace
will remain. And to appreciate
this is not worth the days
passing so swiftly, the years, so long ago.
And it's not even worth
vanity of vanities.
The main thing is the trace.
That it's evening, dark. That it's late.

[November, 1991]

Yuliya Kunina

Translated by Richard McKane

Inconsistent Self Portrait

I am half Russian, 30, almost got my MA,
1 metre 67, on the list and registered,
fragments of an encyclopaedia, excerpts from a dictionary,
three languages, to synopsise.
Here are my eyes: people say they're beautiful.
Here is my long nose.
My lips are plum-coloured, or bilberry coloured, or
    lipsticked,
whatever.
Here is my profile: people say it's Nubian,
or perhaps Jewish, or really Russian,
the devil knows what the devil's mixed together.
Here is my thieving magpie's habit.
Here is my decisive chin,
although what is it decisive about?
Here are my shoulders – shoulder blades protruding. – I like to
compare them to Natasha's, but they are more like a bird's:
you can squeeze it in your fist, just fluff and feathers.
The journey down, of course, conceals temptations.
I am made out of differing and different
old girls and interesting ladies,
Renoir women and dubious personages,
suffragettes and faithful wives, and these, whom I don't know
who were humiliated in the prefeminist era.

But this is, so to speak, bragging, or rather a hide,
pimply frog skin,
loved by Jew and fool
which I am telling you about.

And so, I crawl, smouldering in ash,
like a serpent or tortoise,
commanding the thunder with my mind.

Evgeniya Lavut

Translated by Yuri Drobyshev and Carol Rumens

About Love

Your hat smelt of dead moths. Your flabby fingers
Betrayed that vulgar shopkeeping hook.
To want to touch your absence of a torso
With my own hands, seemed a kind of joke.

But when my life lacked you my life lacked bread,
Though in your presence food grew rancid, cold,
As if an angel stretched the sky to spread
His knees apart, and pissed into my world.

In the body of the town I'm a pupil

In the body of the town I'm a pupil.
I wander along its entrails,
with my pack, at an easy pace
from place to place.

I know like my own five fingers
where things are – the smelly things,
the flowing things, where the tramps
get moved on, where they linger.

In the body of the town I love to settle
like pubic lice in trousers.
In the body of the town I'm a monk
for whom there's nowhere to kneel

and as long as the place is possessed
by its crazy thunder-storm,
I'll wander round, an alien
microscopic life-form,

leaving a stubborn trace:
I gasp, grow speechless, go grey.
I'm sorry I don't belong
– but my vision is my own.

Elena Lazutkina

Translated by Robert Reid

The wind's mane

The wind's mane
in the blue pasture.
Its muzzle in the skybald horse's eye.
And with smoke over the barns
how will I find my dream book?

I stand and inspect the phenomena drawn up

I stand and inspect the phenomena drawn up,
as once Dubrovsky stood,
debating – to kill or not to kill
the next squire on his list.

Ruined so many romances

Ruined so many romances,
destroyed so many smiles,
wasted an ocean of time, then disappeared

how can he be
Chinese?

Inna Lisnianskaya

Translated by Ruth Fainlight

Ode to the Computer

For you, little friend,
I gave thousands of greenbacks
and made a green salad
of my stanzas' last lines.

On the pithy meat of reason
with rhyme as trimmings,
from the last provisions
you and I shall feast.

What do I care about money,
fame and magical pageants?
You are the last distraction
of my century.

Echo, mirror, envoy,
ghost and double,
why have you come to trouble
my last days?

Between hope and failure

Between hope and failure –
and trees with foam on their lips –
the bed remembered how the night passed.

The notebook recollected how the day passed,
how life passed: snow and fallen petals.
How death passes, dust and ashes will not forget.

Like the earth turning, I creak, and dream

Like the earth turning, I creak, and dream
of a return to the Garden of Eden

where reptiles, people, birds and beasts,
as I recall, were always glad to meet.

Triptych of Reflection

1

Your whole life is a parallelogram
without bisectors.
A superannuated schoolboy
brought you daffodils,

and spring-flower reveries
revived in you.
You smoke, not changing position
in an official armchair.

The lime-tree breathes its bribe of honey
into existence through a hotel window
like the venom of fame
– or a life without limits.

2

I am the reflection of every mirror-
like, living and unliving,
animate and inanimate thing:
brooks and basin-taps,
paradisal wings and infernal
polished relics.

I reflect like the lid of a grand piano,
like a negative,
and my universal sorrows
scarcely belong to me.
They are only a reflected myth.

In this there would be no drama
if I could crawl out
of the annular iambic pit
where there are no reverses
or angles, and amalgams of Spring
blur the surface of the glass.

3
How can one know
who is reflected into the world
and if this reflects well or badly
into your heart.

Try hard not to look
at anything that shines:
not foil nor tin nor copper,
not even into the mirror

hanging here, where life
exists like a heart grown quiet,
where all my verses
Come now to die.

Sveta Litvak

Translated by Daniel Weissbort

Shadows of the plane tree leaves

Shadows of the plane tree leaves
along the wall of stone
play like a close-up
of red and blue barrels.

They move the shutters aslant,
opening just a chink,
as if a crooked scythe
had brushed against the stone.

A spurt of tiny drops
leapt clean over the fence,
gets entangled, and misses
the deftly scurrying rakes,

aimed at a striped awning.
On the slope, mould and ivy
and on the neighbours' side,
children playing quietly.

What they're after is trout
or feeding the little donkey.
Bird on the old fir tree,
a weathercock on a pole,

a child's broken chair.
About to drop from above,
a roof tile, cracked and loose
has missed its chance to do harm.

A lizard has frozen there,
the sun in a circle turns,
the little girl might have fallen,
had the mother not grabbed her arm.

I catch the smell of beans

I catch the smell of beans
Sit silently in a chair
I'd like to add some salt
I'd like to cook some noodles

I'd like to attend a meeting
The one in the *Mutualité*
O, take away from me
What's standing there on the stove

I've already learnt how
To listen to Maurice Thorez
To look at Fernand Léger –
to scrub spuds and slice them up

Proudly to demonstrate
With a little bag and wearing a wig
I was born a foreigner
In Russia in my own small town

A thread of scattered beads
A bow that's untied itself
It's not just a question of taste
But brains and talent as well

Weakly the flame of the burner
Flares up and dies away
The urchin's a pain
Skittish my festive steed

Olga Martynova

Translated by Elaine Feinstein

What does the river know of its own bed

> *At the heart of this black world*
> *Covered by endless gardens –*
> *Look: at one unopened morning*
> *Rose, and this, shut in the evening.*

What does the river know of its own bed,
Or the spider of the web?

What does a canvas know of a painting?

Who knows what anyone understands or needs?
In this dark abyss, everything
is frightening and gentle at once.

What does the backing cloth know about silk?

We are in a dark, hidden
hollow full of songs, moans, whistling
and the click of fingers.

Listen.

Night unwraps the true stuff of the world

Night unwraps the true stuff of the world:
Poorly clothed houses, shadows in a back street,
Lorries and limetrees on the boulevardes –
All sleep under the rain; their black and white
Faces show bewildered discontent. What still holds
Of their comfortable life? Is this new look
Deception or reality? Electric words
Suddenly flash their alphabet. Night
Moves, lit only by itself. And until
The light of early morning, you can
Repeat the letters of the night-time world.
Now, a sign flashes in a passing headlight,

Then somebody's whisper, menacing footsteps,
God knows what else – as the black scene shines.
Day clothes this nakedness and
Hides the evidence of it within our flesh.
Language turns into babble, and then,
Sitting on a bench in the boulevard
You try helplessly to remember what remains
Once night has gone, more than
A worn-out negative of how things are
Under the heels of the rain.

Larisa Miller

Translated by Richard McKane

The light cross of lonely strolls

The light cross of lonely strolls
O. Mandelstam
I write poems, what's more in Russian
and I don't want any other work load,
I don't want any other job.
Honestly I don't want to shoulder
any other enterprise.
The time of the year involves me,
the moment of risk, the hour of the soul . . .
I sharpen my pencils with them.
Pencils. Not knife or teeth.
The silver trumpets sing
in the frail neighbouring forest
where I will carry my usual cross
of lyric-making strolls.
Each backstreet is full
of the torment of the soul and yearning
for feminine and masculine rhymes.

[1993]

Let's fill in the form: date of birth

Let's fill in the form: date of birth –
that's the start of the delusion,
the start of delirium or dream . . .
The problem is clear, it seems.
And in the box below the date
we give our address and phone number;
on the left – our sex, lower on the right
we give our nationality,
then the signature. Well, is life clearer
now and how to manage it?

[1995]

The heavens are playing with the earth

The heavens are playing with the earth,
teasing, threatening a landslide,
they threaten to set fire
to the dwellings and forests – in a fantastic fire.
But on a dull day they hang again
over this mortal world
like a grey, humble shroud
and there's no soothing the tears of the heavens.

Tatyana Milova

Translated by Robert Reid

Sometimes, not often, its true

Sometimes, not often, its true,
    an old man comes in on the mail coach
    Under the small town's principal arch
And, reclining against the dashboard, the driver smokes and reads
      his paper
    But a harp is concealed in his bosom;
The inn is closing up, the church is quite silent, the shopkeeper won't sell
      his kerosene
    Nor anything else besides.
The old man adjusts his dickey-bow, his hanky traps a sneeze, his pocket
      yields a harpsichord
    Which he puts together to the sound of trumpets.
The distant rumble of a tuning-fork, storm-like disturbs our eternal
      repose
    The air of which is windless and bitter;
The last flies are trooping, and gather on the horse's backside and a
      flourish of its tail accidentally
    Sounds the triangle under the shaft-bow;
In melodious embrace all intertwine: reverberating bronze and
      horsehair, and a noble cedar
    Sawn up out of eyeshot;
And we, stuck to the tarmac and barely awake, still manage to listen to
      the orchestra
    Beneath our unsetting sun.
And this is the only reason behind all that we do in our small forgotten
      town,
    Its forgotten houses and little cinemas;
And the children run after the coach empty-handed, or almost – with a
      doughnut if they're lucky
    Legs dappled with iodine;
Carelessly clad, outlandishly red of face, hair tousled beyond all combing,
    Or parting or ribboning, they run . . .
. . . To where there's hope of loving one another, of flying, aching,
      vanishing away
    To the thunder of their drums.

. . . I've overslept my stop . . . the train will spit me out . . .
The halt is deserted. I'll panic, that's for sure.
The wind is wet and drives me from the platform
And tears and tousles me until I speak.

Wind, if I'm a sail, then where's my boat?
If I'm a treetop, wind, show me my roots.
What am I to you? I'm asking calmly, nicely.
Distant clanking. Buckets? . . . Distant neighing. Horses? . . .

'Silly' comes the whisper nice and calm,
'We know your niceness and we know your fables
But what are you to me? – a Chinese lantern or a sparkler.
If I can, I'll huff and puff – you'll gutter and go out.'

Wind, you're master here. And I'm the guest and will be silent.
Ruined tractor. Gravel pit. Rusting stove-pipes.
The smell of the river sticks in my throat like a bone.
You're master here. It's hard to deny.

The train has come and I am leaving.
God Save the Wind! The houses echo and the fields are bare.
I'm strange to them and whether it's my fault's
Too late to say. There's nowhere for me here . . . no word for me here.

Elizaveta Mnatskanova

Translated by Gerald Janecek

Note by Gerald Janecek: *The poem here presented is representative of Mnatskanova's musical approach to writing, involving numerous variations on a set of themes. The words grow from one another and circle or spiral back again in an obsessively intense way with new thoughts and verbal associations added.*

Childhood Adolescence Solitude Youth Vale of Life Freshness Death

The Description of a Life without Death

Twelve short Recollections

Recollection No. 1
And he recalled a tree, a maple, in the rays of the long sun and on the corner of a street half-forgotten in tears.

Recollection No. 2
And he recalled a tree: a maple in the rays of the lengthy sun on the corner of a forgotten street, in tears.

Recollection No. 3
And he recalled: a maple tree in the meadows of a distant sun, in the rays of a vale of light, in the candles of a lengthy sun.

Recollection No. 4
On the corner of a street half-buried in tracks he remembered a maple tree. On the corner of a distant light-world in the meadows of the sun.

Recollection No. 5
On the street corner he remembered a maple tree. He remembered it long, lengthily, eternally. He remembered it outside the window: it called, nodded, laughed, gladdened. Outside the nursery window. He remembered in the tears of the distant sun. He remembered, recalled, called, would call lengthily, eternally.
Through the leafage it was green, draughty.

Recollection No. 6

Through the leafage it was draughty, could be seen lengthily, could be seen long: through the leafage. He remembered long, lengthily, marvellously, long ago he remembered, far away, farther and farther. Outside the window. The window of childhood, farther and longer. The window glows, glows with sun on sun, in the rays of the long sun, in the tears of the valley sun. In the tracks: a shadow in the rays of the yellow sun, tracks of shadow in the rays, the tracks of evening fall on the sidewalk in rays. Lengthily in the rays they fall, eternally. Ah, mama, mama dear, dead mama, how dear! how dead! how lengthily in the rays, how long in the rays I recall, she calls eternally! And the shadow, a long shadow, a dead, lengthy shadow of evening falls in the rays. Your shadow, mama, an endlessly long dead lengthy shadow in the shadow of a long dead tree. It dies long, eternally.

Recollection No. 7

That life was long, long without death. And the tree on the corner stood lengthily, stood long, nodded, gladdened. A maple tree, a long tree without death.

Recollection No. 8

But once it also had a love in life once. Once, long, at one time. It also had a love at one time. Long it was, lengthy, long ago, at one time. That love was in winter, lengthily in winter. And the sun glowed. With an evening eternal light the sun glowed on the window, on the glass, on the window of glass, on the glass of the window it glowed.

On the window of glass it ignited, turned red, went out without a word. And there also was love.

Recollection No. 9

Outside the window of childhood of the room he remembered long marvellously remembered the maple tree: the tree bowed, it bowed, straightened out, stood, remembered. The tree called, recalled. And he recalled the tree, in the rays, in the fields of the marvellous valley sun. The tree bloomed, the children bloomed, played in the meadows. Whose children? He forgot. He didn't remember.

Recollection No. 10

And the candles once glowed. With the golden fire of an eternal sun. On the window of childhood they shone, went out without a word. Also love. For he also had a love in childhood at one time. The window glowed with the winter sun, turned red, farther and farther. Long was that love, an evening one, eternal. And the window flamed and burned with an evening, eternal light. An eternal light.

Recollection No. 11

Long was that life, a long life: without death. And the tree the endless tree without death: on the corner of the sun. So they both stood there without death. And the shadow. The lengthy, evening, eternal shadow. A shadow in the shadow of the tree. And both shadows in the shadow of mourning, the sidewalk in shadow. Ah, mama, your lengthy, long shadow in the mourning lies long, runs long, straightens out. The tree straightens out, the tree in the sun, glows, is green, trembles. And a track. On the sidewalk. A mourning track. And in the tears of a forgotten street. Of a street forgotten by someone in tears.

Recollection No. 12

Long was that light-world: the lengthy sun. The evening shadows fall in the shadows endlessly. And they run back and forth, they run endlessly: a lengthy shadow, long, endless is that shadow. In the irretrievable shadows.

And he recalled a maple tree or cedar cypress or bush or tree on the corner of a street someone could not forget.

[Vienna, 24-26 March 1978]

Yunna Morits

Translated by Daniel Weissbort

Face

I would like, my father said,
to see your face once more!
Before me a blind man sat,
with pupils blueing over.
My father said: Understand,
there are clouds before my eyes.
With my lips and with my hands,
I want to see your face.

He reached into the air
his sun-browned arms and hands.
Anticipation, fear
played round his smiling mouth.
But my spirit would not submit!
The wild beast in me rose up.
I slammed the door. I fled!

. . . Adrift from poplar trees,
the fluff clung to my face,
in the lilac I sank my head.
My father, it must be said,
was out of luck that day!
Now, turning to the wall,
he closed his sightless eyes,
and the visions standing there
made the tears start in mine.

Leaves, grass, grit I rubbed
into my cheeks, my brow.
Things, it must be said,
were not going father's way!
It was in a secret place
I hid my love, as such –
Old sir, this is my face,
this lake. Touch!

A Memory

They threw the children
from the burning train
out onto the grass.
I slithered and swam
in a bloody trench
of bone, gristle, guts.

The pilot who flew overhead,
this scion of the brownshirt blight,
grinned like an invalid,
finally out of his mind.
He hovered in his airborne cage,
pressed to the cockpit glass.
I saw the swastika on his arm,
the sweat on his brow, the rage.

And I saw, too, the red circle
of the locomotive's wheel.
And fear robbed me
of the strength to exclude
everything I had seen'–
because the engine was motionless,
yet the blood-red fumes
rose from the wheels, turning still,
and the iron lever groaned –
it was like an arm, crooked at the elbow,
torn from the trunk it served,
to keep the locomotive's wheels
posthumously going round!

This was in the fifth year of my life.
The Good Lord rescued me
for the long way that lay ahead . . .
But in my blood, like mercury,
is the dread that entered my flesh!
And now, in the moon's view, as I sleep,
so wildly do I lament
that the very wall where the memory
is stored streams with tears.

On the Other Side of the Wall

He said I love someone else.
Don't cuddle up to me, dear.
I am in her clutches now,
She is going to be my wife.
And with her I shall leave this place,
So I do not have to see,
dear Lyuda, how each day,
You take my child to the creche.
As my new bride has commanded,
I shall cut myself off from you,
So my heart should not grieve overmuch,
Or try to find a way back.

She whispered: Dearie, Don't you fret!
Get up and pour us some wine.
My heart is weary of you,
You needn't feel sorry for me.
Nor is it in my power
To make you do anything, friend.
Your fancy and your loving's
As firm as the passing snow.
And it bores me, to tell the truth,
Means nothing at all to me.
I'd much rather this goodbye now,
Than to purr like a cat on heat!

He said:
Here's to you, then!
Good health and good luck as well!
And a fifty-rouble bill
He laid by the child's sleeping head.
And, like a wild creature, Lyudmila yawned
Gnawed through the invisible strand,
And dozed for a thousand years
Before washing down the porch.

Crow

A crow came to our house one time
to our window for its pittance.
Crown, alas, does not rhyme
With Crow, His Sombre Indigence.

This shininess and braggadocio,
Awful voice and effigy,
Is nothing but a hungry crowdom,
which has survived three centuries.

Three hundred years to fight for food,
Three hundred years to snatch and grab –
What can one do but caw, my friends,
and out of boredom go quite mad!

Perhaps the very crow that does
its thieving from your board,
knew Sir Isaac Newton once
when it was a fledgling bird.

But it does not earn its keep
By granting sundry interviews –
The crow knows what is good for it,
as it makes huge eyes at you!

Between Scylla and Charybdis

*To be a woman poet in Russia is harder than
to be a male poet: the unit of female power
in Russian poetry is one akhmatsvet*

With a rattle we are walking
Round the cradle, flowering, fading.
Between the Arctic and Turkmenia,
Between the Polish lands and China.

With a deep sob we abandon
Clouds above the Lycée puddle –
Between Oedipus and Lear,
Between Julius and Brutus.

We keep our reason healthy,
Dim the light above the folio,
Make a crib for naked phrases,
Between Pushkin and Alighieri.

Highlighting the reprises,
We find a vast connection
Between Blok and Persian Hafiz,
Between the Muse and Cassandra.

And breathing, hyperborean,
We sail through, caravel-like,
Between Zhenya and Andrei,
Between Bella and Novella.

But like a gory bullfight,
The ancient path is threatening,
Between Scylla and Charybdis,
Between Anna and Marina.

Between Scylla and Charybdis,
Between Anna and Marina,
He whom the gulf has swallowed
Was spat out by it likewise.

Consequence became a cause.
I'll explain this odd idea:
He whom Marina swallowed,
Was spat out then by Anna.

In all our born days, never
Did we command the Golden Mean –
Between Anna and Marina,
Between the Polish lands and China.

And above our native chasm –
Who knows how! – look, we are flying
Between Anna and Marina,
Between the Polish lands and China.

Note: 'Akhmatsvet', a compound, derived from the names of Anna Akhmatova
(the sound "akh" recalls the outbreath) (1889-1966) and of Marina Tsvetaeva
(1892-1941).Zhenya, Andrei, Bella, Novella are Evgeny (Zhenia) Yevtushenko (b. 1933),
Andrei Voznesnesky (b. 1933), Bella Akhmadulina (b. 1937) and Novella Matveeva
(b. 1934), popular public poets of the generation that includes Morits.

Excerpts from an Interview with Yunna Morits

by Daniel Weissbort

Your father, you said, went blind.

He went blind, but gradually. When I was seven years old my father was beginning to lose his sight. He wore glasses. By the time I turned sixteen, he was blind. What makes it even harder is that I've similar eyes to my father. I look at how my father was and sometimes, when nobody's there, I shut my eyes and try to see what my father saw as he was walking. I try to walk with my eyes shut. [. . .] My father washed his hands frequently, because they were his eyes. I do the same. I cannot bear long fingernails, because if the nails are long I can't feel things properly. I have to feel exactly [. . .]

Pianists keep their fingernails short.

And when I came to your country, your city [*not strictly mine, but the interview took place in Iowa City, USA!*] I tried to touch all the simple natural objects, because my sense of touch is keen.

Do you relate this to poetry?

Yes, of course.

Touching with sound?

It is very important. Sometimes I can touch things through my drawings.

I was struck by that image of your father, in the poem, where you describe his reaching out to touch you and your running away from him. [. . .]

We have a proverb, that the eyes are afraid but the hands are not. When a dead man or woman, in our folk tales, comes out of the grave and moves in your direction, you must turn, face them, and then they vanish. Because when you can touch something, you are no longer afraid of it [. . .] I believe that when people are dead, they have no hands, no legs, no heads, but they can still touch, move, feel. Because we have a strong tactile memory. Through memory we can touch without hands, move without legs, understand without heads [. . .]

What did your mother do?

My mother was very well educated. But she couldn't have a job, because she had to help my father. So, my mother and father were like a single organism, because they both went to father's work. Without mother father couldn't do a thing.

What did it mean being a Jew, having Jewish parents?

From childhood I knew I had to be better than others, cleaner, more honest . . . Because many believe not only that the Jews killed Christ but that they drank the blood of Christian children, and so forth. Also that Jews dream only of making lots of money. So, I knew I had to find a different image for myself, a different kind of profession. I was very talented at drawing . . . But I chose literature. My parents were not thrilled. I chose literature because I *knew* it wouldn't bring me riches; I also knew it *would* bring me many troubles! A typical Jewish kind of choice!

Did you have any sort of Jewish education?

None. We couldn't speak the Jewish language, celebrate Jewish holidays. And we couldn't have friends among Jewish immigrants. I was maybe five years old when I already knew about this, because of the war with fascism. I knew that the fascists were liquidating the Jews. I knew about all that [. . .]

During the war you left Kiev.

We were evacuated from Kiev very late in the day, because the Nazis moved so quickly.

In one of your poems there's a description of how the train you were on was bombed. Was that when you were leaving Kiev?

Yes, it's a true picture from childhood. It was when we were leaving Kiev, my sister, my mother and myself. And after this, well, our mother was taken ill and removed from the train. Three weeks later she managed to find me and my sister. I was four. My sister was fifteen [. . .]
    When my father was arrested, my sister understood everything, because at school some of the children and teachers told her she was the daughter of an "enemy of the people". But I didn't understand, because I was only a little child [. . .] My mother didn't tell me my father was in prison, because she thought children couldn't understand such things

[. . .] I knew about my father being in prison only after Stalin's death, in 1953.

How long was he there?

Two years. And after that he got work, but was under constant supervision.

I suppose you have a vivid memory of Stalin's death. Were you in Moscow at the time?

No, I was in Kiev. And I didn't properly understand what was going on. So many people I loved were upset, wept, and wondered what would happen to us, as if without Stalin there could be no country! [. . .] Only in 1956, when Khruschev began to reveal some of the truths about the Stalinist oppression . . . And then I got to meet some of the people who returned from the camps [. . .]

So, you returned to Kiev after the war, and then went to the Gorky Institute in Moscow to study literature?

Because, although I wanted to study at Kiev University, they said I had no talent for literature and was not admissible to the Slavic Department. I went to evening classes instead.

When did you start writing poetry?

I wrote my first poem at the age of five [. . .] My mother knew lots of poets and recited poems to me from memory. So, I loved poems through my mother's voice – she read beautifully. I loved poems before I loved books, because there were no books around during the war, and after the war we couldn't afford them . . .

You have to understand. [. . .] We had one room, for mother, father, sister and me. And there were three beds, one for my sister, one for father, and one for mother and me. So, I slept with my mother in one bed until I was nineteen. And it was only when I came to Moscow, to the Literary Institute that, for the first time in my life I had my own bed.

Did you have your own room?

No room of my own! I shared with eight other women! But I did have my own bed, for the very first time. My sister was studying architecture and worked on her projects in the evenings. [. . .] I had to stay outside, in the street, because when I walked around in the room, my sister couldn't be accurate, since the room shook. [...] Winter, summer, rain or snow. Sometimes I had to be in the street in the middle of the night. [...]

So, I would sleep in the daytime in the city park, when the sun was shining. And when I began travelling to the Arctic region, it wasn't so hard for me, because I'd known a hard outdoor life before! *[Morits lived for some time in the Archangel region; an early book of poems was about life in that harsh environment]*.

I was meaning to ask you about that, because I first came across your poems, in the mid Sixties, in a book called Mys Zhelaniya, *which was set in the far north.*

Well, I was so young then that I was not really able properly to convey what I experienced. Still, I understood something about the place, a great sadness. I witnessed such difficult relations between the people who lived in the Arctic. [...] There were lots of tiny islands and of very lonely people. Three or five to an island, in small houses, with half an hour of daylight. It's very hard on people's nerves. So much so that sometimes they even killed each other! When I saw what this life was like, I realized that Moscow wasn't the centre of the universe, that it was a very special place in which people had it easy. In the Arctic I met lots of young people, boys and girls, without parents, moneyless. They'd come there to make money, hoping afterwards to be able to get themselves a house, maybe a higher education. But in the Arctic they drank a lot, and then they were incapable of any higher education. They took the money and went south, to the Black Sea, for two months in the Summer, and spent it all, and then returned to the Arctic. [...]

What was the native population like?

[...] These people don't know anything about any historical process. They don't know there was a Revolution. They don't know who the leaders are [...] They are far removed from all these problems.

So, probably their life hasn't altered much. The Revolution hasn't made much difference.

[...] All that's to be seen there is snow. And very few flowers. All the same, I have to say, there are some beautiful flowers, wonderful little flowers, in the snow. Nothing like it in Moscow. [...]

How long did you spend in the North?

Maybe five months in all. I worked in the library, on the ship. Sometimes

I helped with the cooking. [. . .]

How about literary influences? Who were you reading?

Lermontov . . .

I suppose, then, that when your mother read to you, she read the classical authors?

Yes, but modern classics as well. Maybe even some of the decadents, like Nadson . . .

Blok?

Blok. And Pushkin, of course, Tyutchev . . . Mother knew lots of poets. She was very artistic as well and only had to observe someone for a minute to be able to give you a picture of that person, a sort of instant portrait. My mother showed me what I was like! I could see myself, like in a mirror. She was my mirror. [. . .]

Did you, for instance, know a poet like Gumilev? [Nikolay Gumilev (1886-1921), husband at one time of Anna Akhmatova, arrested and shot for alleged involvement in an anti-Soviet plot.] Did people know about him, or was he simply forgotten?

No, I heard about Gumilev and was able to read some poems by him, when I was about sixteen. But I first read Pasternak only when I was nineteen.

You describe Zabolotsky. [Nikolay Zabolotsky (1903-1958), major Russian poet and translator. He was arrested and spent many years in a Far Eastern gulag. I was interested in him, having myself translated his poetry for some thirty years.] There is that poem of yours in which you talk about your "teachers". And you say at the end that he, Zabolotsky, was like a wall behind you.

He read some of my poems and told me that with a talent like mine I would not be able to make a normal living. He said that I should take up translation and he also passed on to me some of the secrets of translation.

Such as? And when was this?

In 1956. I didn't meet with Zabolotsky so often – maybe ten times in all. But he told me about translation. [. . .] For instance, that you can translate with the help of a *podstrochnik* (ad-verbum version) without knowing the language and that this is not necessarily a bad thing. You can take a dictionary and read, and get a sense of the poetic lexicon, and also consult books on the source culture. He told me that people may know a language wonderfully well, but still not be able to translate from it. And he also told me that I should not translate word for word, line by line, but look inside the language and the thought. If, for instance, there is a significant word or image, object in line seven, it's no crime to transpose it to line eight. He told me, too, that if I encountered a word that was specific to the culture, I might embody in the translation an explanation. [. . .] You can change the order of the lines too. When you translate word for word, it is a false translation, because you inevitably lose the spirit. I'd always assumed that you had to translate line by line.

Pasternak was a great translator, they say. Did you discuss translation with him?

Yes. Pasternak and Zabolotsky were accused of straying from the original. They translated not from the original text, but from literal versions.

What was Zabolotsky like as a man?

He was very ill when I met him, after the camps. The one who paid most attention to my poetry was Arseny Tarkovsky. [*A well known poet, father of the celebrated film-maker.*] He took me into his home when I was nineteen. Akhmatova listened to me. She told me my poems were good, but very hard, stiff. She tried to make them softer, telling me: "Well, you're so hard, it's impossible for you to make it softer!" The psychology of young people is such that they always want to do the opposite of what you suggest! She helped me to find a style. When young people come to me for advice, I use the same trick. [. . .]

Any comment on your poem 'Crow'?

The crow is a very common bird in our country, because we have filthy streets. Winter and summer crows are cawing. And they watch us on our balconies. That rhyme I have, "korona-Vorona" [literally: "crown-crow"] can't really be translated. You see, when I write, I use good rich rhymes, but the crow is poor, poor and black, so that the rhyme too is, as it were, poor! You can change it, if you like [. . .] "Voronstva" [*I translate it as "crowdom"*] is a neologism. Do what you like with it. There's that novella by Pushkin, 'The Captain's Daughter'. In it a crow lives for three hundred years. Of course, the poem is about my life and that of my friends. For three hundred years we had to fight for food and so forth. It is impossible to survive without crime, impossible without going crazy too [. . .]

So, the poem is about you and . . .

Yes! And maybe this bird really did meet Newton and . . . Of course, it is also about you! [. . .]

And there's that poem you wrote about a favourite teacher?

We kids loved her so much, no man could possibly ever love her as much, and so she remained alone. She never married, because we loved her too much. It was our fault! She wrote a dissertation on Platonov, by the way. [*Great Russian modernist writer.*] She lived in Kiev and had cancer and died at home. And when she died, I felt that I had to write about this, about children loving someone so much. [. . .] You know, it's for sure that people do not die. I've spoken to many doctors who prepare people for death. [. . .] Our walking about, talking, our friendships, are a preparation for the work of death. And when we die, that's all that's left, these experiences. We can touch without hands, walk without legs, speak without mouths. We can do everything without the body. Only the body is not lost, the personality, the feelings, memory. And our parents, friends are with us, because we can recognize each other without the body, without faces [. . .]. I am preparing my spirit for this work, because it's the same world after death, as here. [. . .] We are not lost to one another after death. But it's hard work. [. . .] All of this in my poetry. Life after death is neither hell nor paradise. [. . .]

As for that teacher, it was difficult for her, because she had such a lovely experience with the children, and this was before she knew any man. This is a special psychological problem, because she had no sexual experience. [. . .] She is pure, without a sexual imagination.

And then there's that other poem, about a woman, a simple peasant woman . . .

An urbanised peasant woman! Hard to translate, because the language is tough folk language, yet at the same time very emotional. [. . .]

In it, when the man is leaving the woman, he puts a fifty-rouble note near the head of the sleeping child. He doesn't just place it there, but strokes the note, as you might some material, straightening it out, smoothing it down. He thinks it's a lot of money.

All he has in mind really is his life, but the woman's only concern is the child, not the man. Her work may be dirty, but her heart is pure. She doesn't want to hold this man. But the children . . .

By the way, the woman is clever. [. . .] After the war women lived without men. They had lots of children. They were not prostitutes. We had many women and very few men. This type of woman is no prostitute. She's not interested in sex, but she does want children. So a man is found for one night, three nights. They know very well, those women, that the man will leave. It doesn't matter. She's not afraid of hardship. [. . .]

[Iowa City, September 1992]

Negar

Translated by Richard McKane

Forgive me that I opened your door silently

Forgive me that I opened your door silently,
without knocking entered your fate,
that I lit the fire but then turned cool,
that I searched but did not find.
Forgive me that I trusted, did not know shame,
that I charmed you with my boldness.
Forgive me that I became now and forever
an indelible scar on your soul.
Forgive me for laughter, forgive me for tears,
forgive me for sincerity that you didn't accept.
Forgive me, my dear, for rosy dreams,
for your never understanding me.
Forgive everything in the present,
forgive everything in the past
which by chance followed on your heels,
for my once opening your door,
well, now I'll slam it behind me.

Olesia Nikolaeva

Translated by Catriona Kelly

*

Once I used to study languages dead for millennia,
Losing sleep over the other-worldly verbs:
My voice broke on the fall of a line-break
As it tried to keep up with night's bolting car.

Once I was a confidante of midnight, a rival of day's plain-speaking,
I tried to curb my gestures and rein up sight:
But still I took a flame-red stallion to water
And I'd dive into his jet-black shade.

I shivered in fever heat as I walked onward,
Toward things that hated me – the coffin, the mausoleum,
The day of judgement. And the earth swam under my footstops
Slick as an ice floe on the deafening waters of spring.

Now my lips are set hard, and my eyes like paper:
So dry. Once a week, with my hand on an armchair's spine,
I teach university students to write their verses,
Unhobble their rhythms, and close a thought with a rhyme,

Make the voice fly up en pointe, clean out the odd passage
That jangles – the sound of Anon filling in a lost line –
Bracketing earth-bound passion not metamorphosed
Into words, in the margins, I press down my pen.

So, with a glimpse of myself reflected – a demon
In the depths of a polished gold mirror – I ask no gift:
Put me in a closed coffin and burn me to ashes,
Or fix a dragon's jaws to the top of a stake.

*

You can go on holiday now, you can dabble in verse,
Or buy yourself a red coat with buttons in shocking pink:
You can make good money, or bad, or worse;
You can do the Lotto, you can take your friends for a drink.

You can get your house seen to, get your car fixed, or your teeth:
You can demonstrate, stop the world going down the drain;
You can say what you like about politics, or the police,
Or sit and look all morning at the falling rain.

You can rig up a darkened mirror on your own window-sill
To tell your fortune by the stars, draw down the kindly light:
You can pack up a parcel with a purple wax seal
And send it to Chile, or doodle with ash off your cigarette.

Now there aren't any rules and we've torn up the script
You can do all that, and more. But what's the point?

Rea Nikonova

Translated by Gerald Janecek

*

The earth is burning
But the fibre of laughter
is indissoluble

*

Six charred leaves drift
fools down the road
touching their damp roots
to the acrid warm earth

Sick barred leaves
drink transparent water
so that temples of fallen stems
can be raised up as a crown

*

Along the threads of veins
run mice

Along the spines of songs
crawl groans

*

I sit over grief
I warm myself . . .
I sit over grief
I chop into a log
I sit I say nothing over grief
while it seethes

Vera Pavlova

Translated by Maura Dooley and Terence Dooley,
Jason Schneiderman, Steven Seymour, Derek Walcott,
and by Daniel Weissbort

Sun

How, when the sun first rose,
how frightened everything was.
The grass burned blue, the shadows
lay down, far from where they chose.
Whole armies of angels
demon hordes arose, took flight
in fiery whirlwinds
whirring left to right.
Now trees are blind as moles
now shrubs and grasses close their eyes
that once had razor vision and were wise.
How empty-eyed the rivers are and hills.
Now you and I we train our best
field-glasses where the sun sets, on the West.

Grass

Oh praise the lowly stalk
that will not sing alone
enfolds its single talk
in general conversation
commingles with the lawn
and, neighbourlike, will share
the shade, the rain, the air
and, standing tall, will hide
the unofficial mint,
the bridegroom and the bride.

When flakes of white are blent,
and no-one is beside,
then stands alone the blade
as if it never leant,
and reaches to the skies
for seeds of paradise.

Heaven and Earth

You began with the heavens
formed from the primitive darkness
as an ice-breaker breaks ice

    You began with heaven and earth
when darkness was over the earth
and might have overwhelmed it

if you had not made both

And the spirit of God
moved on the face of waters
uncreated, still distant
and the rusty firmament
rose above the waters

    before it was time
and disbelieved it was, in fact,
a mountain on dry land, as in the book
because the book
dissolves into the dark
original waters as before

    and does not
reflect His face
and there is no Law
and the burden of eternal night
drags on, until the awful moment
when, through the universe,
explodes the light.

[MD and TD]

from **Signs of Life**

> *Syllable – a sound or combination of sounds,*
> *pronounced in one push of exhaled breath.*
> *(Ozhegov's Dictionary)*

Fate

In forty-one, the Blessed Virgin appeared to Grandma,
came through the window, transparent, and said:
«Don't cry Anna, your man will come back!»
End of quote. The beginning of a long hope.
Matvey came back. The Blessed Virgin didn't come back.

Cancer

In half a cup of hot sweet tea –
half a cup of cheap vodka. And – chug.
The drink was called «The Cocktail according to Matthew».
Matvey wouldn't sit down to eat without one.
30 December of some year
Matvey and Sashka sat down to eat.
Matvey said: *Last time I drink,*
drank the cocktail according to Matthew and died
according to Throat Cancer.

Juice

My parents were virgins.
At 22 – even then it was a bit much.
Yes, Papa had a reputation as a skirt chaser around the women's
                    dormitory
but he «went» to the women in order to eat a little,
because he lived on his stipend . . .
He starting going to Mama also in order to eat.
And when there started to be talk of a wedding at the Institute,
they slipped her a copy of
«How a Girl Becomes a Woman».
Mama threw it out unopened.
It was scary for them to make me.
It was strange for them to make me.
It was painful for them to make me.

It was funny for them to make me.
And I absorbed:
To live is scary.
To live is strange.
To live is painful.
To live is very funny.

Counting Rhyme #3

I call out to dualism for a duel
I aim-I aim, but in the eyes, the target doubles
and in frustration, I fire at random.
From the sky, an angel's feather falls.

Mother

Funniest of all was birth.
– Go, – growled the nurse
and waved her
out into the hallway.
She held her stomach from below, and walked out.
Walked, walked, suddenly – a mirror,
and in the mirror – a belly
in a shirt to the navel,
on thin, shivering,
lilac legs.

She laughed for five minutes.
After another five she gave birth.

[JS]

This is the way a row of official tulips

This is the way a row of official tulips
commands you "Do not pick the flowers",
hoping that they'll be picked up when it gets dark.

This is the way a girl's vagina, weeping
from virile fingers, pleads for mercy
hoping that mercy will never be granted.

This is the way I pray "Don't let me live in Russia"
knowing well my prayers will not be answered.

[DWalcott]

And God saw

And God saw
it was good
And Adam saw
it was excellent
And Eve saw
it was passable

On the way to you

On the way to you
was writing verses about you
done with writing realized
was headed in the wrong direction

Armpits smell of linden blossom

Armpits smell of linden blossom,
lilacs give a whiff of ink.
If we could only wage love-making
all day long without end,
love so detailed and elastic
that by the fall of night
we would effect at least five exchanges
of prisoners of war between us two.

[SS]

from **Letter from Memory**

9

We are not slaves,
we are slavettes.

12

Those who refused to meet
earned the right to make a date.
Those who wouldn't be embraced
earned the right to an embrace.
Those who said no to sex
earned the right to sex.
Beloved, come tomorrow morning
so as to be instantly deprived of these rights.

13

The body sat
the body ate
glanced at the alarm-clock
and leapt to its feet
and began to sweat
put on clean underwear
and tore along
and flew in the air
and hardly made it
didn't want tea or coffee
sang huskily to a guitar
and loved someone's body
sadly, tenderly and uneasily.

17

What's lovelier
than your shoulders?
Your forearms.
Than your forearms?
Your palms.

Than your palms?
Your fingers.
Than your fingers?
Your fingers
squeezing
my fingers,
palms,
forearms . . .

Place me there like a seal.

To come on each of your fingers.

33

You paint my profile
I you – from behind.
Both from nature,
without opening the eyes.
What did I achieve?
A death mask of the back of the head
And you? My
self-portrait asleep.

[DWeissbort]

Interview with Vera Pavlova

by Gleb Shulpiakov

How do you relate to the expression: "women's poetry"?

"Womens' poetry" is almost a genre definition, a bit like "The woman's novel". There is "women's poetry" and there is poetry, written by women. There's hardly any connection between them. The first doesn't interest me in the least, and the second I find enormously interesting.

Are there any subjects particular to women or to men in poetry?

It's not a matter of subjects – they both write about the same thing.

I know, but surely they treat them differently?

Not the point either! That's not where the bone is buried!

So, let's dig it up!

One has to be circumspect. As I understand it, poetry at the beginning of the nineteenth century sounded male, but towards the end of the century, even though verse writing remained a man's job, it became more female. At the beginning of the twentieth century, women's voices began to be heard, but they had a masculine sound to them. Tsvetaeva's or Gippius's voice is more male than, say, Mayakovsky's!

Well, Mayakovsky – but he's a sort of hysterical woman in pants . . .

And Gumilev? Blok? Men became so female, that women had to take on the male part themselves. How did all this resolve itself? Towards the end of the century, women poets became far more radical than men. Stylistically and spiritually. That is, if one attempts to define poetry according to theme and gender – I would prefer to consider the radical experimentation rather than suffixes. And this radicalism has a definite female character. Who has gone further than Rea Nikonova, for example, in the performance genre? And stylistically, who has gone further than Shvarts or Fanailova? Or Iskrenko? Men have grown accustomed to hiding behind "schools". Look, there are no women either among the ironists, or among the conceptualists. But when it comes to direct statement, women are always in the forefront.

And what is the role of gender in experimentation?

The paradox is that the deeper you immerse yourself in your sexuality, the better you understand the other. We speak of the femininity of Mayakovsky, and that's why there are no women in his poems. His woman is that "six-foot tall acquaintance, who doesn't say anything" from the tragedy 'Vladimir Mayakovsky6'. As for Pasternak, for me one of the most courageous poets, he writes 'The Childhood of Luvers'. Generally speaking, you see the world more clearly from the depths of your sexuality. The lower (in all senses), the more you press on the diaphragm while breathing (singers will understand this), the higher the notes you can reach. On the contrary, if you ignore sexuality, you inevitably narrow your range.

What poetry, written by a woman, has impressed you most?

The selection of Inna Lisnianskaya's poetry in *Znamia*. She writes about her love for her ninety-year-old husband, how she washes him and so forth. Amazing poetry. A Song of Songs, written by an aged Shulamite.

Has your poetry changed with the fall of the Communist regime?

Somehow I never took account of the regime. There was Communism in school, but I just went there for show – I came to life in music school. And what's Communism got to do with music? This spectre passed me by. So, I feel neither nostalgia, nor hatred.

Are you often asked to pronounce on "women's questions"?

Yes. On this subject I have something ready, a poem: "M F. / Mortally sick – Fervently alive. / Delete where necessary". In art the basic distinction is not between male and female, but between dead and alive.

What are the main critical views of your work?

They go from one extreme to another! On the one hand, I'm regarded as a sort of male invention. On the other, I'm an earth mother, concerned with gynaecological matters and not metaphysics. Also there is the psychoanalytical view, which says my poems are a clear case of inter-sexuality.

What's that?

All I could find in a dictionary was: "Intersex, an organism in which there are no clear indications of male or female gender."

So, a sexual zero! And what follows from that?

That there's nothing especially female or male about poetry.

How comes a prose publisher like Zakharov published you?

The proposal originated from Zakharov himself. He is an adventurous man, and decided that putting his reputation behind me might be effective.

And commercial.

Above all.

And how has it worked out?

The book sells four thousand copies a year.

Do you know what your audience is?

As far as I can tell, my reader is not only or even so much someone who knows about poetry. People who hitherto were unfamiliar with poetry read me. It seems that for them my poems are not quite poems. That's how I feel about them too. So, I'm pleased.

You must have a lot of imitators?

What I get are basically parodies. And the writings of people who before this didn't write. Seduced by my "non-poems", they start to write something in that spirit.
More often M or more often F?

Believe it or not, more often M! Maybe I've taught men how to speak?

So, after all, you are "intersexual" . . .

Let me tell you . . . My most loyal supporters are men. And my most rabid ill-wishers are women.

We were talking about voices. Your favourite opera voice?

Maria Yung . . . Callas . . . But that's like talking about Pushkin . . . Of operas, above all, *Don Juan*; next *The Marriage of Figaro*. A while ago, I'd have said *The Queen of Spades*, but now I'd say *Onegin*. I'm very fond of Debussy, his opera *Pelléas et Mélisande*.

And subjects – gender. Can you listen to Wagner?

Well, if you go to the theatre, it's wonderful to watch a Wagner opera. But at home, no, at home I listen only to orchestral interludes. 'The Death of Isolde' – music I'd like to be listening to when I die.

Auden said that he'd like Siegfried's Funeral March at his own funeral.

Too grandiose. I'd make do with the slow movement of Mozart's A-major piano concerto.

Which composer would you have been prepared to marry?

I'd have married Handel, the most masculine of all composers. I might be unfaithful to him with Haydn.

How about poets?

Nabokov.

Hmm. And which female poets would make good wives?

I'm afraid there may not be any. Well, perhaps Emily Dickinson?

So we can't really get away from the male/female divide?

I'm afraid not . . . It would be convenient simply to say that the division on gender lines is rubbish, but that's not the case. My experience tells me that even memory has a clearly defined gender character. If I sort through episodes that have remained in my memory – from childhood, adolescence – I see that they are all connected to an awareness of myself as female. "A maiden's memory" is not amnesia, but a kind of censorship in the service of sex, of realising oneself in sex.

So, there are no asexual voices in poetry?

In poetry there is everything and more besides. I can only speak for myself. For me, the clearest, most evocative things in life are connected to the way a woman develops out of an asexual child. Self-awareness as such is directly connected to awareness of oneself as a woman. It may be only the first step, but that's what I feel now.

In that case your poems, do they just record or do they transcend this condition?

Isn't it the same thing?

But surely with poetry there has to be a direction, a vector? Don't you sense a space, female, poetic, whatever, in which you and your poems figure?

Ask me that in a decade or so. We'll see.

Agreed.

[Translated by Daniel Weissbort]

Alexandra Petrova

Translated by Dennis Silk

Tarantino's languor and dreaming back

Tarantino's languor and dreaming back.
The cooling hoop of Jerusalem
Throbs.
Dull scales light up for a cruel look:
Hashishnik, child of the East.
He recoiled,
Saturnine bubbling by in grooves of drains,
Till she pumped into him one two three four slugs.

Snake croaked but by daybreak
Reddening bands of scales.

O cinema dragon, I take in your fumes,
Shadowy bodies pour from your darkening screen,
Immediate injection into your heart.

'Recognize it ?' This snake city! – your brother.
Lumière's finger twitches on the trigger.
Waiting the night army of roaches.

*

Again sick.
Just now somehow paler.
Saxophone riff carrying blues along spiral
In undrawn curtain twilight –
This keen light –
X-ray or ultra-sound screen –
With its eddying silhouette
More rarefied than tedious.

Above the spool of the intestines,
Scheme of channels and sluices –
A dim angel, abandoned god,
Lit up by rotating blues.

Syncope flash
Forces your eyes open.

Pillow smile.
Attempt of it.

In Juda desert

In Juda desert,
in sunkness,
Marusenka washed white legs.
Green slime swam.
Three toads sat.

II
"Slime, where are you going?"
"Nowhere, I'm concentrating."
"Toads: friends. And you?"

III
The toad-singer with the pea in the throat
had a guttural sound:
By the mountain we guard
the frosty body
of time.
It swells more,
we face down more.

The time till it's decoded
is called expectation
it flies so fast
with a drawing of smiles
on the fire-pollen.

Yet the double-unity rim
displaces toward dead brother,
past people past things
jostling in the wrinkles
of its body and face.
How stuffy it is!
Hollow "was"
begins to be more than "will".

Here, at earth's sonorous origin,
we'll set out the clock.
Sandstorm will spread the grain
and life-scales be equal.
Isn't it all to be obedient?
Let's stalk on with an uplifted lantern
and in redundant space
find the day that rolled under.

IV

But Marusia, heeding the desert creatures,
hesitated.
Look for what? Here's mussel or crab –
At the dead house but alive.
We're like that –
        not living is our shield
without it we're lonely.

V

Ach, Mariya always humble,
look at the receding ball.
D' you see the redfoam
fire from its retreat?

The times of a verb change on the move,
now they're in the past, the pillar of salt
looks at the blinded, naked, voiceless
vampire time cleaned out.

Mariya sat down, her sad
palms warmed her feet,
and the creatures, choked with the wet trill,
were silent and a long way off.

The mere legs of Mariya
rayed pallor.

Liudmila Petrushevskaya

Translated by Daniel Weissbort

*

the cloud's gone away
the blossoms have blown away
the wind
the grass is flat
a train far off intones its song

all of this happened
and was over
me
I'm the only witness

apart from me not a soul
in this
theatre

what'll happen
if I turn my back

everything done for
weepy sobby
covering its face
curling up
cat-calls

but I'm here

and the boss, the director
is a smooth operator.

Poor Ruth

seems she was called Ruth
though the carpenters wondered

the nurse
you remember
she drowned herself

hid
the bottle from her old man

he didn't find it
in the water barrel
out in the kitchen-garden

he found Ruth
she was sticking out of the barrel
of water

only it was
her legs sticking out

Ruth was small
and it was raining that evening

the barrel was running over

obviously she climbed up there that evening
to look for a bottle in the barrel

felt around
couldn't reach it

couldn't stand it
dived in

poor Ruth
the carpenters
laughed put out

you can imagine
what sort of
funeral

poor
Ruth
really

*

the telephone
we hurry
through the village
enter the house

"Moscow's put the phone down"

we sit wait

a heavy sort of atmosphere in the hut
the owner sits there
inactive

"Having a rest at last?"

"No, the cow's ill"

waiting for something here
that's why there's this heaviness
the dear creature's lying there
stretching its neck

cut its throat
or it'll get even thinner
or wait a bit

they wait

wait

Olga Postnikova

Translated by Richard McKane

Archangel Cathedral

The coffins of great Russian princesses stand
in the basement of the Moscow Kremlin. They
were brought there in the 30s from the
destroyed Voznesensky Monastery.

There where the angels weave the sky,
where there is the triumph of the last dream,
where the cellar secrets conceal,
I asked myself: For whom

have I lived and suffered this life?
I didn't fall prostrate in prayer,
I always sang my own words
in the dark storehouse of useless tsaritsas.

Here, under the gigantic splinter-bar of walls
there is disparagement of forgetfulness.
I stand over poisoned Glinskaya,
her pillaged tomb.

And over us now red flags,
now the alcoholic madness of the country.
Only timid bones can be seen
through the robbers' hole in the sarcophagus.

In these cracks of the royal masonry,
in this mould of terrifying corners,
there are the denouements of chronic illness,
the revelation of prophetic words.

By the high iconostasis
by the column, by the coloured trunk
I will say before the pupils of the Saviour's eyes
in my great shame:
'Why did I live?'

So that breathing in the celestial blue
someone remembered the forgotten,
and someone heard, how a peasant woman wailed,
falling on the zinc coffin.

Irina Ratushinskaya

Translated by CJK Arkell, Daniel Weissbort,
Alan Myers, and by Lydia Stone

Thus you lived your life without regret

Thus you lived your life without regret,
Hands warmed against a kettle caked in soot,
Gaudier than cheap-jack kiddies' sweets,
The daring trash of sages on the streets,
Dressed in tinsel and torn lace, surrounded
By the stenches of a travelling zoo,
By evening, you'd grown princes, known to few;
At night you'd ask "Why follow me?", astounded.
Tomorrow the white raven laughs, and where
The noise is loudest of kids' shouts and curses,
You'll find in a new town a well to share
And give clean water to your weary horses.
The circus leaves, the posters fade and wash,
The tearaways who raved about your thrills
Will make their different ways in life. Your bells
Will not change the world. Hush, now . . . hush.

How, my girl, could you ever dream to follow?
The rib cage of the circus tent subsides.
Our women age so quickly. Far and wide
They sorrow; there's not one who does not sorrow.
 Ignore the embroidered shawls that seem so rich,
The baubles spangling on the sweaty saddles;
So often were they wronged, their smiles are raddled
Grins that harden on their lips like pitch;
Their cheeks are eaten by cheap rouge, their breasts
Are sucked to rags by babies every year.
I'm leaving you, no need to lie, I can bear
This slap in the face. Forget me, it's for the best.

If God's paradise exists, my old
Parrot surely lives there – he who told
Half of Europe's fortunes, who abused
All mundane authorities, and used
To swear in every language known to man,
Who took his final breath cupped in my hands,

Who pitied no one any more at all,
And I was the only one he called a fool.

[CJKA]

from **Pencil Letter**, *Bloodaxe, 1988*

The heron walks in the marsh

The heron walks in the marsh,
Its legs like a pair of compasses.
The cold, like a greenish shadow,
Lies upon the forest.
The air, dense and grey,
Itself lies down under its wing.
Above is the twilit sky,
Below, a network of plants.
Who is playing there with the wind?
Who, altering his voice,
Has called from the forest,
But has not ventured forth?
A ray of forgotten light
Gingerly tests the water.
Now our endless evening
Has gone off on its circular course.
Beasts, people and birds,
And voices, and specks of light –
We pass through all like ripples,
And each one disappears.
Which of us will recur?
Who will flow into whom?
What do we need in this world
To quench our thirst?

[Kiev, 9 October, 1986]
[DW]

Penelope, the screaming is all over

Penelope, the screaming is all over,
Put aside that cushion!
He's returned, your broad-browed ocean rover
To son and kingly station.
And his horses too, and his retainers,
Bed made out of olive . . .
The enchantress could not long detain him,
Nor those on Olympus.
The blade now wiped, see rage to sweetness alter,
A lion breathing . . .
And since his mighty sword-arm did not falter –
No innocents lie bleeding!
Punishment descended on the wicked
With proper lawful sentence.
Slaves will wipe the blood off the mosaic –
Then happiness commences.

[AM]

Where was I when I saw a wet branch against pavement worn grey

Where was I when I saw a wet branch against pavement worn grey
Or a woman with fantastic blooms on her hat selling cherries
Or a wrought iron angel above the door of a café?
Where was I when I saw?
What impossible queries!
I cannot recall dates I read carved into marble and stone
Nor hear sounds of the city that longs for my step.
It is time to go
All else I must postpone
For some night, endless years hence
When I haven't slept.
Tears for those shores, that once cooled when sun set
And a wave kissed my hand and then died
All the roads to the moon turned the colour of jet
Yet the one that led upward stayed white.
Though the sounds from the windows came up, from the street;
Slowly voices of children and insects grew still
And it seemed that the silence was perfect, complete,
Though a trolley car whined on the hill.

[LS]

Tatyana Retivova

Translated by the poet

Elegy to Atlantis

Your mainland split
Surges within me
With Pythian ecstasy

And antediluvian recall
Of the Oracle at Delphi.
Erupting from the wrath

Of Jehovah, you, oh
Umbilicus orbis terrarum, who
Simulated the atomic splitting,

Spasmodically vulcanizing,
As if you had contintentally imbibed
A lethal dose of heptyl.

Since the first high priestesses
Of Hera from Argos, I have been doomed
To declaim in hexameter the contents

Of theogonies, catalogues of ships,
Goddesses, and inventories
Of Poseidon's antebellum.

And to remember how between
The pillars of Hercules would slide
Scythian and Phoenician vessels,

Smoothly floating from Tauria
To Peru and the Mississippi valley
Kurgans, and back along Iberia.

Cypress and tree resin.
Myrtle, cane, and cedar smoke
In burners on board the ark.

The half gods having shared
Food and lodging
With the gods, desecrated demos,

The ten Atlantic kingdoms,
And have sunken you into the depths.
Mud hailed from the nethers

Across the heavens, overthrowing
Semiramida's gardens, Hesperides apples,
With the help of all four elements.

Your seven rivers changed their courses,
Mare tenebrosum swallowed the land,
Minting itself in metallurgical shreds.

The marbles of Patros, eddas,
Cuneiform writings of the Chaldeans,
The Aztec codex of Chimalpopoc

All testify to the crack
Of your splitting backbone
Along sea cliffs to the ridges

Of the Appalachian mountains.
In the mysteries, the golden age's defeat
Flames in the blushes of maidens

From Samiya who sacrifice
Their hair to Hera's temple,
Dreaming at night of Chronos.

They often attribute to me
A hyperborean provenance.
My predictions from time

Immemorial have been copied
By five scribes, direct descendants
Of Deukalion. Bathing

In Castalian waters, with laurel
Leaves in my mouth, I predict
The future to the past, the past

To the future over the burning
Pyres of Python, who emerged
Out of your flood slime,

Until I myself will be consumed
By the flames of my own prognosis
Of the erupting Vesuvius in 1737.

After the deluge

by Tatyana Retivova

The past decade has been pretty dry for me as the years of writing in a vacuum (five of which I have spent in Ukraine) began to add up. It was not until a year after Iosif Brodsky's death that I felt compelled to write again, resulting in my 'Ode to an Untuned Lyre' in his memory. Then again, the vacuum, the silence. Tick, tock, the clock of one's mortality tailoring itself to one's heartbeat. And then, like swallows after the longest winter you ever saw, a little over a year ago, the words started coming back, forming themselves suggestively in preparation for articulation. The "antediluvian legacy" was born, it all started with those two words and the desire to come to grips with time. I did not quite understand what the message was, what antediluvian legacy? And even after I wrote it, it still was not clear to me. However, I felt I had hit upon something like a dormant volcano, and it would just be a matter of time until it erupted into something coherent and graspable ("... Years later I erupt / Like some Vesuvius in a frigid land.") So I waited with clenched teeth, as there was the bombing of Yugoslavia, which pretty much made writing impossible for me.

Then the dog day afternoons were upon us, and suddenly the legacy began to make itself heard in my mother tongue (this being my borrowed tongue), and I felt the stirring within me of some kind of archetypal fish off on its endless journey. To spawn or not to spawn. Every summer I become obsessed with rivers and am rendered totally useless as I dream of them and long for them and can find no respite but in currents. I even would read about fish, and like a child I would marvel at the complicated habits of the sturgeon, the sevruga, the beluga. In my notes, I had once written: "Beluga (*Huso huso*) (what a great classification! Huso, huso, so evocative of a kind of lightning quick, primordial motion through the seas), ash, white, Caspian, Black Sea, spends most of its time in the sea, goes into rivers only to spawn, not nec. every year. After spawning, returns to sea along w/ its young. The bigger it is, the farther away it will go to spawn, from the Black Sea to the Mediterranean or the Adriatic. Most sturgeon, belugas, sevrugas entering the sea in the spring are young, those that winter in the rivers are older and ready to spawn up river in the spring."

And so I metamorphosed myself into a kind of beluga in search of its river of origin, usually they return to it for spawning. What prompts them to travel such great distances is unclear. Yet it is somehow familiar, having covered great distances myself, for no apparent reason. But as I had no intention to spawn, I had to rely on some other image that would fit into my personal mythology, and so emerged the gutted beluga, gutted for her fish eggs, which like pearls are cast to swine. This rang home, the ageless solution to the spawn or not to spawn dilemma. And I think I rode it out to "the end of the road". But still, I was hesitant to let this Beluga Dream be, she seemed so raw and exposed, so I locked her up and threw away the key.

And then I entered upon another beluga-like journey, less virtual, in the search of an author, Mark Kostrov, who like some river God reigns over all the water routes of Novgorod. I had read some of his essays in *Novy Mir*, and urgently wanted to find him. Just like that, to find him. Why? Well I presume it is because of this common obsession with rivers, though mine is much more greenhouse-like in its domestication. And what would I say if I found him? I really didn't know, maybe I would ask him to draw me a sheep. I just knew that it suddenly became a matter of life and death just to find him. It was useless to try via *Novy Mir* as their mailboxes are overflowing. So I searched via the Internet, I tried to find his address through Novgorod directories, without luck. I spent hours searching and searching for him all over creation until I stumbled upon a certain site that posts his works in translation. Breathless like the beluga in her obsessive course up multiple seas and rivers, I finally had reached a kind of shore, unfamiliar though it was, and knock-knocked a cryptic, desperate SOS out to its editor with something to the effect if I don't find this Kostrov soon I will just asphyxiate with my gills exposed to air (hush, Mx: poetic licence!). Said editor was a bit surprised to receive such a cryptic message and responded in a flash by sending me Kostrov's translator's e-mail address, and in an aside to my aside was curious to hear that I had written a book called *In My Borrowed Tongue*.

Sometimes it takes just one good reader to break the entropic spell of the vacuum.

And then came the deluge.

And here is its culmination.

'Dedications' was born in my mother tongue, as a thing in itself, *sui generis*, without predecessors in my borrowed tongue. As opposed to the Russian beluga that had for predecessor my 'Antediluvian Legacy', which also dealt with the image of the spawning beluga split open by caviar smugglers. My beluga *ex machina*.

'Dedications' came about out of something anthropomorphic, a need to acknowledge certain things, symbols, phenomena in a deeper, more personal context than usually is acceptable. A desire to alight upon that which makes up one's immediate, intimate inner world. It began as a kind of haunting, a self-haunting. A coming to grips with being at the mercy of something other than the visible, outer world. I did not need to go calling in search of a cast, they found me, one by one, in fact, they were just waiting for my third-eye projector to come around and focus on them. The lares of the hearth, what I call *domovoy* for lack of a better term, was my first experiment in the *sui generis* voice in the mother tongue. The context was new, intimate, personal, and served to bridge my two selves. I exposed myself in a way that I rarely would have done in the borrowed tongue, fraught as it is with irony. And upon translating myself into English, I was pleased to find that "Dedications" are indeed *sui generis*, and they were not translations of translations of translations of words or contexts. They had emerged as a kind of primary source. I had created my very own primary source in my mother tongue out of God knows what kind of poetic alliance! It begged to differ with my translation, as the context was no longer that of my borrowed tongue. And the translation could barely do justice to the original.

Created with the presumption that there is an Other, but that Other is shattered throughout the various strata of this inner world . . . After all, if one were to study the genealogy of the gods, one would surely find that however many generations after the age of Hera but before the Trojan war, the Muses did not precede poetry, they emerged once poetry began to manifest itself in various genres. In the beginning, there was the Delphic Oracle, and the Sybils waxed prophetic in hexameter. Therein lies the origin of the oracular nature of poetry. There were no muses to speak of then, muses became necessary only once the oracular nature of poetry was lost.

And it is the pre-muse inspiration that I have been trying to get back to. Perhaps because the most ultimate muse I ever had was that voice which is no longer. "My muse is gone, and with him goes my voice . . ." And in the absence of such a voice that had held my attention for so long, I finally came to find that everything had shattered into this kaleidoscope of multiple others, and that one could find one's muse in anything. A leaf of grass! In fact, what is the Other other than a kind of Holy Ghost or *Sofia Premudrost' Bozhiya* that permeates everything? A piece of wood with the depiction of the deeds of the apostles is the metonymical image of the real thing. Amassed, the Other is the *animus* for women, and *anima* for men. Logos, in the latter case, and the eternal, undefined feminine, in the other. And, as Jung wrote, "Whereas the man has, floating before him, in clear outlines, the alluring form of a Circe or Calypso, the animus is better expressed as a bevy of Flying Dutchmen or unknown wanderers from the sea, never quite clearly grasped, protean, given to persistent and violent motion" (*Aspects of the Feminine*).

In other words, the guardians of the conscious threshold or the muses. The twain to meet only in an alchemical *mysterio conjunctium* of sorts, perhaps. One's poetry becomes a pony express with no final destination, a kind of journey for the journey's sake, without really caring whether or not the message ever reaches the intended addressee. Then there was this other thing, this layer upon layer of being split in two. The Cold War served as a convenient background for my own personal dialectic with myself and the occasional bevy of Flying Dutchmen. It seemed that once the Cold War passed, it too would pass, the internal dialectics. But no, I found that the chasm had grown deeper and had taken on Oceanic proportions. It kept threatening to break out and become a chronic leitmotif. (". . . But first I must be ripped asunder / from the metal-working god / who has rendered my malleable parts / null and void. I am no longer / his angular wishbone to be / split after the feast of Thanksgiving . . .") I felt I needed to investigate and figure out from where doth it spring, this split? One thing was becoming clear to me, in a pythian kind of way, the split that I had in mind was much deeper than any entertained this "past" millennium. It seems to stem from some kind of old wound from time immemorial. I thought perhaps it could be mirrored in the Graeco-Roman duality, in that Russia had inherited the legacy of Byzantium which, willy-nilly, had Greece for its foundation, whereas the Anglo world had inherited the legacy of fiddling while Rome burned and all its declining and falling attributes. A Platonic caveat.

As Jung writes: "Just as outwardly we live in a world where a whole continent may be submerged at any moment . . . so inwardly we live in a world where at any moment something similar may occur, albeit in the form of an idea, but no less dangerous and untrustworthy for that. Failure to adapt to this inner world is a negligence entailing just as serious consequences as ignorance and ineptitude in the outer world." As I attempted to neglect neither the inner nor the outer world, or the deeper I dug my route from the inner world to the outer, the more it all came together, namely that there was some kind of inherent connection between Atlantis, the Delphic Oracle, and the Hyperboreans in this web that I was weaving, and that the split that worried me had actually occurred not only before the Cold War, the Civil War, the Napoleonic wars, and the Greeks and the Romans, but right before the deluge.

There were ten kingdoms that were ruled by Atlantis. The Scythians, the Hyperboreans, the Scandinavians, the Gauls, the Celts, the Greeks, the Mayans, the Aztecs, the Mexicans, the Phoenicians, the Aryans, the Chaldeans, the Egyptians, and the Berbers all had similar legends about the flood, and there is evidence of pre-deluge contact among them.

The first Sibyls were said to have been Hyperborean. The first Delphic Oracle was founded over the smoking remains of the Python slain by Apollo. This Python was born out of the slime that remained from the sunken continent of Atlantis. It was this smoke that made everyone who came near go berserk, and which prompted the creation of the Oracle right then and there.

And the rest is poetry.

Olga Sedakova

Translated by Catriona Kelly and by Robert Reid

Letter

To Professor Donald Nicholl,
'Rostherne',
Common Lane, Cheshire

Here, in this country, Donald,
that you so loved, and never visited,
in this country that makes us sick
at heart – or somewhere more fundamental,
in this unbearable country,
I remember your house
standing by its English common,
the plain, dignified house of someone steeped in work,
and Dorothy bringing tea on a tray,
and your radiant death.

Holy Russia was what you talked about:
the drowned city of Kitezh,
where Saint Sergius shares his bread with a bear,
where at Easter the blessed Serafim
says, Good morning my delight,
where his smile lights stars in the noon sky,
where prisoners pray for their guards.

Maybe now they'll come to greet you, Donald.
They must do, when you believed in them so.
Blessed Serafim, Saint Sergius, the multitudes from Mogadán
            and Kolymá,
without number or name, those whose faces,
as you said, would fuse into one,
the face of the Holy Spirit.

But, Donald, my heart is as hard
as earth scarred by the passing of tanks.
If anything grows there, it'll take years –
centuries, two centuries at least.

Your words about how
everything passes into a single inexorable whole

like waters into the sea,
how everything will be changed, forgiven,
flowing into one immeasurable ocean,
the infinite depths of mercy
whose existence we sense –

your words won't sink deep.
This exterminated soil
can't sustain the growth of stray seeds.
It's suffering of that ugly kind
you asked about with the persistence
of someone used to talking to God.
It's not anger or affront, Donald:
that passes quite quickly.

But now,
in this late wet autumn
full of misery and reconciliation,
irrational misery, irrational reconciliation,
I remember you
and your voice talking in another language
about the blessed Serafim greeting Easter,
about St Sergius and his bear,
about the prayers said in Solovkí camp,
about the infinite depths of mercy
resounding like the Northern seas.

Note: Donald Nicholl (1923-1997): Catholic layman
and theologian, whose works include *Holiness*,
The Testing of Hearts, *The Beatitude of Truth*, and, of
special relevance here, *Triumphs of the Spirit in Russia*.

Rain

"It's raining,
and still people say there's no God!"
So Granny Varya,
an old woman from round us, would say.

Now the people who said there was no God
are lighting candles in churches,
ordering masses for the dead,
shunning those of other faiths.

Granny Varya lies in her grave,
and the rain pours on,
immense, abundant, relentless,
on and on,
aiming at no-one in particular.

Sant'Alessio, Roma

Roman swallows
swallows of the Aventina,
you fly here and there,
eyelids tightly furled

in a scowl. For ages I've known
that all creatures with wings are blind,
and that's why birds cry, 'O Lord!'
in a more human voice than ours.

You fly here and there,
who knows where from, where to,
where to, where from, who knows,
past the branches of orange and stone-pine . . .
The fugitive returns to his parents' house
like water to a deep old well.

No, not everything is lost,
not everything vanishes.
That, "what's the use of it?"
That, "oh what does it matter?"
That something even a mother, a wife
will never find out – that won't disappear.
How good to know, in the end,
how good it is, that everything
people want, people beg for,
everything they'd give their all for
turns out not to matter at all.

So no-one recognised it? How could they?
After all, what does last?
Nothing but putrefying flesh and bones,
bones bleached dry, as in the valley of Jehoshaphat.

[CK]

Note: "valley of Jehoshaphat": Also known as the valley of Kidron, to the East of the Jerusalem Heights, and used as a burial ground since ancient times. It is mentioned in Jeremiah 31, 40 as the "valley of the dead bodies, and of the ashes"; in Orthodox tradition, it is the valley where the Last Judgement will begin, as anticipated in Prophet Ezekiel's vision of divine doom, read during the vigil for Easter Saturday.

In Memory of a Poet

It's grandeur of design that matters, as Joseph puts it.
(From a letter by Akhmatova)

1
As the glaze takes into
its upswirling reek
goods, chattels, things unclaimed,
and all before it,
staring into the blue,
into empty features
into the straitened, clamped
azure of blindness, –

as the sepulchral sting
of the Pierides
absorbs the lap of the lagoon,
sight, sound and aroma,
while trying to fathom
the muteness of the singer
on the edge of
exile, beyond the edge of the end –

2
Just so, closing his book
the dead one bears off
those last days of autumn
whose name is "with him",
that tower, that arch,
that wonderful porch,
that square of St Mark,
where the three of us walked.

3
Neither friend nor companion
(nor brother? nor other?)

in the jangle of harmonies
of his own melody
holding fast,
like one
who's already resolved
that life
won't beguile
and death
will not daunt, –
　　　　as the wheel
　　　　to the helmsman,
as rain to the rider,
　　　　as a nook
　　　　of earth,
　　　　as stars are to travellers:
　　　　all passes, all wanes:
　　Sound is a strange thing: Me-
　　lchior. Balthazar.
　　Turnpikes. Uplands.
　　A cryptic connection,
　　sound's a strange grief:
　　it is serving the Muses.

　　What was it he sought,
　　that all-forsaking soul:
　　the horn that trusted Charlemagne?
　　Smoke, searching: higher!

　　4
O, yes, we were hatched
in other fields
with broken backs
and blind to the living,
　　under old-style compassion
　　for such as ourselves
　　(not the Virgin of Shame:
　　the dark lumbering mass) –
　　　　the forgotten,
　　　　and downtrodden.
　　　　those murdered for nothing,
　　　　or driven beyond the point of madness . . .

death is no Russian world.
How did Paul put it?

Death is a German world
But prison has a Russian accent.

5

The slave in his galley,
the ogre in chains,
the convict in infinite,
infinite steppe
       their longing consign
       to the all-burning fire:
       higher!
       things are unbearable
       without it: higher!
Or else
that cannibal shame will dine out
on our endless negations,
your knife and your pot.

6

Like an open cage
to a woodland bird,
like a heart,
ill-disposed to the pull of the earth –
like a raft unfettered
by gravity's robe.
And who'll remain fixed
when he is afloat?

7

This smoke's not from bonfires,
nor mountain assaults
nor hamlets exhaling
their souls in the gloom,
nor smouldering,
cinders, nor torments by fire,
a hundred-armed Shiva.

8

It staggers at first
its feet thickly wrapped,
it puffs, and it clings and it hides
in the bushes –
       and above the destruction
       the valleys of tears

O, thanks be to God
– for it kindles at last!
it rises and kneels
like the heart of kings,
the blessed smoke
of earthly altars.

9

... The sea at evening,
Sappho's delight,
star after star,
verse after verse ...
They no longer recall there
who's living, who's not.
The hireling's exhausted
the oxen unyoked ...
     What is purer than that
which has burned into nothing?
     This: the stars have no number
     the vault has no bottom ...

10

Like children playing:
'It's my turn first!'
on the edge
of the universe, in a land out of sight –
     Oblivion's poppy,
     memorial honey,
     the one who goes first
     let him take these alone –
to a place where the surf
offers sisters welcome,
where there's sky and an island
and "sleep, my dear"!

[1998]
[RR]

Author's note: As the reader will immediately note,
this piece is modelled on Akhmatova's 'Through all of Earth';
Tsvetaeva's devices are also discernible. I wanted these two
Russian muses to participate in verse dedicated to Brodsky.
Brodsky himself, in his verses on the death of Eliot, took
Auden's 'In Memory of W.B. Yeats' as his model.

Excerpts from an Interview with Olga Sedakova (May 1994)

by Valentina Polukhina

Now that time has put some distance between us and the 1980s how does the poetic landscape of that decade appear to you?

In the Seventies, the illegal "second" culture separated from the official culture in much the same way as oil separates from water; there was hardly any confusion. Towards the end of the Seventies things began to be shaken up again.

Official literature began to lose its aesthetic coherence, and many discoveries of the "second" culture, at home and in emigration, were adopted (for example, there was a growing fashion for imitating Brodsky, among already established writers).

With the arrival of Gorbachev the picture grew still more confused. The generation of the Sixties merged completely with the Establishment at about that time, while as it were trying to arrange for a second debut, as persecuted artists. New names? It seems that the commanding heights were occupied by the Conceptualists and the more moderate "ironists"; apparently they were what became known as the "poets of perestroika".

Who do you feel closest to among the poets of your own generation?

Really it is not so much a matter of feeling close to anyone; more, whose work excites and attracts me ... First and foremost there is Elena Shvarts, a powerful poet with rare gifts; Ivan Zhdanov – his complex world, his imagery was something new in Russian; Sergei Stratanovsky has created a sort of poetic equivalent of Platonov's prose; Viktor Krivulin, Sergei Chegin, Aleksandr Velichansky, Vladimir Lapin . . .

Let us talk about your own poetry. Close reading of it suggests that, in a way, you are emulating God in His creation of the universe, taking as the basis for it the elements: air, water, earth, fire.

I was not aware of that thematic thread in my work until you pointed it out a few days ago! But I do recall that from the very start, I felt more attracted to the non-human world or, rather the non-social-human world. Remember Batyushkov's: "I love my neighbour but thou, mother-nature, / art dearest to all in my heart". When I was fifteen I was writing about the same things, but not as well as "gentle Batyushkov": "And this is why I feel more intimate / with the language of the boughs, the language of the tree trunks..." or, differently put, this is a world where you can more easily lose your consciousness of self; people always force you to remember.

Among the thinkers of modern times that I've encountered, there is a deeper feeling for the natural world in Goethe. This feeling can engender not just elegiac lyric poetry but also scientific theory building. It is a sensing of the elements as meaning, as structure... For me the most disturbing element, the one I was least fond of, from childhood, was earth. It frightened me. Earth, when the snow has melted, out there on the other side of the garden fence... It is too alive, too like us, sensitive to pain in the same way as we are. I remember being scared to tread on it, especially in early spring; I would only want to use an already existing path. Most frightening of all was its too obvious vitality, its corporeality ... My favourite element was water: static or flowing, it drew me like a magnet. The sight, the sound, the touch, even the smell. There is an early poem of mine: "... and it was just that little bit lighter thanks to the smell of water..."

Perhaps it is only happenstance. Then again, maybe it is contact with the extra-human world of nature, always one of the functions of art, because forgetting about that contact is not only commonplace [...] but also has to do with our religious tradition, at least the Judaeo-Christian strain. Demands on one's humanity almost always concern those closest to one; the eternal theme is always People, People in history, People in society [...]

Is not that the provenance of your own particular commingling of the four elements: "And water is the ashes of unknown fire" or "In the aerial water", "on skyey earth".

Your observations are provocative! Why do they change, one into the other? I think it's because that is how it really is; Heraclitus knew it. But, generally, I have no great liking for final judgements. One result of such finality is tautology: water is water, fire is fire and so on... I would like every possibility to remain open, so that everything can be itself and something other and have the potential of transforming itself into something as yet unknown.

Do you see it as part of your artistic mission to bring harmony where harmony is almost unachievable? The trivial daily round — stale, boorish and vulgar — how can you bring harmony to that through the use of the word?

No, that is not my mission, not now, nor has it ever been. Perhaps this is precisely why I find myself in such a lonely position in the contemporary scene. Even those poets who are closest to me – Elena Shvarts, Ivan Zhdanov – [...] In Dublin I was asked by Carol Rumens what I felt about Sylvia Plath's idea that poetry should be all-inclusive. My answer was that it was a question of your attitude, whether you were looking for extensivity or intensivity. Let us take Pushkin's 'Tale of the dead tsarevna': for me that is all-inclusive. And it's still true of the Sapphic fragments, just a few words – even Ezra Pound's stylization of that sort of fragment in his 'Papyrus' ("Spring . . . / Too long . . . / Gongula . . .") manages to get everything in. You can "include everything" without even mentioning anything harsh, ugly or vulgar.

The inertia of downward movement is very apparent to me. That has been the vector which art has been pursuing for centuries now, "speculation about degradation". It seems that even in Renaissance times, art attempted to extend the realm of the aesthetic into the non-aesthetic, transmutation into a new, more complex, more spicy harmony which can barely be harmonized . . . But that movement in one direction alone has become senselessly inert . . . When Baudelaire discovered the beauty of the trivial, of evil even, it grabbed his reader's attention as a widening of experience, in its own peculiar way an act of kenosis. It is no accident that in Rilke, the *poète maudit* is confronted by the image of St Julian, bestowing a kiss upon a leper.

You must understand that when I say that art is free not to find its subject matter in chaos, the gutter and so forth, I do not mean that it should exclude them completely and that we should return to writing idylls about Chloe and anthology pieces about roses. That would be simply dishonest. No, I think that, bearing all that in mind, knowing about it, you can express new experience through the very intensity of language. What does excite me is the intensity of a word, its semantic, phonetic, grammatical force, and it is there that I see new possibilities. [. . .] Ugliness, evil, chaos lack a well-defined image and for that reason our consciousness is incapable of dealing with them. "I looked and went on", as Virgil advised Dante in the *Inferno*.

Is there any one particular poet you feel breathing down your neck?

Your question seems to have been prompted by Brodsky's famous image of emulation as a stimulus to poetic growth. Poetic emulation is an ancient tradition, as ancient as the legend of the duel between Homer and Hesiod. I got to know Elena Shvarts's poetry in 1975 or 1976 and it made me very envious. A great poet and living. I sensed her poetic primacy, the purity of her tone. But I knew it was another world and, though I felt less pleasure in my own, I could not follow in her steps. She made me feel freer in my world and that was invaluable and encouraging. I first encountered Brodsky's poetry in *samizdat* (at university) in 1968.

His themes, his music, were alien to me, but you sensed the inspiration, at its most intense in those early poems of his.

But to return to rivalries and influences. The most powerful influence of my youth was Mandelshtam. What could one write after that? It was not a matter of writing post-Auschwitz, as they say now, but of writing post-Mandelshtam, writing in the wake of that new intensity and beauty, all that he achieved in his late poems . . . My next idol was Rilke, in whom I saw the Poet par excellence. In order to read him in the original I learned German. To read Dante I learned Italian. To read Baudelaire I mugged up on my French. *Les Fleurs du mal* had a major influence on me, which comes out in my book *The Wild Rose*. Of Russian poetry, Pushkin, who has always been more than a poet for all of us – as it were, the genius loci or the Orpheus of Russian literature.

What do you consciously reject, stylistically, thematically?

First of all I can tell you what I have not felt the need to reject, because it never attracted me. An emphatic style with inflated lines, with wilfully deformed imagery, anticipating, if not requiring, a certain response from the reader: a style which wants to lord it over the subject and the intended audience . . . But no less unattractive is inflated expression, or its polar opposite, over-smooth writing, what is generally called the academic style, "correct" writing, conforming to a standard that is somehow neither too laboured nor too fine. I find that style really just as aggressive as the other. And what both of them exclude is the accidental, the unexpected, air and open space . . .

When I think about what I have had to reject [. . .] Perhaps my own prejudices. There were quite a few. I was afraid of anything lengthy, narrational. Short poems, things with a maximum of tension – there was a time when I could not imagine another kind of poetry for today. Then certain themes, certain words seemed to be unusable. Politics, street talk [. . .] At the same time I was afraid of being too elevated, employing too hieratic a vocabulary, the sort of thing you find in Blok: blood, love, roses etc. Generally speaking I have had to "consciously reject" my own purism in its various manifestations.

How do you manage to eliminate the first person singular in poetry?

It is an illusion! I think I use the first person as much as anyone . . . In the final analysis, it is only a narrative strategy: you can talk about yourself in the third person. Nobody is really fooled as to the identity of the "sick man" in Pasternak's 'In hospital', nor the identity of the "lodger in the raincoat, with a bottle of *grappa* in his pocket"in Brodsky's 'Lagoon' and the same goes for the hawk in his 'The Hawk's Cry in Autumn'.

[. . .] But there are examples of an upwards escape route, away from the romantic "I". Rilke and his subjective lyrics . . . Or the "I" of TS Eliot, choral and representative. [. . .] It is not a matter of eliminating the first person singular and achieving some sort of impersonal point of view – that is a utopian task, even for a scholar. It is really a question of having something to look at from your own point of view, in order to avoid thinking about yourself – either judgementally or self-admiringly – like shielding one's eyes with one's hand, which hides the whole world. As it says in a Hasidic parable: "The world is so large but a man can hide from it with his own little hand." [. . .]

Could you be more explicit about what you mean when you say "exceed yourself" in relation to poetry? To present the world with a new vision of things, to achieve self-betterment in the process of giving birth to the poem, or to improve the language?

We are accustomed to thinking that the poet at the moment of inspiration becomes greater than himself, another being altogether . . . But another postulate was known to classical antiquity, that a work of art is no greater than its creator. This presupposes the essential unity of personality and, as it were, the impossibility of transcending that personality. It seems to me that this antinomy does not require resolution; both poles are equally true. In reality an artist transmits through his work not only his talents but also his weaknesses; all that remains at his command when "silence falls upon the sacred lyre". And we, I mean the readers, are able to recognize those weaknesses; particularly in the idiosyncrasies of form, which is where an author has least control.

And what does exceed oneself mean? I can, probably, only answer in a negative way and only by having recourse to someone else. Eliot talked of "the expurgation of intentions". You approach things, unaware perhaps that your motives are not entirely pure, the best being, let us say, the perfectionist desire "to create something sublime", to make an impression, please those in the know, overwhelm the reader. However, any deliberate motive is bound to spoil your work . . . All that remains is intention or, if you are not afraid of big words, service.

Service to whom or what: language, one's talent, God?

That is the question! If I could answer it . . . But, it seems, nobody can, neither poets, nor philosophers, nor theologians, trying to determine the status of art in the spiritual hierarchy. Strange as it may seem, that old theme, the condemnation or justification of artistic creation from a spiritual standpoint, has now taken on a very particular reality. Apparently it has to do with our return to the Orthodox fold. Some of our enthusiastic new Orthodox zealots have declared war on Apollo; free creation seems to them to be the devil's work, art is somehow at odds, in a big way, with piety, obedience, humility, what have you . . . It does seem to me though that when art is harshly repressed, it is religion that suffers. It is reduced to moral precepts and more or less closes itself off from the whole surrounding ocean of existence. It is left without the poetry of life, without the latter's play and openness.

What role would you assign to poetry in Russia's present rebirth?

[. . .] Poetry's role? In the dead years, independent poetry circulated in manuscript. Along with the living, Mandelshtam, Tsvetaeva, Khodasevich, Kuzmin and others were both cherished and vital as never before. They bore witness to the fact that our language was not dead, that man had not yet been transformed into an Orwellian cipher. Poetry foretold the end of that nightmare – and, in its daedalic way, led to it.

Do you see any specific problems facing Russian poets in the century's final years, problems which did not trouble them at its beginning?

At times it seems to me that the potential of Russian poetry, for all its great achievements, has scarcely been touched. That there are many paths that have not yet been explored. That – and please forgive the anachronism – the soul of Russian culture has not said all that is to be said, and that much remains unexpressed. At the same time, there are many things that, to me, seem to be exhausted.

You have translated such major poets as Dante, Rilke and Eliot. When translating, do you see yourself as the poet's ally, double, rival?

Our tradition of translation, as you know, unlike here [in Britain] demands the complete reproduction of the original form. When Ezra Pound did that, the result was published as his original production. Really, the need to preserve both meaning and form is over-ambitious. Yet there are many in our country who have mastered the art of doing precisely that. What to translate is mostly a matter of reading and thinking, "It's a pity that's not in Russian!"

As for the authors, personal contact, I don't think about it. The poem is the thing . . . But accuracy *is* a problem. In reproducing the form you are forced to deviate semantically from the original. You have to change things selectively, but in which direction do you go? From what resources do you draw your changes? [. . .] The inner connections between images can be understood only through a knowledge of your author's work as a whole: in translating a single poem you really ought to keep in mind the whole poetic world.

There is yet another side to translation. It satisfies the actor in one to speak in the voice of a man, a wise man, like Rilke, or in the voice of a holy friar. When an actor works he uses his body; the poet-translator uses his state of mind. Of course the range of roles in my repertoire is limited. There are many styles and meanings I cannot play. But in choosing an author I seek not a reflection of myself (even an idealized, imaginary reflection), but what I lack – the firmness of a Dante or a Rilke, let us say, or the dryness of Eliot, Claudel's sense of lofty comedy, St Francis's purity. [. . .]

[Translated by Chris Jones, with Valentina Polukhina]

Evelina Shats

Translated by Daniel Weissbort

Like Casanova

In the miserable interior
with candlelight
the solemn attributes
of seduction,
a
"little boy"
he called
all the women
who in delight or with longing
skated over his
fate
as
on an ice-rink.
Was he open?
not a bit of it –
He was lonely
and loved the female body
like Casanova: so
a mechanical doll of the
settecento
became a mechanical orange
in the XXth, to complete
this ancient
scenario.

A rose

A rose
a
shameless
red
rose
ultra
sensitive
flesh
exploded

in
fearful
black
thorns

how
love
dies

The End

patiently I do not finish the phrase
omission points amount almost to
patience
it's dreadful putting a full stop
in the space of absence
new thoughts are born
but an end without an end
is a chinese torture
this is when
I prefer the guillotine
to finesse

Sleep soundly, dear poet

*"I don't like men who leave behind a smoking trail of
weeping women."*   (Auden)

I shall stop weeping
shall not leave, weeping, a smoking trail
so love should not annoy Auden
so Joseph can sleep soundly
a genius's sleep and save the world with his
rigorous – almost delirious –
desperate dedication to the word

[Sicily, 15 May 2002]

Inerview with Evelina Shats

by Daniel Weissbort

Is there a difference – apart from the obvious linguistic one – between what you write in Italian and what you write in Russian?

Heidegger said: "Language is the house of life". Each person renders it habitable in his or her own way. When I left Russia, not being an active dissident, I still tried to free myself from the grip of an exhausted Russian language. I wanted to think in a different way. Italian requires a new mentality, so to speak, clarity, which comes from Latin, an intellectual structure. Liberation from the naivety of an obsolescent system of rhymes, from the simplification of the text that results. Russian? I returned to it twenty years later. I wanted to be able to sing! A poet's native language is his, his one and only. But he may also use other instruments. And perhaps Italian is the language of reason, Russian that of the soul? Anyway, words, in their depth and density, transcend the rules of this or that language. As for poets, they all speak in several languages.

How do you relate to other Russian poets, Russian women poets?

If there's no connection with poets, an ideal connection with *texts*, there can be no poetry. As with culture, there is probably a sort of divine hypertext for the universe. I'm always sleeping with some poet or other! Emily Dickinson, Gottfried Benn, René Char, Paul Celan, Amalia Rosselli. As you see, I like contemporaries. Russians? I simply get lost because of the abundance of contacts, all the excitement. At different times, different poets have been bedside reading for me: Tsvetaeva, Akhmatova, Mandelshtam . . . And especially – Khlebnikov, Brodsky. Khlebnikov is my university, Brodsky for me represents a kind of unconscious love, hard to understand, like all love, crazy.

You also produce books yourself. How did you get into this? How does your art or craft relate to your poetry?

How did I start working on making books? To find Samizdat! A brilliant school of book creation! Add to that, spoiled sheets, general literary bric à brac. Yes. I simply collected that kind of junk, and then for pennies I bought volumes of contemporary Italian poets. What can I say? Samizdat is humankind's salvation. Of course, I wanted to laugh it off. I often say that my handmade books are for fools and collectors. In them you'll find childish love for picture books, the history of Russian visual literature, popular literature, futurist hand production, Italian indifference to the printed text and in general to the text as such. The wish to seduce, to entice people into reading. To make something emotionally alive, something rather like a relic.

What do you think about our collection, a collection devoted to Russian women poets? Don't spare our feelings! You wouldn't be the first to object . . .

For me large-scale epic poetry is male. What characterises women's poetry is a laconic quality, brevity of exposition. Of course, you can divide people into brunettes and blondes, short and tall; there are differences. If poetry is distinct from prose on account of its economy, then women's poetry is doubly distinct. Take Emily Dickinson – a brilliant neo-classical voice, a voice of contemporaneity! Perhaps this indicates reserve, which is linked to a certain lack of confidence in herself? Still, reserve of this sort leads to an "ecological" awareness, a semiotic rationality and lends the text a naturally contemporary form. Women have entered the history of poetry in an extended front.

Once, when I was asked at a poetry evening what being a female poet meant today, what sprang to mind and what I blurted out was: *Poeta sempre femina* – The poet is always female. Then I remembered how my friend, the artist Alvaro once exclaimed: "You've two quadrangular balls in your noddle!" That's Blok and Tsvetaeva, the female and male principle. So, let's see, what about this special issue of *MPT*? In general any ghetto nauseates me. I agreed to take part, because to be translated into English was seductive, in this case to be translated by you!

This may seem a bit out of context, but you said you were thinking of compiling a book of your own poems dedicated to Brodsky. Can you say what Brodsky as a poet means to you?

For me he is the eternal interlocutor, the *other*. I'm often in dialogue with him. Yes, it's time to collect all the poems to JB written over the last twenty years.

A naïve question, perhaps? What's it like writing Russian poetry outside Russia?

Well, of course, a poet's country is his poetry. Thank goodness, the earth has long ceased to be square, when everybody knew exactly where to go. One can travel in one's own shell, wherever one's nature leads one.

You told us that your father called you goika. *Presumably, then, you've some Jewish blood in you.*

Once upon a time, the Austrian prime-minister Kreisky said that every Austrian was a third Jewish. I don't know whether that's so, but every European has got some Jewish blood, if you consider that our blood is the culture, and that religion is its primary material. My love for the Italian language, for the world of the Mediterranean, isn't it the product of Jewish antecedence and of having been born in the amazing cosmopolitan city of Odessa? Anyway, as Tsvetaeva said: All poets are Yids.

[*Venice, May 2002*]

Tatyana Shcherbina

Translated by Derek Walcott, Daniel Weissbort and by J Kates

About Limits

The cicadas, the cicadas are singing, Rameses.
The hemlock, Socrates, pour me my just amount.
Let the others apply to their Central Committees.
No, my brother Reason, I'm the soul, and I can't.

The buildings, my idol! Look at the buildings!
Are we really insects, with our shrivelled wings
who throw down our bodies on the bunks of the hive
and drape our rags on the chairs they provide us with?

Discover her, Columbus, discover her anew.
Your descendants have grown tired of their own shadow.
What way lies open now to the stumbling Jew?
What road will tell that tired remnant where he must go?

My friend, my mutant, pliable, unstiffened,
my crazy colleague, it will come to an end.
There's a limit to vomiting and diarrhoea.
So here they are, have a good look. We've made it, my dear.

[D Walcott]

They cut off my hot water

They cut off my hot water,
love's juice, the verbal flow.
I'd like to complain to the nation,
but they'll shut me up, too, long before.
Without moisture, I'll dry out,
along with the dirty dishes and the washing.
I'll get mouldy, gather moss,
I may even graduate to long-forgotten!

What's it you're howling, siren-telephone

What's it you're howling, siren-telephone,
why don't you whisper some fairytale in my ear?
So, even eternity passes:
went berserk, re-stocked.
But I invested in it years
of designer and model expertise,
looked for new approaches,
wrote "prick" on the drapes.
I spent an eternity in the doorway,
in telephonic angst.
It was always in place,
its undoubted homespun place.
And now even this has passed
and the sacred spot is empty, hazy,
the whole of eternity marks time –
hasta la vista. *

* Spanish: Until we meet again / Goodbye.

Where's the future's clawlets?

Where's the future's clawlets?
Scratches on the street
pointing the way, like spires, arrows.
And the decoys
which captured us in parentheses?
The demon of wild entertainments
had such success with just a log in the fire,
making one want to keep changing places.
Suddenly, a pause, endspiel spire-ends, post-space,
suspended there like a low ceiling.
If the computers fall into a trance,
the claw will scribble things, like inverted commas.
The world is pressed between them, traffic-wise,
in context, in the fixed habit
of running backwards.

Tell me, Comrade God, how can life, over this stretch

Tell me, Comrade God, how can life, over this stretch,
go from tolerable to such a pain,
when everything is not as it should be,
weather, ecology, men.
And even the barking of dogs, it's not the same dogs
that beethovenly, chopinly tickled the hearing.
The grass egged on the act of love
but that was grass, not senna leaflets.
My God, it's like you're not mine, because
finally even you went over to the khazars
abandoned our side, for which –
and I'm speaking for the market place –
the deeper into the forest you go, the more the wolves howl.

[D Weissbort]

Except for love everything

Except for love everything
can be bought. Can be stolen,
snatched, bullied, asked for nicely.
Dear, you can even be converted to Buddhism.
changed from a man into a woman or just into drag.
A hag can turn into a ravishing beauty,
an old lady knock off half a dozen years,
a black become white, or a citizen of Siberia
black, wandering through Africa.
Babies can be made in test-tubes, in the blink of an eye,
New York be reduced to dust, men fly to Mars.
Except for love
in every act of will greater than the will of fate,
the baritone sings countertenor.
Except for love and death and, okay, talent
everything's in our control. Win the battle
or fall under the foeman's blow,
but neither give up nor take the alien outpost ll
Ove.

[JK]

Tatyana Shcherbina

Drafts by Derek Walcott

About Limits

The cicadas, the cicadas are singing, Rameses.
The hemlock, Socrates, pour me my just amount.
Let the others apply to their Central Committees.
No, my brother Reason, I'm the soul, and I can't.

The buildings, my idol! Look at the buildings!
Are we really insects, with our shrivelled wings
who throw down our bodies on the bunks of the hive
and drape our rags on the chairs they provide us with?

Discover her, Columbus, discover her anew.
Your descendants have grown tired of their own shadow.
What way lies open now to the stumbling Jew?
What road will tell that tired remnant where he must go?

My friend, my mutant, pliable, unstiffened,
my crazy colleague, it will come to an end.
There's a limit to vomiting and diarrhoea.
So here they are, have a good look. We've made it, my dear.

Cicadas. my (dear) Rameses, cicadas   a
Pour me the ~~poison~~ hemlock, Socrates   b
~~Go to the Central Comittee~~   a
Should I get in touch with the Central
                 comittee   b
No little brother of mine, I will not
                be the soul

of reason, address to another level
           but the soul does not.

B

(A)

ABOUT THE LIMITS.

The cicadas, dear Rameses, listen to the cicadas?.
~~Hemlo~~ The hemlock, pour it out for me Socrates.
~~Apply to the Central Comittee don't you apply~~ you
~~Don't apply to the~~
Aren't you going to apply to the
                  Central Comittee?
             & aren't you going to
                 apply?

No. My brother reason, I, (the soul wont.
                   will not)

            nor I, nor I

No, brother Reason, I'm the soul, nor I.
           I have a soul.

Concerning ⊕ Limits.

The cicadas, dear Rameses, listen to the cicadas: ↘
The ~~pitiless~~ hemlock, ~~pour out~~ Socrates, pour
~~some out for me.~~
out my ~~portion.~~
amount

~~Tot them apply to~~
~~Arent you~~
. Let the others apply to their Central Committees
But me, my brother Reason, I am the soul
~~not it.~~ ⌐
and I can it.

My friend, my pliable mutant, my untameable
colleague,
There's a limit to even vomit and diarrhea

plaint untameable, insane

(2)

with our

Buildings, my idol, look. The buildings.
Are we really insects?. Who they
Their bodies down on the bare bonks in the hive
and to drope our rags on the chairs they provide
us with.

(B)

my friend, mutant (not old) pleant
my colleague, untameable, insane,

Let'
Vomity and diarrhea have a limit.
and there they you are. Yes. There they are
dear.

(3)

Discover her, Columbus, discover her
more quickly.
The your
Your descendants are tired of leading earthly:
lifes lives.

To what=where
the poor Jew
wretched
To where does our remnant unfortunate
our natural-remnant
any path left direct for the remant to go.

(4)   pleant

My friend, "   soft

①

The cicadas ~~are singing, Rameses, the cicadas~~
Rameses, the ci-

The cicadas are singing, can you hear them Rameses?
The hemlock, Socrates, pour out my amount.
the ~~Let~~ others apply to their Central Committees.
No, little brother Reason, I am the soul and I
Can't.

The buildings my idol, look at the buildings
Are we really insects with our useless wings
who throw down our bodies ~~and in the~~ on the bunks of the hive
and drape rags on the ~~stools~~ they provide us with?

Discover her, Columbus, discover her
more ~~quickly~~ anew
Your descendants are tired of their ~~weary lives~~ miserable shadows
what path lies open now to the
That remnant stumbling ~~wandering~~ Jew?

④

Discover her, Columbus, discover her anew.
Your descendants are weary of their own shadows.
What path lies open to the stumbling ~~Jew~~
~~That remnant~~
what path will ~~tell~~ that remnant where to go?

Discover her, Columbus, explore her anew.
Your descendants are weary of their own shadow.
What path lies open to the stumbling Jew.
What path ~~tell~~ that poor remnant where ~~is~~ he
                                    must go?

My friend, my phant mutant.

Even vomiting and diarrhea have a limit.

Look, here they are.   this is it

Discover her, ~~my~~ Columbus, explore her ~~self~~ self.
Your descendants are weary of their own shadow.
What path lies open to the stumbling Jew.
What road ~~tell~~ the more remnant which way
he must go now.?

My friend my.

~~Even vomiting and diarrhea have~~

There's a limit even to Vomiting and diarrhea.
And here they are. Have a look We've
arrived my dear

Discover her, Columbus, discover her all anew!
Your descendants have grown tired of their own shadow.
What path lies open to the stumbling Jew?
What road tells the tired remnant where to go now?

unstiffened
My friend,
There's a limit to even vomiting and diarrhea.
So, here they are. Have a good look. We've
made it, my dear

My friend, my mutant, pliable, unstiffened
My crazy colleague, it ~~will mist~~ will come to an end
rr hoea
There's a limit to even vomiting and diarrhea.
So here they are. Take a good look. We've
made it, my dear.

Discover her, Columbus, discover her anew:
Your descendants have grown tired of their own
                          shadow.
What way lies open ~~now~~ now to the stumbling Jew.?
What ~~road~~ ~~will~~ tell that tired remnant where
                          he must go.?

There's a limit to even vomiting and diarrhea.
~~And~~ So here they are. Have a look.
~~good.~~   We've made it, my dear.

To Tatiana

love

Derek

ABOUT LIMITS.

The cicadas, the cicadas are singing, Rameses.
The hemlock, Socrates, pour me my just amount.
Let the others apply to their Central Committees.
No, my brother Reason. I'm the soul, and I can't.

The buildings, my idol.! Look at all the buildings.!
Are we really insects with our shrivelled wings
who throw down our bodies on the bunks the hive
and drape our rags on the chairs they provide us with?

Edwin.

CONCERNING THE LIMITS

Cicadas, my Ramses, cicadas are singing. — a
Wing your circuituous way to me, Socrates. . b
Swing to the Central Committee, will you please? b
No way, my soul brother. Soul am I and will not. a   I am a soul

Look at the building, my idol, look at the building.
Don't we turn into insects in order to fling
our bodies down on unoccupied bunks in the hive
and hang up our rags on the stiff-legged chairs they provide us with

Open, Columbus, open up quickly,
your offspring sweated to lead their earthly lives.
Where will it lead the impoverished Jews,
how will it point out the way to our wretched refuse?

My friend, my soft-shelled genetic sport,
my crazy colleague whom nothing can thwart!
We reach our limits at puke, diarrhoea:
Here they are. Take a look, we've arrived, my dear.

Interview with Tatyana Shcherbina

by Yuliya Lukshina

Tatyana, you use an expression, Columbus Complex. What does travel mean for you?

Travel is an attempt to penetrate into another time space, different customs, different people. Practically speaking, we know nothing about this world, about history, about the cosmos. When we approach it we bump our heads against the ceiling. We make vague guesses and we call this religion. So, what is history? Recently I wrote about a Portuguese poet, Pessoa, who had fifty-three different personalities. Every day he woke up as one of them and didn't remember the others. He wrote his poems under the name of three of them and these three names are inscribed on his statue beside his actual name, Fernando Pessoa, the meaning of which is precisely "personality". [. . .] We treat history by uniting events and facts around an axis: here is the beginning, this is what follows, and this is what comes after. When you travel you see that there's no single history, but a multiplicity of histories [. . .]

My problems with travelling are global, ontological: time and history. Columbus's personality interests me. I feel some sort of kinship. He discovered America and changed the course of history. When I discover something it helps me to understand history. I visited all the places Columbus knew: Genoa where he was born, Portugal, Cape St Vincent – the end of the then world. When Columbus reached this cape and said: "There, beyond the ocean there is land. Equip an expedition and I will find the land", they laughed at him. I was in Sagresham, where there's the naval school, in Andalusia, in Seville, where Columbus is buried against his wishes. True, the Spaniards followed his will literally: he said he was not to be buried on Spanish soil, so they set his coffin on a platform. History treated him shabbily. He died in poverty and America was named after another voyager. But the life of his soul after his death seems to me just as marvellous.

Would you like to be someone else?

In principle I can easily imagine myself as somebody else but it is not important. I am sorry that in this life, by definition, it is already impossible for me to achieve certain things, know certain things. Contrary to the well-known saying, I am not lazy and I am curious.

Tell me about your life in Paris. You have a very close relationship with that city.

I studied French for many years, first in a special school, then Moscow State University. When I was allowed to travel, I went to France, after visiting many other countries. Finally I was invited to a literary festival. There I met a French publisher who offered me a contract. As a matter of fact, I suffer from what is called topographical idiotism; I can hardly ever find my way anywhere. But when I got to Paris, for the first time in my life I had the feeling that everything was clear about the city. Most likely because at school, god knows why, we studied the map of Paris. And since Paris, I've been able to find my way much better in other places as well. Also, in Paris, I experienced a sensation, unknown to me hitherto, which is usually defined, vacuously, as happiness. I was happy, wandering about and speaking French. Language, for me, means self-awareness. I soon began to think in French, and I have even written a collection of poetry in French. I wrote a few articles for *Le Figaro* and received a grant to put together an anthology of contemporary French poetry, for which I won a prize. Paris was my home for three years. When you speak a foreign language, you activate a psychological mechanism which is dormant in your native country. The French language is so different from Russian. I remember, in Russia, they always said that the Russian language was the richest in the world (and also the greatest and most powerful!). I think French is richer. It has more nuances and is more sensual. In general, Parisian life is such a gentle life, with overtones that don't exist in Moscow. At first I was very surprised. Many of my French acquaintances complained of depression and they took lots of anti-depressants. I thought they must be crazy! After two years of Parisian life, I also began to experience depression and soon I realized I had to get away. In Paris I restructured myself as regards feelings I didn't possess and I couldn't control this. I experience violent mood swings, whereas in Moscow my mood is more even. And this has to do with language. I'm organically at home in Russian; my nervous system is accustomed to it.

What makes you happy?

In general positive emotions dominate. So, almost anything can make me happy. But there are things which irritate me, like television, or music in supermarkets or on the street. This is almost a physical torture for me. But I do my best to ignore it, because what's the point of getting enraged? It's much better to shut it out. This is what home's for, one's burrow. I bring everything I like there ("The imperfection of my home doesn't disturb me/ but somebody else's imperfections irritate me").

What I don't like about my home is that it needs redecorating. But I don't want to waste my time and energy. This means it is not annoying me to such an extent and I can live with it. I am totally indifferent to country homes and nature in general.

There is a view that the female poet is a creature entirely unequipped for life.

I don't understand that. Probably it's what they say about all creative people whose brains have overdeveloped right hemispheres, which are responsible for intuition and abstract thinking. As for me, I'm ambidextrous. In my childhood they tried hard to make me right-handed. Now I hardly remember which hand I use better. I use my left hand for shooting, and I draw with my left; also I eat with the left hand, but I write, usually using a mouse, with my right. This means that both parts of my brain are active. So, the analytical part of me co-exists peacefully – sometimes not so peacefully – with the emotional side.

From Atmosfera, *No. 3, 2002, Moscow*
[Translated by Daniel Weissbort]

Elena Shvarts

Translated by Stephanie Sandler, and by James McGavran

Memorial Candle

I so love the flame
That I kiss it,
I stretch out my hand to it
And wash my face in it.
Tender spirits live
In its flower bud,
A circle of delicate forces
Rings around it.
This is their home,
Their shell, their joy.
Anything else would make
Too crude a place for them.

I burned my hair,
Singed my eyelashes,
I thought you were there,
Trembling in the flame.
Maybe you are trying
To whisper a small word of light to me.
The low flame trembles,
But in me there is only darkness.

*

Reason quickly leaps
Through the small window that opens to the stars.
Where are you going, my mind, my little mouse?
A sad black cat is guarding us.

O reason, my little one! Don't even try!
You will never make it past the curtain of darkness.
You went strolling around – now off to your little burrow.
A crumb of time and a crust of space await you there,
And a bitten slice of memory – so here, gnaw on that all night.

Conversation with a Cat

'I'll have a drink, you take a bite,'
I say to the cat, and she
Answers with a quick
Lash of her furry tail.
"And let them that weep be as though
They wept not – puss, was it St Peter who said that?"
No answer. Instead she gnaws silently,
Steadily at her piece of fish.
Not a word from the dead, which is strange:
Is it so hard to dig a tunnel out from death?
She purrs and hangs her head,
Not once lowering her watchful gaze.

A Child in the Ghetto Surrounded by Letters

Aleph never came back today
But yesterday he was leaping all over me,
Calling me to play in the old oak tree,
The tender-coarse gold tree.
I bore him in my hand,
Tilting back and holding him out in front of me.
Aleph, you are smarter than I am,
I was born foolish and silly.
'What's wrong, Basenka, why are you shaking?
Open your eyes, go wash your face.'
With a groan, little *omega*
Fell onto my finger like a ring.
Outside the window the willow tree rocked low to the ground,
Suddenly through the wall, a woman's deep voice
Screamed in cold terror, "Hurry,
Hide the child under the mattress."
Everything was gnashing and rumbling all around,
A stupid truck snorted.
And in my heart the letter *shin*
Burned three candles down in one short second.

[SS]

Free Ode
To the Philosopher's Stone of Petersburg
(with two offshoots)

to A Kuznetsova

Why, creator laborious,
Did you build this prodigal city,
Phlegmatic, miraculous, inane and judgemental,
Like an alchemical vessel?
You mixed rum, and blood, and stone,
Raised them to your lips, but suddenly left them
And threw yourself to this crucible.

Then it became nothing new,
And each man threw, like a drop of blood,
His own life to the constricted expanse,
And each was required, at the entrance,
Under the pupil of the malicious frost,
To lick the axe.
And hundreds of tongues fell
To your train-stations and gardens,
And writhed, and chattered
In the ears of the Future.

I busied myself with a simple game,
And perhaps it was a bit childish,
I will tell you in plain language –
Where lies the stone – the treasure.
Like coal it is languishing in latent mist,
Swampy, crimson, metallic,
While it remains dead.

There where the murdered tsar Rasputin,
In a caftan of bright-emerald,
Gnaws his own skull, his eye-sockets
Locked shut with bolts,
Behind them it lies – that miraculous stone,
Faded, wrinkled, broken.
Along the kind buildings I pass,
Along the enduring stony growths,
I pull apart their buds –
And there such shadows roam,
And bombs are produced like *pelmeni*,*
And the explosion's noise reverberates.

---

* a kind of dumpling

There lies a priest strangled by a calloused hand,
And January's blood under the Winter
Flows and turns like an ark.
There Ksenia, arriving home,
Shakes snow from the bare steps.

What then, like a worm, for a long time I lay,
And the knight of the tsars trampled me.
But suddenly the voice of the Stone called out,
And here I stood up before you
And I did not run away.

Go then, tsar, to the "palace of crystal",
To drink with a shorn schoolgirl,
You cannot defeat me.
I will raise up my heart to the heights
And arduously wring out your violet,
That the stone might drink in the deep darkness,
And mumble about itself.

For this not much is needed –
The tiniest trifle or glance,
An owl, perhaps, on the corner,
Or simply – that the forces of hell
Draw a cross on top of the snow.

1

Dawn grows, grows.
Finishing the opus,
I notice that I
Have been flying a long time in the abyss.

Whether I myself stumbled
And slipped from the edge,
Or somebody sneaked up
And pushed me – I don't know.

On my head is a weight,
On my torso – steel,
Revolving, I fly
To the place of the Grail.

A whirling of downcast rocks,
A gorge of solitude,

But this is not a fall,
Rather a long pilgrimage.
At home people rise from the darkness,
Ponderous, like towers,
To the Holy Land we are flying,
And we are not afraid.

Knight of the fall,
Of icebergs of stone,
The glove of creation
A paladin wears.

2   *Where the Stone may be*
In the eye of the gryphon,
In the clenched paw of the giant lion,
In the love of the Sphinx.
Here comes a man,
His brain more dappled than a peacock.
He is not at all afraid.
He remembers himself and everyone,
He will up and leap from the tower,
Fulfilling
The walnut's fate.

A Portrait of the Blockade
Through Genre, Still Life and Landscape

1   *Eyewitness Account (Genre)*
Past Andreevsky market
A man walks in the blockade.
Suddenly – an incredible vision:
The aroma of soup, a soup apparition!
Two stout babas
Pour the soup into plates,
People drink, and huddle closer,
Staring down into their reflected pupils.
Suddenly the police –
Knock plates out of hands,
Fire into the air:
People, you are eating human flesh!
Human meat!
The babas' chubby arms are bent back,
Led to the firing squad,

They walk and quietly howl,
And from their eyes wolfs' paws
Claw the air.
The passerby is too late to share in the soup.
A bird pecks it up from the ground – she is worse off.
And he leaves, stepping over the dead
Or walking around them, like puddles.

2 *Still Life*
Garbage dusks lap at the window.
A youth is hunched over impatiently,
Glancing at a casserole restlessly . . .
Inside it a cat gurgles!
You arrive, he calls it "rabbit",
You eat, he laughs so savagely.
Soon he dies. In the air you quietly
Trace with coal a *nature* (o indeed!) *morte*.
A candle, a fragment of carpenter's glue,
A ration of bread, a handful of lentils.
Rembrandt! How one wants to live and pray.
Even if frozen, even if ossified.

3 *Mixed Landscape. Stairway, yard, church.*
(paper, coal, raven's blood)

Neither a brother nor a father anymore –
A shade they lead,
Their guns pressed against his tailbone.
A naked bulb dangles similarly,
A draught presses in from the basement.

Behind this damp blue paint – there's yellow, behind it green,
Do not scrape to the void, there's no need,
There stand plaster and vapours of hell.
Here, eat up, a potato pink colour.
You have nothing more, blockade, my bone!
What have you eaten? Tell me:
Blue frost off of rocks,
Worms, a horse's snout,
A feline tail.
On barrels of human hands and tufts of hair
You have fed. On sparrows, on stars and smoke,
On trees, like a woodpecker,
On iron, like rust.

And in the yard they cut a man's throat with no knife,
Unceremoniously simply.
A voice leaks out of the steaming wound.
It sings of a mustard seed and a crumb of bread,
Of the soul of blood.
Under the weak northern lights
The sky walks on tumours.
The blockade eats up
The soul, like a wolf eats his paw in a snare,
Like a fish eats a worm,
Like bottomless wisdom eats words . . .
O, return all those carried far away
In the body of the flabby truck,
Jingling, like frozen firewood.

Good Friday. Empty, hungry church.
The Deacon's voice desiccated, he is barely alive,
Echoing shadows bring in the shroud –
The Priest rocks back his head:
"O, now I have seen, I have grasped –
You awoke from sick death,
And cannot recover, it's ruin for us all."
My blood becomes icy wine,
Ouroboros bites through his tail.
Teeth are scattered in the sky
In place of cruel stars.

[JM]

On Elena Shvarts
by Stephanie Sandler

Elena Shvarts writes poems that mix the fervour of Dostoevsky with the
formal clarity and freedom of Mikhail Kuzmin. She shares the religious
quest of the former and the mystical stylizations of the latter. She brings
the city of Petersburg to life much as they did, but also sets her poems in
a timeless, boundless arena where values are transcendent, aspirations
infinite. Her poems can exude the polyphonic characterizations of
Dostoevsky, and her long sequence of Lavinia poems from the 1980s has
the feel of a novel. The intensity of her short lyrics and her longer
narrative poems is Dostoevskian as well. In the poetic tradition, Tsvetaeva
or Mayakovsky are closer models for her sense of drama and romance.
Other poets have attributes she sometimes displays – Khlebnikov's

surreal juxtapositions, Zabolotsky's urban clangour – but Shvarts inevitably sounds like none of these predecessors, despite all the ways that she lovingly and compellingly speaks from within the traditions they established. She is among the best-known poets of contemporary Russia, a poet who performed her work in the Leningrad underground in the 1960s and 1970s and emerged to a wider audience in the glasnost and post-Soviet eras. Twelve volumes of her poetry have appeared in Russian, and a two-volume set is in preparation as of this writing. She has now travelled abroad many times to festivals and public readings; she has been honoured with the Andrei Belyi (1987) and Petersburg Northern Palmyra (1999) prizes, among others. Shvarts continues to flourish, writing poetry and prose at an impressive rate, and, more than thirty years into her career, she is still growing as a writer in interesting and unpredictable ways.

The spiritual qualities of her work continue to deepen. She has never been content with traditional notions of the soul, still less with poetry's ideas about the self. In the lyric and narrative poems she has been writing since the 1970s, she has asked repeatedly what makes a soul, whether it can be known. She has been unwilling to oppose the spirituality of the soul to the physicality of the body. And so it is no surprise that in the last few years, when Shvarts has written more often about death, she has sought images and allegories that might express the fate of both body and soul after death. She wants to make the soul visible, to give it the kind of substance and materiality that confirms its existence. That materiality results in extravagant language that can work as palpable rhetorical equivalent to a poem's themes. Shvarts's language is precise but adventurous, letting her draw on vocabularies that mix as vividly as do the rhythms and forms of her verse.

Translating that language into English poses special challenges. The delicate formal features can be hard to reproduce, even such simple iambic lines as are found here in 'Memorial Candle', and 'Conversation with a Cat'. In the latter, the even-numbered lines rhyme in Russian, nicely anchoring the form in a way I could not reproduce in English without wreaking havoc on the immensely calm diction of the poem. Shvarts gets large effects from relatively subtle choices, as in her allusion in this poem to Ivan Krylov's early nineteenth-century fable 'The Wolf and the Cat', where the cat is also questioned but responds garrulously, even speaking the fable's moral, "As you sow, so shall you reap". The dead do not speak, Shvarts fearfully suggests, because she has not earned an answering voice: the dead remain quietly enigmatic, like the cat with whom she would converse. Her poem also quotes from First Corinthians (7:29), when Paul (not Peter, as she speculates) reminds us that our time on earth is short, that those who have shall be as those who have not, and they that rejoice shall be as they that rejoice not. But for

Shvarts, the key division has to do with mourning; her tears in this, as in so many poems in this collection, gain her neither relief nor sympathy.

All four poems translated by me come from her two latest collections, *Solo on a White-Hot Trumpet* (1998) and *Wild Writing of the Recent Past* (2001). The death of her mother is mourned by the poet in these volumes, which cry out in tones of melancholy and grief heretofore unheard in her poetry. In *Wild Writing* we find poems that are infused by this sadness but take up other themes, some of them historical – the remarkable cycle about the Leningrad blockade and the last poem given here, 'A Child in the Ghetto Surrounded by Letters', among them. Such poems point out the way of the future for this fascinating poet. We may look forward to new forms of wild writing about Russia's present and its past, and about the passions of heart and soul.

Mariya Stepanova

Translated by Richard McKane

Airman

When he returned from there,
where he screamed in his sleep and bombed towns
and spirits appeared to him,
he used to get up to smoke and open the window,
our ragged clothes lay together in a heap
and I gathered up a bag for them in the darkness,
but that is nothing yet.

He didn't begin to and forbade me
to dig the back garden by the big house –
food and income for the family.
He put on weight, got angry, brutalised, then got thin
and rolled his own home-grown.
But life went on.

When he returned from there,
where the vessels of the civilian fleet fly,
from the heavens beyond the clouds,
when he had really come back from there,
we were all helpless
as children sucking at mama.
But that is nothing yet.

High up there they are singing at the controls,
the flight stewardesses are giving out wine,
trundling their carts down the rows,
but mine can't live up above,
he leans on the Father's shoulders
and I will not give that up.
But life went on.

When he returned forever from there,
a released man from the prison of heaven,
mysterious as a suitcase,
we became servants to the fine night,
a son in arms and a daughter around.
And he hit me in the face.
But that is nothing yet.

Like a moist blush at the word love
his blue-eyed glance slid over his face
while he hurt me.
All our family tree sat on the lawn
and saw the glow, where the horizon was,
where they hadn't yet put out the fire.
And life went on.

He drank for a week, tear after tear,
threatened someone, "Piss off" said to someone.
He held his stomach and wheezed,
then he felt silent and said quietly
that – Up there – he did not look in my eyes –
the Heavenly Daughter lives.
She's a daughter, a woman, a wife
and what she was like under her clothes –
I would have forgiven the lies
but he described painstakingly
her dispassionate as the skies
colourless eyes.
First he saw her, he said,
when the snow-white town was burning
and we had completed our mission
and in her blue skirt and white scarf
she stretched to me in an empty dive
to open the parachute above me.
He added: She is more visible at dawn.
She is always in a pioneer uniform,
a bluish ribbon in her hair.
Then he snored suddenly and woke the house,
now empty, without even a lock,
since we'd wasted all the money.
As for me I have nothing of my own,
but this astral bitch of his,
his commissar of the air
will answer, answer for his every turn
and remember his crashed plane
and what else was fated.
But everything changed. Life healed,
as though everything was bright, more transparent
than glass and nothing was owed it.
My man stopped, looked round
and became a controller for honest trips
on the country's transport resources.

Only once he returned home different,
like before, the same stress in his voice
and looking me close in the face
said that he was fed up with life on earth:
the Heavenly Daughter had appeared to him
on the trolleybus by the ring road.
He lay on his bed and began to die,
picking invisible fluff off the sheet
and died, while I, out of my mind,
was running, screaming to buy Corvalol
and saw: the trolleybus was going round
and at the first window was – She.
She had on a pioneer uniform,
she was blushing to the roots of her hair.
I leant towards the window,
there was a terrible roaring in my ears,
but I made a pace towards the platform
and judgement met me.
. . . Forgive me, although there can be no forgiveness,
for the killing of a twelve-year-old girl,
innocently perishing because,
in the soulless abyss, like a fish in soup,
the Heavenly Daughter is living in sin,
but with whom, no one will ever know.
. . . *And life goes on.*

Darya Sukhovei

Translated by Christopher Mattison

Spring Scales

1

we'll smoke a couple cigarettes
each third a unit of time

toss out a computer
or trade in a hard disk

buy a new mouse and two books
what for what for

2

with a new mouse and two books
in a semitransparent polyethylene
bag

with dreams like a refrain

take the trolleybus take the trolleybus
what for what for

3

hello – insert someone's name here
I won't report anything new to you
absolutely nothing
except for that I have time for nothing

therefore I won't plan to meet you
in the very near future

4

our affairs however require supplemental
agreement and discussion
th-ere wh-ere we get together

I sincerely hope
a cup of tea (martini/mug of beer)
to choose the essentials
they'll be guaranteed

5
you know material complexities
I look through the window to the sky

the mini-bus is twelve roubles, metro six
I have to buy two books a month
a computer mouse polyethylene bag
shoe repairs analgesics contraception

6   a continuation of the enumeration
quick noodles
cigarettes telephone bills rent
flowers

it's not yours to worry about

as usual our everyday things are fine
I'll tell you my news when we meet

7
a signature *sincerely / regretfully*

what for what for

send by fax send by fax
pasting in new names and more new names
discovering new names for myself
which live like me

8
instead of the mini-bus I'll buy a beer

I even have enough for klinskoye
and if there's no klinskoye
then a light bavarian, baltica

eight sixty eight sixty
spring waits won't go winds whistle

9
first spring in the city centre
like an unpretentious colour scale
drink back a beer drink back a beer

too late to experiment with anything else
+
too early to go back
=
something else will work out

10

I go somewhere to argue with someone
I might even go far away
with this very goal

to the other end of the city for example
or to another city
under the same sky

11

strictly speaking there's nothing more I can say

I open the first door I come across
a bar or the scientific institute it doesn't matter

they let me in because of my honest eyes
hair washed in the morning
unfamiliar face

12

I can't even explain why
this text is called spring scales

probably some old inertia
trajectory

previously established laws
of ecumenical equilibrium

13

It's already a sort of egor letov
twenty third of march in club polygon
squeeze an order of tickets an order of tickets
press here

the author indicates the heart
and leaves the scene

Olga Sulchinskaya

Translated by Richard McKane

The Kite

My soul is like a kite
and the thread is in your hands.
It is wild as the wind and disobedient
and the thread is in your hands.
Now it plays merrily with the wind,
soars effortlessly in the clouds,
now it shudders and dies
and catches the air stertorously
and he, below, stands, laughs –
he loves to watch.
The kite threshes, the wind swirls,
wanting to wear through the thread.

Crimea

The cow's moo and the goat's meheh carry down
from the hills and the measured murmur of the sea
like breathing in and out goes off into the distance
until the soul appropriates the experience
of the great day and also observes
how the cloud in the boiling milk
sweetly settles in patterned foam.
It now remembers with difficulty
the completed roads beyond the long day.
It's good here. Where else to go?
The twilight comes. The cricket has come to
and busies itself unlearning its peripatetic sound.
The pupil swims and dilates
looking into the dark-crystal horizon.

*

The wind paces on the lower branch.
There are napkins on our knees.
You eat olives and I shrimps
and together we are wonderful kids.

We drink wine, talk in poems
and we don't know what will happen to us.
We both have families and children
but we are alone in the world.
We'd run away without permission,
had fixed ourselves a Sunday,
without a middle or continuation,
without punishment or salvation.

Vitalina Tkhorzhevskaya

Translated by Daniel Weissbort

Wild Rose

Rose of the Russian nation
you are frosty and wayward
like poetry and prose
in a locomotive's furnace
    like
disaster under the big top
    rose breaking out
    rose of the Russian nation
    thorn of the heart
rose of the Russian nation
mustn't pluck you with the hands
tread you under foot
you're armed with teeth
    you're made of rose flesh
    all silence and menace
    no metempsychosis in you
    a direct route to the heavens you are
of early morning neurosis
filled with an inner luminescence –
like the wonderful and dazzling
moment – Rose

[1996]

He wouldn't sign the death warrant

He wouldn't sign the death warrant
when he read his own name among the names of the condemned
and this question I put: Is he a good judge?

Silence

[This is addressed] to you – A century on,
When you experience despair
And the tremor of fear and anger,
You'll hear my silence.

And you will follow me
Along the flight paths of eagle and hawk,
Where
Bright coloured openings
Leak endlessly.

Direct speech of grief.
The sky
Is covered in crosses.
As to my god-child
I bequeath to you Silence:

Seize it – like
A song,
Whistle
It
In your quiet moments:
We are but a reprise
Of the current of the years

Of blossoming – of twittering –
Of Silence – forever.

Elena Ushakova (Nevzvgliadova)

Translated by Elaine Feinstein

Sold into Egypt, he was altogether homesick

For Joseph Brodsky

Sold into Egypt, he was altogether homesick:
And more fierce, desperate and stubborn
Than the man in the bible. Dear poet,
I don't know whether to use the familiar form

Of "you"– a distinction the English language ignores,
Meanly. They have only the same chirpy word for
What is tender and intimate, like an embrace, or
What is as sedate as a firm handshake –

How can I talk about the golden shadows in Krochnaya
Where your school was, or your home on Pestel?
In December, I see the street lamps there still
Spill out light, like honey, over the Fontanka.

And always on the edge of that canal we felt
The presence of a young unhappiness, warm
Tears of elation. It is the innocent river of your early
Leningrad poems, running under the figured ice.

How much heart you needed to learn an alien tongue.
Yet you adjusted to it, tamed it, held it to yourself,
Until a new character entered your nervous system
Penetrating the tissues with his threads like rain.

To speak of home: it's as if you dragged your own
With you in a suitcase, with clothes trailing out of it.
Or as if a dark wing stretched across the ocean behind you.
You explained all that in your book *A Part of Speech.*

What a piece of astonishing good fortune

What a piece of astonishing good fortune
it was, when under Fleming's microscope
that first speck of penicillin grew –

It could so easily have lodged in
other useless places, just imagine:
some long forgotten coffee cup
on a window sill, for instance, or a rotten
potato, thrown away, pitted with mildew.

But then, would the indispensable
invention of a microbiologist
have escaped us? Would it not exist,
this blessing we all depend on?
No. Someone would make the discovery.
If not an Englishman in twenty-nine
then perhaps a Frenchman –
or even a Russian in nineteen-thirty.

Baby mould, you are like Luck itself:
chancy, spotty, unprepossessing,
nothing to do with work or giving oneself
up to selfless work with dedication –
some moist, cloudy stains appear
as if on a spread-out wet sheepskin
and there it is: a secret meaning,
a treasure, enigmatically concealed within.

Ekaterina Vlasova

Translated by Peter France

A little sympathy

A little sympathy
for the poor birds,
whose wings have grown heavy with snow.
A little compassion
for my own inner I,
who cannot attain this luxury –
wings heavy with snow . . .

On an old grand piano

On an old grand piano
the music was scattered.
But fingers crept out
for a little hunting:
with caresses, with blows,
with rain and with colour,
enfolding in heat
or in sorrowful coldness;
they danced and they laughed,
were braided and bent,
whispered and cursed,
loved and didn't care,
joked and endeavoured,
beseeched and surrendered,
for a while put on airs,
awkwardly smiled
and pretended to be God . . .
And then they flew up,
fluttered off somewhere
(to sounds leaving shadows
that resembled streams) –
to look for new hunting,
for some new tasty morsel . . .
and God tidied the music
and seemed to start weeping.

I see

I see
your hands in my nightmares,
they bring me unbearable pain . . .
and yet they are just wiping the dust
from the pale looking-glass of my soul.

Create me a world

Create me a world
of transparent-green fibres,
of dark-snowy skies,
and opal-smoky heights;
I will depart for ever,
will slip between walls, between windows
into that narrow opening,
that house, behind which is sunrise.
I shall not at all miss
all I leave behind with a smile;
in a diadem of gold
I shall forget the axe marks;
and then, of course,
somewhere at the very end
I shall make myself briefly
come down to you and shout: 'Time!'
But meanwhile I keep silent,
hiding cold hands in red spots,
sails on my back,
and a look of furious hunger . . .
Give me a day:
I shall hear underground noises . . .
whisper of words on the wall:
'The film has been seen, has been dubbed, has been shot.'

There is a way to sew wings on arms

There is a way to sew wings on arms,
the needles are blunted though, the leather
is scuffed, the sword won't leave the scabbard,
the word has vanished into sand.

And to sew wings on arms there is a way,
but sensing danger, the birds flap to death,
and wind blows out the town like a lamp,
and the sun has set before sunrise.

Tatyana Voltskaya

Translated by Catriona Kelly, Emily Hardiment,
Daniel Weissbort and Richard McKane

*

The low clouds, the shreds of dry grass,
Beet leaves tufting behind the decayed fence,
The gravel path staggering blind-drunk down:
This is no English landscape, sleek as fine china,
With ancestral oaks and the family silver of a brook:
No: here the snare of a dropped fir branch
Lies across every path, trees hold charred stumps
In their midst like blackened teeth:
And in fields there's no help from the storm-crossed showers
That have it in for everyone, even God.

[CK]

Snow grows old, like an actor you knew as a child

Snow grows old, like an actor you knew as a child,
It sags like a drape, so that footsteps keep on escaping
The dim mirror of the wind – you're happy, alive or dead –
It's not important, flushed or pale, – here's a make-up artist,
Surging upwards, tracing cheekbones with a powder puff.

Suddenly you're somebody that nobody knows.
Alone on this evening, your every movement will
Dissolve in an instant, without reflection,
Snow falls outside the frame, dark beckons with a nod,
And you lie, curled up, along the edge of the bed.

Without a reflection in somebody, you are without being.
Deaf, and mute, and unseen. Crows' nests are swaying.
The wheel has rolled past, its tracks are silvery scars,
The heavens have torn apart – their edges billowing,
And the moon drifts past in a wide, frozen halo.

Circles have thawed beneath pine trees, as though

Circles have thawed beneath pine trees, as though
Around tired eyes.
The tops of empty birches sway –
Damp bell towers

Bereft long ago of their green and
Deciduous bells –
And overhead the wind, like an axe,
whistles.

And light has decayed, and fits over fields
Like cranial bones.
February has turned scrooge at last, worn and
Money-grubbing.

Yellowed ice glimmers like bone beneath a
Pussy willow candle,
While a crow pecks away at dead snow,
Grey, prophesying.

From bitterness that's flowing in the boughs

From bitterness that's flowing in the boughs,
From gusts of wind that shake away the dust
From wax-white legs, from shouts of criminals
Among the scrub in chain-mail shirts soaked through,
From time, which streams from eyes, and from the fear
That only ever leaves us for a moment in
The lowest depths of an embrace, the place
Where we completely die, or so it seems
When we have moved beyond our bodies' bounds,
And from the horizon, colourless as chalk,
And from the sandy rustle of a paper,
From a friend, who's bellowing at you 'Hallo',
From melting snow, and drunks on metro stations,
And from fate, whose odds are all or nothing,
From those footsteps pounding on the fourth floor,
From the kettle, that's already boiling dry,
From the empty evening stretching out before me,
From my pathetic words, 'Don't leave me!'
From the hundreds of mouths all judging me,
Love is my shield: on it they'll bear me home

The snow has receded, like a sea, and uncovered

The snow has receded, like a sea, and uncovered
The skeletons of dead grass, the shells
Of barns, damp mirages of groves,
At the station sodden sheaves

Of people stand waiting for trains,
Ever delayed in their departure
To follow the sigh of thick smoke still
Lingering, the trail of black bushes.

Tree trunks stick up, like rusty knives,
Sacks are piled in a heap at the market.
The snow has undone embraces, uncovered
All the darkness, all the restlessness of the earth.

[EH]

Rhyme is a woman, trying on clothes

Rhyme is a woman, trying on clothes,
plaiting a rose into her hair.
She splashes in blood, like a naiad,
and surfaces, when not asked to.

Rhyme is a bell, driving away evil spirits
from the solitary guilty soul,
when the wind in the thistle thickets
weeps during the cold night.

Rhyme is a celestial trumpet – that is,
it rouses me from the grave,
when you come, beloved, with shining eyes,
and kiss me on the lips.

Rhyme is a path bordered by wild strawberries,
now here, now gone – so beats the heart.
I walk but don't know where,
I distract death with smooth talk.

[DW]

I want to go with you to the city with a name short as life

I want to go with you to the city with a name short as life,
where the eagle sun circles in the blossoming columns,
undried drops on milky hills, below
the heat squeezes out a tear from swollen fountains,
and in the cathedral-oaks between the petrified branches
the angels have woven their nests in taut gilt leaves,
where more alive than the vine, transparent and warm-loving
the marble burgeons winding itself round space.
I want to go with you to a city where the world was full
of the milk of faltering
speech, where the moist echo is around,
where the arena is empty, but in striped shadows, like a tiger,
under the bridges the yellow, glossy Tiber purrs,
where neither ice nor snowdrift cover the swimming steps.
We will arrive together in the city, in a crown of dill and myrtle.
It will look at us, who are wounded, from under its slow eyelids.
It will give us the thumbs down – or perhaps up.

God is the first snow. He is a leaf, a mosquito

God is the first snow. He is a leaf, a mosquito.
He is Benedict burning. He is sleeping Abelard.
He is a speckled stone at the bottom of a lake.
He is steam over milk. He hides in me.
But not in the ears, catching seduction,
not in depth of eyes that have been fed on dirtiness,
not in the dull, hard coffin of the skull,
not in the skipping fledgling in a ribcage nest,
shouting "Love, love!"
He doesn't dive
in the blood and splash "Catch!"
He is uncatchable for me, in me.
Only two are powerful enough
to cover Him, like a crane
in a magical, fine net of words guiltily left unsaid and movements.
Then He is here – not everywhere –
but in the fingertips and the tips of breasts
with which I softly touch you,
standing barefoot on tiptoes.
Inasmuch as this moment is fired and pure
like a pottery pitcher, like a narrow broom leaf

God breathes in it; He is the cold between the shoulder blades,
sparkle of the sun on the shoulder and imprint of a word unsaid on
                        dry lips:
the track of an angel. The track of sun on stones.

[RMcK]

Interview with Tatyana Voltskaya

by Gleb Shulpiakov

"Poetry has a high voice.
But this voice is impersonal."
(Tatyana Voltskaya)

Does poetry have a gender?

I think there are two ways questions like that can be answered. First of all, though, a warning light immediately goes up! All these divisions are good for the bathhouse, and, as we know from ethnography, not for all bathhouses either. In the vast majority of cases, the division of art and literature according to gender, age and so forth is simply a camouflage for the only real division, i.e. between bad and good writing. And by the way – why aren't these fashionable gender distinctions applied to painting or the theatre arts? As soon as it's a question of literature, inevitably there's talk of anthologies of women's poetry or prose.

How about the second way?

I'm reminded of the words of Samuil Lur'e – about how prose and poetry (in the highest sense, of course) have a voice, that of prose being male and that of poetry female, in that it is high pitched: "The higher the poetry, the higher pitched the voice." These remarks about the essence of poetry and prose, its intonation, seem to me true, profound. From this point of view, discussions about female and male poetry seem patently absurd. Although obviously it doesn't follow that only women should occupy themselves with poetry. In the final count, a tenor also has a high voice, doesn't he?

And a soprano?

Exactly. Between tenor and soprano, there's a gap into which talk of female and male poetry might fit.

Are there any particular characteristics attributable to male and female poetry?

As for characteristics, these come from ways of understanding the world which is different as between men and women. I think the male vision shows a tendency to grasp the world as a whole, to fathom out its structure, whereas the female vision is inward, including sensitivity to the actual texture of things; on the other hand, it has some difficulty dealing with abstractions. When I read Rein's or Gorbovsky's poetry, it never occurs to me that a woman might have written it. But when I read Kushner, I'm not so sure. And here's something . . . During the period of Soviet poetry, that is at the time of its general decline, it was the female poets who seemed more worthwhile. Maybe because, under any regime, response to textures (to a leaf, a sleeve cuff, a child's cry, the clang of a streetcar) is truer than the general view of things. There's less room for lying. As always, material reality comes to the aid of women. For that reason, during Soviet times – naturally, I'm not thinking of the poetic heights occupied by the likes of a Brodsky – as well as now, female poetry, in my view, has been stronger than male.

Does poetry have secondary sexual characteristics, and if so, what?

I've already answered that question, at least in part, when I spoke about male and female poetry. I'm afraid I can't be any more helpful. If one ignores grammar and specific themes ("My darling, what have I done to you?"), I have to confess that I personally am hardly able to distinguish, from a gender point of view, between the poetry, let's say, of Svetlana Kekova and Bakhyt Kenzheev, or Yury Kolker and Irina Znamenskaya. It is quite possible that there is a clue to these differences in nature, but I'm not aware of it. With some obvious exceptions, of course, such as Kipling or the aforementioned Rein. Nevertheless, at the very highest level, poetry is simply an elevated voice, and this voice is impersonal; that's the main thing about it, whether it's male or female.

Can one call your poetry female?

I don't know. It's not up to me to say – especially in view of what's already been said. Although I do have some thoughts on the subject. I suppose it was not for nothing God, in creating human beings, "created he them male and female". He must have had something in mind. Not that I presume to peer into the Almighty's mind! I'm simply assuming that there was some intention behind it all – it wasn't just for the sake of propagation, but also for that of voice, intonation, with which to praise Creation. And if the intention was to make me a woman, I'd be the last one to oppose or disguise it – in the way I dress, behave, write poetry. But I see no particular reason to keep harping on it either. Sometimes I imagine that all poets, earlier ones, contemporaries, future ones, belong to a celestial choir. We've no idea even who the soloists are. And in a situation like that, you'd better know exactly what your place is, that's all.

OK. Which poets, in your opinion, coud be said to embody Russian female poetry?

I don't know. The obvious answer, of course, is that the most female poetry is Akhmatova's, and the most male Tsvetaeva's. But looked at from the point of view I've been putting forward, it might be the other way round. Tsvetaeva's voice, whether you like it or not, seems to me the highest (among women, of course) – an agonizingly tense falsetto. It's true that it's often hysteria accounts for a poet attaining such heights, but that's another matter.

What about your relationship to the gender? Don't you think it's just a load of nonsense?

Nonsense, no. But sometimes the theme does seem to me absurd or just trendy, a trinket the scholarly world deploys with shamanistic zeal. Why? That's another story.

And what about the fall of Communism?

There are two sides to the collapse of the Soviet regime, as far as poetry is concerned. Firstly, as with literature in general, poetry stopped performing functions not germane to it. As a result, it lost its artificial multi-million readership, which used to fill stadiums for performances given by sixty-year-old poets. Actually, I believe that interest in poetry as such is unchanged – the situation has simply been normalised. Second, in lyric writing, as in all literature, *everything* now is possible. If editors before had deleted the words "God" and "soul", if the work of those who did not wish to sing the praises of communism was half-contemptuously labelled "quiet lyric poetry", now all poetry in effect has turned into "quiet lyric poetry". No better or worse for that, though. I think that the poetry of women writers was as liberated by all this as was men's poetry. But I have already described how women, in Soviet times, were evidently less damaged – for that reason, the shock was less severe. After Perestroika, many venerable Soviet poets literally took to raising strawberries or chickens; that sort of thing didn't happen in the case of women poets. It was considerably easier for those who wrote on religio-mystical themes – in Soviet times such writing was unacceptable in any shape or form and was confined to the underground. Still, I don't think it matters so much what one can or cannot do; what matters is the degree of talent and what one does with that talent. Of the many kinds of so-called love poetry (particularly with regard to women's poetry) I now get the feeling that, yes, we were able to look into the kitchen sink and sometimes everything there was clearly visible, but that doesn't make for art. Freedom, as we know very well, is not simply a gift; it's a burden as well.

[Tranlated by Daniel Weissbort]

Liudmilla Zubova

Translated by Daniel Weissbort

Let's talk about the weather. It's time, what!

Let's talk about the weather. It's time, what!
That week, you recall, it was hot.
I was waiting for weather like that a whole year –
You and I wanted to go to the forest, yeah . . .

Things aren't so good with me: can't get you out of my mind.
Maybe we can just go on loving; we're parting for a long time.

Let's talk of the weather, since you'll be on your way.
What an ordeal: nothing but rain, rain again.
In Leningrad, no sun, sky overcast – slush.
Surely you'll understand, my dear man,
how good it is to weep when the rain's coming down in a rush.

Let's talk of the weather. The eyes are scared and shifty,
Because now even talk about the weather's not so nifty.

The wind's blasting from the windows, the floor is unwashed

The wind's blasting from the windows, the floor is unwashed.
The table's rickety, and the cupboard's hanging open.
Let's go, visit friends,
And later on we'll tidy up.
Forget it, this house!

We'll visit friends –
have a sing-song.
It's nice there, with its young folk.
You can fool around with the fat cat,
Compliment the hosts. Already it's hard
To remember there's a home back home.

So, why are we sighing, grieving?

So, why are we sighing, grieving?
My sweet, let's make it simple.
Towards August, or maybe Jan,
I'll take myself in hand,
I'll beg myself, give myself a talking to.
Even now I seldom visit you.
When I'll feel all right on my own,
When I can come to you any time,
When I don't remember my own shame,
then, then . . . I don't know what then.

Bibliography

by Valentina Polukhina

Advisers:
Alekhin, Alexei – the editor of *Arion*
Kalpidi, Vitalii – poet, editor of *Ural'skaya nov'*
Kuzmin, Dmitrii'– founder of *Vavilon*
Rogachevsky, Andrei – Lecturer in Russian, University of Glasgow
Sukhovey, Darya – poet and literary curator
Voltskaya, Tatyana – poet and critic

Consulted:
Anthologies: *(Hereafter referred to by abbreviated title only)*
Post-War Russian Poetry, ed. Daniel Weissbort, Penguin, 1974
Russian Poetry: The Modern Period, eds. John Glad & Daniel Weissbort, UIP, 1978
The Penguin Book of Women Poets, eds. C Cosman, J Keefe, K Weaver, Penguin, 1978
Three Russian Poets, tr. Elaine Feinstein, Carcanet, Manchester, 1979
Ostrova, samizdat, Leningrad, 1982
Antologiya sovremennoi russkoi poezii tret'ei volny emigratsii, eds., A Glezer & S Petrunis, Paris-New-York, 1986
The Blue Lagoon Anthology, eds. K Kuzminsky & G Kovalev, 9 vols., MA, 1980-1986
A Double Rainbow/Dvoinaya raduga, ed. M Akchurin, Moskva, 1988
Molodaya poeziya 89, ed. A Tiurin, Moskva, 1989
Child of Europe. A New Anthology of East European Poetry, ed. M March, Penguin, 1990
Novaya volna. Stikhi segodnia, ed. SM Mnatsakanian, Moskva, 1991
Antologiya russkogo verlibra, ed. Karen Dzhangirov, Moskva, 1991
Latinskii kvartal, ed. V. Kulle, Moskva, 1991
The Poetry of Perestroika, eds. P Mortimer & SJ Litherland, Iron Press, Newcastle upon Tyne, 1991
Twentieth-Century Russian Poetry, eds. John Glad & Daniel Weissbort, UIP, 1992
Third Wave: The New Russian Poetry, eds. Kent Johnson & SM Ashby, UMP, 1992
Contemporary Russian Poetry, ed. & tr. GS Smith, Indiana University Press, 1993
Twentieth-Century Russian Poetry: Silver and Steel, eds. A Todd & Max Hayward, NY, 1993
Drugie. Antologiya sovremennoi russkoi poezii, Mt Holyoke, MA, 1993

I vsiakie. Antologiya noveishei poezii, Mt Holyoke, MA, 1993
An Anthology of Russian Women's Writing, 1977-1992, ed. Catriona Kelly, Oxford, 1994
Dictionary of Russian Women Writers, eds. M Ledkovsky, C Rosenthal & M Zirin, CT, 1994
Strofy veka, ed. E Evtushenko, Moskva, 1995
Against Forgetting. Twentieth-Century Poetry of Witness, ed. C Forche, NY/London, 1995
Pozdnie peterburzhtsy, ed. V Toporov, St Peterburg, 1995
Sovremennaya ural'skaya poeziya, Cheliabinsk, 1996
Antologiya russkogo monostikha, ed. D Kuzmin, Moskva, 1996
Sovremennye russkie poety: spravochnik-antologiya, ed. VV Agenosov & KN Ankudinov, Moskva, 1998
In the Grip of Strange Thoughts: Russian Poetry in a New Era, ed. J Kates, Zephyr/Bloodaxe, 1999
Russian Women Writers, vol. 2, ed. Christine D Tomei, NY, 1999
Poeziya bezmolviya, ed. A Kudriavitsky, Moskva, 1999
Russkie poety v Amerike, ed. A Gritsman, Chicago, 1999
Crossing Centuries: New Generation in Russian Poetry, eds. John High & others, NJ, 2000
Russkaya poeziya. XX vek, ed. VA Kostrov, Moskva, 2001
Antologiya russkogo palindroma, kombinatornoii i rukopisnoi poezii, eds. G Lukomnikov and S Fedin, Moskva, 2002

Magazines:
Arion, Chelovek i priroda, Daugava (Riga), *Druzhba narodov, 22, Ekho, Gorod* (Tolyatti, 2001), *Grani, Kommentarii, Kontinent, Literaturnoe obozrenie, Mitin zhurnal, Nash sovremennik, Neva, Novoe literaturnoe obozrenie, Novyi mir, Novyi zhurnal, Oktiabr', Ogonek, Teatr, Domovoi, Yunost', Zolotoi vek, Poslednii ekzempliar, Solnechnoe spletenie, Strelets, Vestnik novoi literatury, Vavilon: Vestnik molodoi literatury, Vestnik russkogo khristianskogo dvizheniya, Volga, Znamia, Zvezda*

Almanachs: *(some abbreviated forms are given in parentheses)*
Krug, 1985; *Molodoi Leningrad-89; Chernovik, Istoki, Petropol', Poeziya, Den' poezii, Al'manakh poeziya*, 1989, 52 (Moskva), *Poryv: Sbornik stikhov. Novye imena*, M. 1989 (Poryv); *Zerkala* (Moskva), *Petropol'*, 1990, 1; *Laterna Magica* (1990); *Indeks-2*, 1993; *Kamera khraneniya; Kliuch. Lit. almanakh*, SPb. 1995; *Novyi Sizif* (SPb., 1996, 8); *Algoritm* (Cheliabinsk), 1997, 2; *Almanakh poezii* (California), *Den' russkoi poezii, vyp. 5*, 2000, SPb. (*Drp*), *Poberezh'e*

Newspapers: *(Abbreviated form is given in parentheses)*
Gumanitarnyi fond (GF), *Literaturnaya gzeta* (Lit. gazeta), *Novaya literaturnaya gazeta, Russkaya mysl'* (Rus. mysl')

Check list of Russian Women Poets; * included in *MPT*

1. Abaeva, Liudmila – *Novyi mir*, 2000, 10
2. Abareli, Avelina – *Nash sovremennik*, 2000, 8
3. Abel'skaya, Natalya – *Pozdnie peterburzhtsy*
4. Afanas'eva, Svetlana – *Nash sovremennik*, 2002, 3
5. Afanas'eva, Tatyana – *Den' poezii*, 2000
6. Afanas'eva, Veronika – *Arion*, 2002, 1
7. Agapova Tatyana (Murmansk) – *Drp*, 2000, 5
8. Agashina, Margarita (1924, Vologda) – *Rus. poeziya. XX vek*
9. Aidina, Olga – *Istoki*, 1999, 5
10. *Akhmadulina, Bella (1937) – *Struna* (1962); *Stikhi* (1962); *Skazka o dozhde* (1962, 1975); *Moya rodoslovnaya* (1964); *Prikliuchenie v antikvarnom magazine* (1967); *Oznob* (1968); *Uroki muzyki* (1969); *Stikhi* (1975); *Metel'* (1977); *Sny o Gruzii* (1977); *Svecha* (1977); *Taina* (1983); *Sad: Novye stikhi* (1987); *Stikhotvoreniya* (1988); *Izbrannoe* (1988), *Poberezh'e* (1991); *Larets i kliuch* (1994); *Griada kamnei* (1995); *Zvuk ukazuyushchii* (1995); *Samye moi stikhi* (1995); *Odnazhdy v dekabre* (1996); *Sozertsanie stekliannogo sharika* (1997); *Mig bytiya* (1997); *Izbrannye proizvedeniya*, 3 vols.; *Vozle elki. Kniga novykh stikhotvorenii* (1999); *Metropol'*, 1979; *Fever and Other New Poems* (1969); *The Garden: New & Selected Poems* (1990); *Znamia*, 2001, 1; *Post-War Rus. Poetry; Russian Poetry: The Modern Period; The Penguin Book of Women Poets; The Poetry of Perestroika; Twentieth-Century Rus. Poetry; Contemporary Rus. Poetry; Anthology of Rus. Women's Writing; Rus. Women Writers; Rus. poeziya. XX vek; In the Grip of Strange Thought; Den' poezii 2000; Znamia*, 2001, 1
11. Akhundova, Alla (1939, Moscow) – *Belyi svet* (1969); *Voskresnyi sad; Rus. poeziya XX vek*
12. Aksel'rod, Elena (1932, Minsk / Izrael) – *Novyi mir*, 1997, 3 & 1999, 7; *Strelets*, 1997, 1
13. Aksenova-Bernar, Tatyana – *Arion*, 1999, 1
14. * Alaverdova, Liana (USA) – poems sent by fax
15. Alatartseva, Irina – *Den' poezii*, 2000
16. Alchuk, Anna (1955, Moscow) – *Dvenadtsat' ritmicheskikh pauz; Chernovik; Dekarotivnoe iskusstvo; Ural'skaya nov'; Poeziya bezmolviya*
17. Aldarova, Milana (Moscow) – *Otsroch'te sud!* (1988); *Antologiya rus. verlibra*
18. Aleeva-Matiazh, Alevtina (Ivanovo) – *Den' poezii*, 2000
19. Alekseeva, Elena – *Den' poezii*, 2000
20. Alekseeva, Marina – *Nash sovremennik*, 2000, 6
21. Alekskandrova, Tatyana (1953) – *Tikhaya osen'*; *Drp.*, 2000, 5; *Den' poezii*, 2000
22. Aleksandrovich, Mariya – *Istoki*, 1999, 5
23. Allaverdonts, Evrika (1973, Moscow) – *Antologiya rus. verlibra*
24. Andreeva, Yuliya – *Arion*, 1996, 2

25. Andreevskaya, Mariya (1936-85) – *Strofy veka*
26. Andrianova, Mariya – (Moscow) – *Antologiya rus. verlibra*
27. Andriurs, Valentina (1956, Dal'nii vostok) – *Bukhta svetlaya; Rus. poeziya. XX vek*
28. Andronova, Tatyana – *Oktiabr'*, 1999, 4 & 2001, 3
29. Anistratova, Irina – *GF*, 1992, 29
30. Anosova, Sasha (1983, St. Ptb.) – *Zvezda*, 1997, 4
31. *Anserova, Vera (1958, Donetskaia obl.) – *Antologiya rus. verlibra*
32. Antonova, Natalya – *Ot raya i do ada*, 1991
33. Anufrieva, Natalya – *Den' poezii*, 2000
34. Aref'eva, Olga —*Kovcheg* (1996), *Znamia*, 1998, 8
35. Arishina, Natalya – *Novaya volna; Soglasie*, 1993, 5; *Novyi mir*, 1993, 5 & 1999, 9; *Antologiya rus. verlibra*
36. Arkatova, Anna – *Arion*, 2001, 1
37. Artikulova, Liudmila (Tol'iatti) – *Gorod*, 2001
38. Asoyants, Irina (Moldaviia/Canada) – *A bylo tak ... –* (1998); *Almanakh poezii*, 4, 1997
39. Astaf'eva, Natalya (Moscow) – *Novaya volna; Antologiya rus. verlibra*
40. Artikulova, Lidiya (Tol'iatti) – *Gorod*, 2001
41. Averianova, Viktoriya – recomended by D Kuzmin
42. Azarova, Liudmila (Riga) – *Stikhi ob otravakh, zveriakh i ptitsakh* (1980)
43. *Avvakumova, Mariya (1943, Archangel'sk/Moscow) – *Severnye reki* (1982); *Zimuyushchie ptitsy* (1984); *Neosedlannye koni* (1986); *Iz glubin* (1990); *Novyi mir*, 1989, 2 & 1991, 10; *Nash sovremennik*, 2000, 3; *Novaya volna; Dvoinaya raduga; Strofy veka; 20th Century of Russian Poetry; Rus. poeziya. XX vek*
44. Baboshina, Veronika (Rybinsk) – *Istoki*, 1999, 6
45. Bakanovskaya, Elena (1968, Khar'kov)'– *Kontinent*, 1992, 70
46. Bakhareva, Galina (1961) – *Den' poezii*, 2000
47. Barakhtina, Larisa – *Kommentarii*, 1995, 6
48. Barbas, Liudmila (SPb) – *Neva*, 2001, 6
49. *Barskova, Polina (1977, SPb./Berkely, USA) – *Rozhdestvo* (1991), *Rasa brezglivykh*, (1994), *Memory* (1996), *Evradei i Orfika* (2000); *Arii* (2001); *Novyi Sizif*, 1996, 8; *Zvezda*, 2001, 3; in *Crossing Centuries, Lit. gazeta*, 3-9 Nov. ,1999.
50. Barykina, Liudmila – *Istoki*, 1999, 5
51. Bashkirova, Tatyana (Kolomna) – *Moskva*, 2002, 3
52. Bashmakova, Tamara – *Den' poezii*, 2000
53. Baturina, Tatyana (1947, Volgograd) – *Ekho* (1973); *Cheremukha* (1973); *Pis'mo* (1973); *I vse vokrug moe* (1978); *Polden'* (1985); *Rus. poeziya. XX vek*
54. *Bek, Tatyana (1949, Moscow) – *Skvoreshniki* (1974), *Snegir'* (1980), *Zamysel* (1987), *Smeshannyi les* (1987), *Oblaka skvoz' derevya* (1997), *Uzor iz treshchin* (2002), *Novyi mir*, 1992, 2 & 3; 1995, 9; 1997, 1; 1999, 12; *Zvezda*, 1997, 3; *Arion*, 1996, 1; 1998, 4 & 9; 1999, 1 & 2001, 3; *Kontinent*, 1999, 101;

Znamia 1997 / 98; 2000, 4 & 2001, 11; *Novaya volna; The Poetry of Perestroika; The Grip of Strange Thoughts; Rus. poeziya. XX vek*

55. Bekkerman, Natal'ya – *GF*, 1992, 17

56. Beliaeva, Viktoriya (1966, Moscow) – *Antologiya rus. verlibra*

57. Belianchikova, Marina (1955, Moscow) – *Put', usypannyi slovami* (1992); *Molodaya poeziya* 89; *Rus. poeziya. XX vek; Den' poezii.* 2000

58. Belorusets, Tamara (Odessa / S-Francisco) – *Ya pamiatyu boleyu* (1995); *Almanakh poezii,* 1997, 4 & 2000, 7

59. Beloshchina, Tamara – *Den' poezii,* 2000

60. Belosinskaya, Nina (1923, Moscow) – *Moi dorogoi chelovek, Poslednii sneg; Kontinent,* 1990, 64

61. Bel'skaya, Nina – *Den' poezii* (L., 1989)

62. Berdicheva, Anna – *Kontinent,* 1992, 70

63. Berezina, Liubov – *GF*, 1992, 13

64. * Berezovchuk, Larisa (1948, Kiev / SPb.) – *Kompozitsiya* (1999), *Mitin zhurnal,* 1990, 35; *Lit. gazeta,* 22-28 Dek. 1999

65. Berk, Nina – recomended by D Kuzmin

66. Bernadskaya, Anna – *Zvezda,* 1988, 7

67. Bernadskaya, Marta – *GF*, 1993, 11

68. Berseneva, Galina – *Zvezda,* 1996, 12

69. Berzina, Liubov —*Den' poezii,* 2000

70. Beshenkovskaya, Olga (1947, SPb / Shtudgard) – *Den' poezii,* L., 89; *Kontinent,* 1990, 65; *Mitin zhurnal,* 1992, 17; *Lit. gazeta,* 25.3.1992; *Zvezda,* 1992, 3; *Den' poezii,* 2000; *Neva,* 2001, 6; *Oktiabr',* 2001, 6; *The Blue Lagoon Anthology,* 5B; *Peremenchivyi svet* (1987); *Podzemnye tsvety* (1996); *Pozdnie peterburzhtsy; Strofy veka*

71. Besprozvannaya, Polina – *Kluch. Literaturnyi al'manakh,* SPb.,1995; *Pozdnie peterburzhtsy*

72. Bessonova, Liubov (1958, Tolyatti) – *V zerkale dozhdia* (1991); *GF*, 1992, 17; *Rus. poeziia. XX vek; Gorod*

73. Bessorabova, Elena – *Lit. gazeta,* May 2000

74. Bezrukova, Galina (1948, Tver') – *Raskleishchitsa afish* (1978); *Rus. poeziia. XX vek; Istoki,* 2000, 7

75. Blinova, Olga (1955, Tomsk) – *Den' poezii,* 2000

76. Biriukova, Marina – *Arion,* 1996, 3

77. Bliznetsova, Inna – *Antologiya sovremennoi rus. poezii 3-ei volny; The Blue Lagoon Anthology,* 3A

78. Bobkova, Zoya – *Druzhba narodov,* 2000, 5

79. Bode, Veronika – *GF*, 1994, 2

80. Bodrova, Aleksandra – *Arion,* 1999, 2

81. Bodrova, Nina – *Grani,* 1985, 138

82. Bochkareva, Izabella – *Arion,* 2000, 3

83. Boiko, Lidiya – *Istoki,* 1999, 5

84. Bondareva, Era (Vladivostok) – *Antologiya rus. verlibra*

85. Borisova, Maya (1932-1997, SPb.) – *Na pervom perevale* (1958); *Vechernie okna* (1961); *Belyi svet* (1963); *Izbrannaya lirika* (1965); *Kamennyi bereg* (1969); *Gribnoi dozhd'* (1970); *Ravnovesie* (1977); *Malaya Nevka* (1978); *Den' poezii*, L. 88; *Rus. Poetry: The Modern Period; Novaya volna; Twentieth-Century Rus. Poetry; Pozdnie peterburzhtsy; Rus. poeziya. XX vek*

86. *Boroditskaya, Marina (1954, Moscow) – *Molodaya poeziya; Arion*, 1998, 4, *Novyi mir*, 2000, 8 & 2001, 8; *Ya razdevayu soldata* (1999); *Odinochnoe katanie* (2000); *God loshadi* (2002); *Strofy veka; Rus. poeziya. XX vek*

87. *Boyarskikh, Ekaterina (1976, Irkutsk) – *Ne stolichnaya literatura*

88. Bozhor, Nataya – *Istoki*, 2000, 7

89. Bromlei, Anna – *Istoki*, 1999, 5

90. Brudne-Wigley, Eva (Milan) – *Novoe rus. slovo*, Jan. 1999

91. Brykalova, Marina (Taganrog) – *Den' poezii*, 2000

92. Bulgakova, Natalya – *Arion*, 1998, 1; *Arion*, 2000, 3; *Den' poezii*, 2000

93. Bukina, Liudmila – *A Double Rainbow*

94. Bukovskaya, Tamara – *Otchayanie i nadezhda* (1991); *Pozdnie peterburzhtsy; Zvezda*, 2001, 4

95. Bushkevich, Tamara – *Drp*, 2000, 5

96. Bushkova, Galina – *Arion*, 1995, 1

97. Bushman, Irina – *Strofy veka*

98. Bushueva, Katia (1973, Ekaterinburg) – *Sovremennaya ural'skaya poeziya*

99. Bychkovskaya, Tania (1963-2001, Achinsk) – *Lit. gazeta*, 11-17 July, 2001

100. Bykova, Zinaida – *Znamia*, 1998, 4; *Arion*, 1998, 4; *Nezrimye ptitsy* (2000)

101. Chagina, Evgeniya – *Istoki*, 1999, 6

102. Chaika, Mstislava (1971, Kiev) – *Raduga; Smena; Vozrozhdenie; Istoki; Antologiya rus. verlibra*

103. Chastikova, Elvira (Moscow) – *Dva gorizonta* (1990), *Antologiya rus. verlibra*

104. Chebotar', Sofya – *Oktiabr'*, 2001, 12

105. Chekmareva, Kira – *Den' poezii*, 2000; *Moskva*, 2002, 3

106. Chernavina, Rimma (Moscow) – *Arion*, 1998, 1 & 2000, 2; *Antologiya rus. verlibra*

107. Chernobrova, Susanna – *Zvezda*, 1997, 3 & 1998, 10 & 2001, 11

108. Chernykh, Natalya (Cheliabinsk/Moscow) – *Crossing Centuries*

109. Chertok, Larisa (1947-95) – *Osen'; Den' poezii*, 2000

110. Cherygova, Tatyana (1955, Izhevsk) – *Istoki; Poeziia; Antologiya rus. verlibra*

111. *Chizhevskaya, Vera (1946, Obninsk, Belorussia) – *Chekanka* (1990); *Antologiya rus. verlibra*

112. Chizhova, Elena (1957, SPb.) – *Tragediya Marii Stiuart* (1991), *Peterburgskie dushi* (1993); *Anthology of Rus. Women's Writing*

113. Chubatareva, Liudmila – *Istoki*, 2000, 8

114. *Chulkova, Svetlana (1958, Moscow) – *Molodaya poeziya 89; Antologiya rus. verlibra; Rus. poeziya. XX vek*

115. Chupurina, Evgeniya (Kiev) – *Neva*, 2001, 6

116. Danchenko, Elena – *Stikhi* (1995); *Etot sluchai nazyvaetsia*... (1998); *Druzhba narodov*, 1998, 5; *Den' poezii*, 2000

117. Danilova, Darya —*Arion*, 2002, 1

118. Dashkevich, Tatyana (1968, Belorussiya/Moscow) – *Molodaya poeziya 89; U zerkala* (1991); *Rus. poeziya. XX vek*

119. Davydova, Rigoletta – *Istoki*, 1999, 6

120. Denisova, Olga – *The Blue Lagoon Anthology*, 3B; *Arion*, 1995, 2

121. *Den'gina, Svetlana (1968, Samara) – *Osennee ravnodenstvie* (1992), *Antologiya rus. verlibra*

122. Dergacheva, Irina – *Den' poezii*, 2000

123. *Derieva, Regina (1949, Odessa/Izrael/Sweden) – *Pocherk; Uzel zhizni; Antologiya rus. verlibra, The Inland Sea and Other Poems*(1998), *In Commemoration of Monument* (1999); *Instructions for Silence* (1999); *Begloe prostranstvo* (2001); *Poslednii ostrov* (2002); *Zvezda*, 2001, 4

124. Diagileva, Yanka (1966-1991, Novosibirsk) – *Russkoe pole eksperimentov*, 1994; *Crossing Centuries*

125. Dinulova, Lidiya – *Golos serdtsa; Den' poezii*, 2000

126. Dizhur, Bella (Sverdlovsk/USA) – *Shadow of the Soul*, 1990; *In the Grip of Strange Thoughts*

127. Dmitrieva, Vera – *Den' poezii*, 2000

128. Dmitrieva, Olga – *Novyi mir*, 1998, 4

129. Dobroserdova, Elena – *Istoki*, 1999, 6 & 2000, 7

130. Dobrushina, Irina – *Arion*, 1994, 3

131. Dokolina, Galina – *Den' poezii*, 2000

132. Dolgodrova, Lidiya – *Istoki*, 1999, 6

133. *Dolia, Marina (Kiev) – *Sirotskie pesni* (1998); *Mezhzerkal'e* (1999); *Znaki na stene. Concherto Grosso. Pamiati I. Brodskogo* (2000); *U vorot* (2001)

134. Dolina, Veronika (1956, Moscow) – *Moya radost'* (1988); *Ili kot ili ptitsa* (1988); *Vozdukhoplavatel'* (1989); *Nivingrad* (1993); *Novaya volna; The Poetry of Perestroika; Strofy veka; Rus. poeziya. XX vek*

135. Dolzhikova, Olga (Kiev) – *Istoki*, 2000, 7

136. Drozdovskaya, Valentina – *Den' poezii*, 1989

137. Drozhzhina, Irina – *Drp.*, 2000, 5

138. Drubachevskaya, Galina – *Arion*, 1994, 3

139. Drunina, Yuliya (1924-1991, Moscow) – *V soldatskoi shineli* (1948); *Izbrannoe v 2-kh tomakh* (1989); *Polyn': Stikhotvoreniya i poemy* (1989); *Sudnyi chas: Posmertnaya kniga* (1993); *Sovremennye rus. poety; Rus. poeziya. XX vek*

140. Dubovskaya, Sofya (1933, SPb.) – *Molodoi Leningrad-89; Antologiya rus. verlibra*

141. Dubrovina, Elida – *Den' poezii* (L., 1989)

142. Dubrovskaya, Elena – *Istoki*, 1999, 6; *Arion*, 2001, 3
143. Dunaevskaya, Elena – *Den' poezii*, L. 89; *Kontinent*, 1989, 59
144. Dyachenko, Tamara – *Istoki*, 1999, 6
145. Dyakonova, Kseniya (1985, SPb.) – *Zvezda*, 2002, 2
146. Dyakova, Olga – *Moskva*, 2000, 6 & 12; 2002, 3; *Nash sovremennik*, 2002, 2
147. Dyshalenkova, Rimma (Magnitogorsk) – *Den' poezii*, 2000
148. Dzhuna (Evgeniya Davitashvili) – *Antologiya rus. verlibra*
149. Egorova, Irina – *Istoki*, 1999, 6
150. Egorova, Natalya (Smolensk) – *Den' poezii*, 2000
151. Egorova, Tatyana – *Drp.*, 2000, 5
152. Egorova-Nerli, Irina – *Istoki*, 2000, 7 & 8
153. Efimova, Nadezhda – *Druzhba narodov*, 1998, 11
154. Efimovskaya, Valentina – *Drp.*, 2000, 5
155. Efremova, Olga (Moscow) – *Antologiya rus. verlibra*
156. Efremova, Liudmila (Nadym Yanao) – *Den' poezii*, 2000
157. Elagina, Elena (SPb.) – *Mezhdu Piterom i Leningradom* (1995); *Zvezda*, 1988, 7 & 1996, 1; *Novyi mir*, 1998, 4; *Arion*, 1999, 4
158. Elfimova, Liya – *Istoki*, 1999, 5 & 6 and 2000, 7
159. Emelyanova, Nadezhda (1947, Orenburg) – *Zimnie uzly*; *Teplo ruki*; *Pora* (1990); *Rus. poeziya. XX vek*
160. Entina, Alla – *Den' poezii*, 2000
161. Erges, Viktoriya – *Antologiya rus. verlibra*
162. *Ermakova, Irina (1951, Kerch/Moscow) – *Provintsiya* (1991); *Vinogradnik* (1994); *Steklyannyi sharik* (1998); *Oktiabr'*, 1998, 8; *Arion*, 1996, 3; 1999, 2 & 2001, 1; *Rus. poeziya. XX vek*
163. Ermolaeva, Olga (1947, Novokuznetsk/Moscow) – *Podmaster'e* (1966); *Nastasya* (1978); *Tovarniak* (1984); *Yur'ev den'* (1988); *Al'manakh poeziya*, 1989, 52; *Novyi mir*, 1996, 9 & 1999, 3; *Soglasie*, 1993, 5; *Rus. poeziya. XX vek*
164. *Ermoshina, Galina (1962, Samara) – *Okno dozhdia* (1990), *Oklik* (1993), *Vremia gorod* (1994); *Chernovik*; *Znamia*; *Oktiabr'*; *NLO*; *Russkii zhurnal*; *Druzhba narodov*; *Antologiya rus. verlibra, Crossing Centuries*
165. Erges, Viktoriya (Moscow) – *Antologiaya rus. verlibra*
166. Eroshevskaya, Lira – *Den' poezii*, 2000
167. Eskina, Marina – *Neva*, 2001, 8
168. Evdokimova, Vera (1935) – *Ne pereiti pole*; *Den' poezii*, 2000
169. Evgenyeva, Anna – *Svetliachok* (2000)
170. Evseeva, Svetlana (1932, Tashkent/Minsk) – *Zhenshchina pod yablonei*; *Novolun'e*; *Evraziya*; *Poslednee proshchanie*; *Zovu!*; *Rus. poeziya. XX vek*
171. Evseeva, Margarita (SPB) – *V Nadezhde na schast'e* (2000)
172. Ezerskaya, Kira (1963, Moscow) – *Studencheskii meridian*; *Antologiya rus. verlibra*; *Arion*, 2002, 1

173. *Ezrokhi, Zoya (1946, SPb.) – *Kontinent*, 1987, 53; *Den' poezii*, L. 89; *Koshachya perepiska* (1993); *Shestoi etazh* (1995); *Na vsiakii sluchai* (2002); *Pozdnie peterburzhtsy*

174. Fal'kova, Zoya (Leningrad / Cleveland, Ohio) – *Samoe-samoe* (1993), *Russkie poety v Amerike*

175. *Fanailova, Elena (1962, Voronezh Moscow) – *Puteshestvie* (1994); *Teatral'nyi roman* (1999); *Sosobym tsinizmom* (2000); *Transil'vaniya bespokoit* (2002); *Rodnik (Riga)*, 1990, 1991, 1992; *Mitin zhurnal*, 1992, 42; 1993, 49; *Arion*, 1996, 3; *Zerkalo* (Tel-Aviv, 1997); *Znamia*, 1995, 1996, 1, 1997, 1999, 1998, 3 & 2002

176. Fediakova, Natalya (1960) – *Laskovo skazhu*; *Den' poezii*, 2000

177. Fedotova Larisa (Pskov) – *Den' poezii*, 2000

178. Fedorova, Natalya – *Arion*, 1998, 3

179. Fedos'kina, Irina – *Oktiabr'*, 2001, 12

180. Fedosova, Larisa – *Den' poezii*, 2000

181. Fel'dman, Mara – *Russkaya mysl*, 21.4.1989

182. Fel'dshtein, Evgeniya – *GF*, 1993, 3

183. Fetisova, Tatyana — *Istoki*, 2000, 7

184. Filatova, Tatyana – *Poryv*; *Molodaya poeziya* 89

185. Filippova, Elena – *Den' poezii*, L., 1989

186. Fokina, Olga (1937, Vologda) – *Syr-bor* (1963); *Rechen'ka* (1965); *Alenushka. Stikhotvoreniya i pesni* (1967); *Kopeshnik* (1973); *Makov den'* (1978); *Pamiatka* (1983); *Izbrannoe* (1985); *Matitsa* (1987); *Dvoinaya raduga*; *Rus. poeziya. XX vek*

187. *Gabrielian, Nina (1953, Moscow) – *Molodye golosa*, 1981; *Trostnikovaya dudka* (1986); *Zerno granata* (1992); Proze collection, *Khoziain travy* (2002); *Arion*, 1995, 2; *Antologiya rus. verlibra*; *Rus. poeziya. XX vek*

188. *Galina, Mariya (1958, Tver' / Moscow)' – *Yunost'*, 1990, 9; *Arion*, 1998, 1 & 2000, 1 & 2000, 4; *Vizhu svet* (1993), *Signal'nyi ogon'* (1994); *Poetry-non-stop*, *Lit. gazeta*, 2001-2002.

189. Galkina, Natalya (1943, SPb.) – *Den' poezii*, L., 1989; *Golos iz khora* (1989); *Okkervil'* (1990); *Pogoda na vchera* (1999); *Strofy veka*

190. Galunova, Irina – *Istoki*, 1999, 6

191. Gamper, Galina (1938, SPb.) – *Den' poezii*, L. 89; *Strofy veka, Arion*, 2001, 1

192. Ganopol'skaya, Elizaveta (Tiumen') – *Antologiya rus. verlibra*

193. Gariunova, Galina (Rybinsk) – *Istoki*, 1999, 6

194. Gasheva, Kseniya – *Arion*, 1999, 4

195. Gasimova, Elena – *GF*, 1992, 1

196. Gedymin, Anna (1961, Moscow) – *Kashtany na Kalininskom* (1985); *Vtoraya lastochka* (1990); *Poslednee liubliu* (1992); *Sto odno stikhotvorenie* (1994); *Molodaya poeziia* 89; *Arion*, 1995, 1 & 1997, 2; *Istoki*, 1999, 6 & 2000, 8; *Den' poezii*, 2000; *Rus. poeziya. XX vek*

197. Georgadze, Marina (NY) – *Marshrut* – (1998); *Chernym po belomu*

(2002); *Poeziya*, 1990, 56; *Teplyi stan*, 1990; *Novyi zhurnal*, 1991, 183-185; *Postscriptum*, 1997; *Kontekst-9*, 2000, 5; *Slovo/Word*, 2001, 31-32

198. Gerashchenko, Larisa – *Istoki*, 2000, 7

199. Gerasimova, Olga (1949, Moscow) – *Mgnovennyi sled* (1989); *Rus. poeziya. XX vek*

200. Giliarova, Elena – *Novyi mir*, 1993, 7

201. *Glazova, Anna (1972, Moscow/Chicago) – *Vavilon*, 1999, 6; 2000, 7; *Chernovik*, 1999, 14; *Stetoskop*, 32, *Paris*, 2001; *Kommentarii*, 2002, 21

202. Glushkova, Tatyana (1939, Kiev/Moscow) – *Belaya ulitsa* (1971); *Vykhod k moriu* (1981); *Razluki net* (1981); *Snezhnaya groza* (1988); *Stikhotvoreniya* (1992); *Vsiu smert' poprav* (1997); *Russkie granitsy* (1997); *Rus. poeziya. XX vek*

203. Glybochka, Olga – *Istoki*, 1999, 6

204. Godik, Anna – *Molodaya poeziia* – 89

205. Gol'dman, Rimma (SPb./California) – *Stikhi* (1999); *Almanakh poezii*, 4, 1997 & 7, 2000

206. Golosova, Evgeniya (1974, SPb.) – Internet

207. Golovanko, Anzhelika – *GF*, 1992, 13

208. Golovanova, Alla (Moscow) – Internet

209. Golubeva, Elizaveta (1985, Sergiev pasad) – *Den' poezii*, 2000

210. Goncharova, Natalya – *Istoki*, 1999, 6 & 2000, 7

211. *Gorbanevskaya, Natalya (1936, Paris) – *Stikhi* (1969); *Selected Poems* (1972); *Poberezh'e: Stikhi* (1973); *Tri tetradi stikhotvorenii* (1975); *Post-War rus. Pooetry; The Other Voices* (1976); *Russian Poetry: The Modern Period; Pereletaya snezhnuyu granitsu* (1979); *The Penguin Book of Women Poets; Angel dereviannyi* (1982), *Chuzhie kamni: stikhi 1979-1982* (1983), *Peremennaya oblachnost'* (1985), *Gde i kogda: stikhi 1983-1985* (1985), *Tsvet vereska* (1993); *Post-War Rus. Poetry* (1993); *Nabor* (1996); *Ne spi na zakate. Izbrannaya lirika* (1996); *Kto o chem poet* (1998); *13 vos'mistishii . . .* (2000); *Poslednie stikhi togo veka* (2001); *Kontinent; Rus. mysl'; Lit. gazeta; Oktiabr'*, 1990, 7; 1992, 11 & 1995, 2; *Znamia*, 1990, 8; *Novyi mir*, 1992, 11; *Against Forgetting; Twentieth-Century Rus. Poetry; Contemporary Rus. Poetry; Sovremennye rus. poety; Rus. Women Writers; Arion*, 1997, 3; *20th Century Rus. Poetry; Neva*, 2001, 5

212. Gorbovskaya, Ekaterina (1964, Moscow/London) – *Pervyi bal* (1980); *Sredi kukol i sobak* (1990); *Molodaya poeziya; Rus. poeziya. XX vek*

213. Goriunova, Galina – *Istoki*, 1999, 6

214. * Gorlanova, Nina (Perm') – *Znamia*, 1994, 3 & 2001, 2; *Novyi mir*, 1999, 11; *Arion*, 1999, 4

215. Gorlenko, Natalya (Moscow) – *Dlia vsekh, dlia vsekh, dlia vsekh, kogo liubliu. Sbornik stikhov* (1996)

216. Gorlova, Nadezhda – *Arion*, 2001, 3

217. Gorshunova, Svetlana – *Arion*, 2001, 1

218. Grantseva, Natalya – *Den' poezii*, L. 89

219. Grechko, Olga (1947-1998, Penza/Moscow) – *Ia shagayu po zemle* (1983); *Zemli i neba krug* (1986); *Predosterezhenie* (1989); *Izbrannye stikhi* (1995); *Lazurnyi sad* (1997); *Antologiya rus. verlibra*; *Rus. poeziya. XX vek*

220. *Grigoryeva, Lidiya (1945, Ukraine/Moscow/London) – *Maiskii sad*–(1981); *Zhizn' moya – svet vinigradnyi* (1984); *Krug obshcheniya* (1988); *Liubovnyi golod* (1993); *Vospitanie sada* (2001); *Ne bednye liudi* (2002); *Arion*, 1999, 1; *Dvoinaya raduga*; *Strofy veka*; *MPT*, 2001, 17

221. *Grimberg, Faina – *Green Weaver* (1993); *Arion*, 1994, 3; *Crossing Centuries*; *Vremia 'Ch'*. *Stikhi o Chechne* (2001)

222. Grudinina, Natalya – *Den' poezii*, L. 89

223. Gruzdeva, Natalya – *Kontinent*, 1992, 70

224. Gutina, Tatyana – *Molodaya poeziya 89*

225. Ignat'eva, Mariya – *Znamia*, 1997/98 & 1999, 9

226. * Ignatova, Elena (1947, SPb./Israel) – *Stikhi o prichastnosti* (1976); *Zdes'*, *gde zhivu* (1983); *Stikhotvoreniya* (1985); *Teplaya zemlia* (1989); *Nebesnoe zarevo* (1992); *Zapiski o Peterburge* (1997); *Kontinent*, 1987, 51 & 1992, 70; *The Blue Lagoon Anthology*, 5B; *Novyi mir*, 1994, 10; *Ogonek*, 1993, 9-10; *Znamia*, 1999, 9; *Strofy veka*; *In the Grip of Strange Thoughts*

227. Ilatova, Raisa – *Den' poezii*, 2000

228. Ingberg, Olga - *Lit. gazeta*, Sept. 2000 & 18-24 July 2001

229. Isaeva, Elena (1956, Moscow) – *Mezh mirom i soboi* (1992); *Molodye i krasivye* (1993); *Sluchainaya vstrecha* (1995); *Lishnie slezy* (1997); *Rus. poeziya. XX vek*; *Vremia i my*, 2001, 152

230. * Iskrenko, Nina (1951, Saratov –1995, Moscow) – *Molodaya poeziia*– 89; 22, no. 67, 1989; *Referendum* (1991); *Neskol'ko slov* (1991); *Ili* (1991); *Pravo na oshibku* (1995); *Arion*, 1995, 2; *Novyi mir*, 1996, 11; *Interperetatsiya momenta* (1996); *O glavnom* (1998); *Antologiya rus. verlibra*; *Novaya volna*; *Third Wave: The New Russian Poetry*; *20th Century Russian Poetry: Silver and Steel*; *Strofy veka*; *In the Grip of Strange Thoughts*; *Crossing Centuries*; *Rus. poeziya. XX vek*; *Znamia*, 2001, 7

231. Istorgina, Aleksandra (Moscow) – *Znamia* 1998, 7

232. *Ivanova, Svetlana (1965, SPb.) – *Ten' na kamne* (1990); *Poyavlenie babochki* (1995); *Nebesnaya Fontanka* (2001); *Stikhi etogo goda*, 1989; *Den' poezii*, 1989; *Molodoi Leningrad*, 1989; *Antologiya rus. verlibra*; *Nezamechennaya zemlia*; *Kamera khraneniya-2*, 1992; *Zvezda*, 1994, 11; 1996, 3; 1997, 9; 1999, 2; 2000, 3 & 2001, 6; *Arion*, 1998, 3 & 2000, 4; *Petropol*, 2000, 9; *Antologiya rus. verlibra*; *Crossing Centuries*

233. *Ivanova, Olga (1965, Moscow) – *Novyi mir*, 1988; *Kontinent*, 1992, 71; *Kogda nikogo* (1997); *Ofeliya – Gamletu* (1999); *P.S.* (1999); *Poste Restante* (unpublished); *Oda ulitse* (2000); *Arion*, 1999, 3 & 2000, 3; *The Poetry of Perestroika*; *Rus. poeziya. XX vek*

234. Ivanova, Elena – *Istoki*, 1999, 5

235. Ivanova-Romanova, Nina – *Den' rus. poezii*, 1989

236. Ivanova-Verkhovskaya, Elena (1959, Moscow) – *Oziabshii muravei*

(1991); *Osennii chelovek* (1998); *Rus. poeziya. XX vek*

237. Iverni, Violetta (1937, Paris) – *Izbrannoe* (1977); *Strofy veka*
238. Izvarina, Evgeniya (Sverdlovsk) – *Po zemnomu krugu* (1998)
239. *Kabysh, Inna (1963, Saratov) – *Lichnye trudnosti* (1994); *Detskii mir* (1996); *Novyi mir*, 1994, 12 & 1996, 11; *Druzhba narodov*, 1998, 3; Istoki, 1999, 6; *Molodaya poeziya 89; Strofy veka; Dvoinaya raduga*
240. Kadikova, Irina (Cheliabinsk) – *21 stikhotvorenie* (1996); *Nesovremennye zapiski*, 1997, 3
241. Kadomtseva, Olga – *Arion*, 1998, 2
242. Kadura, Svetlana – *Dnevnik pererozhdenii* (1992)
243. Kachalova, Ekaterina – *Zvezda*, 1998, 2
244. Kachalova, Irina – *GF*, 1993, 3
245. Kalinina, Natalya (Yaroslavl') – *Zimnii buket. Poeticheskii sbornik*, 2000
246. Kalmykova, Vera (1967, Moscow) – *Rastrevozhennyi vozdukh* (2000); *Prishestvie teni* (2001)
247. Kamenkovich, Mariya (SPb.) – *Reka Smorodina* (1996)
248. Kamshinina, Elena – *Den' poezii*, 2000
249. Kan, Marianna – *Istoki*, 1999, 6
250. Kan, Nina – *Den' poezii*, 2000
251. Kan, Diana (Novokuibyshevsk) – *Visokosnaya vesna; Sogdiana; Baktriiskii gorizont; Den' poezii*, 2000; *Nash sovremennik*, 2000, 10 & 2002, 4
252. *Kapovich, Katia (1960, Kishinev/Boston) – *Den' angela i noch'* (1992); *Sufler. Roman v stikhakh* (1998); *Perekur. Stikhotvoreniya* (2002); *Zvezda*, 1999, 10; *Russkie poety v Amerike; Arion*, 2000, 2
253. Kapustina, Olga – *Istoki*, 2000, 8
254. Kapustina, Veronika – *Neva*, 1992 & 2001, 6
255. Karakmazli, Dinara – *Antologiya rus. verlibra*
256. Karchenko, Irina – *Den' poezii*, 2000
257. Kareva, Elena (Tol'iatti) – *Gorod*
257. Karpishova, Elena – *Den' poezii*, 2000
259. Karpova, Natalya – *Den' poezii*, L., 1989
260. Karpukhina, Mariya – *Nash sovremennik*, 2002, 3
261. Kartasheva, Natasha (Yakutiya) – *Istoki*, 1999, 5
262. Kartasheva, Nina (1953, Ural/Moscow) – *Stikhi iz Rossii* (1991); *Chistyi obraz* (1992); *Rus. poeziya. XX vek*
263. Kasatkina, Tatyana – *Novyi mir*, 1998, 10
264. Kasina, Yuliya – *Mitin zhurnal*, 19
265. Katenina, Ekaterina (Moscow/USA) – *Zvezda*, 1998, 2; *Rus. poeziya. XX vek*
266. Katsiuba, Elena (1946, Rostov/Moscow) – *Petropol'*, 1990, 1; *GF*, 1991, 35; *Indeks-2; Ad Verbum* (1995); *Sobranie sochinenii* (2000); *Crossing Centuries*
267. Katys, Mariya – *Vorozhba* (1992)

268. Kashezheva, Inna (1944, Moscow) – *Vol'nyi aul* (1962); *Moya Ispaniya* (1962); *Ne zakhodiashchee solntse* (1965); *Izbrannoe* (1967); *Belyi gus'* (1970); *Vsegda* (1975); *Segodnia* (1977); *Novaya volna; Rus. poeziya. XX vek*

269. Kazakova, Rimma (1932, Sevastopol'/Moscow)' —*Vstretimsia na Vostoke* (1958); *Tam, gde ty* (1960); *Stikhi* (1962); *Piatnitsy* (1965); *V taige ne plachut* (1965); *Elki zalenye* (1969); *Snezhnaya baba* (1972); *Pomniu* (1974); *Izbrannye stikhotvoreniya* (1979); *Strana Liubov'* (1980); *Probnyi kamen'* (1982); *Vopreki. Novaya Kniga Stikhov* (2002); *Post-War Rus. Poetry; Novaya voklna; Strofy veka; Rus. poeziya. XX vek*

270. Kazakova, Irina (Ufa) – *Nash sovremennik*, 2000, 6; *Vremia i my*, 2001, 152

271. Kazantseva, Elena – *Strofy veka; Vremia i my*, 2001, 152

272. Kedrina, Svetlana (1934, Moscow) – *Antologiya rus. verlibra*

273. *Kekova, Svetlana (1951, Sakhalin/Saratov) – *Pesochnye chasy* (1995); *Stikhi o prastranstve i vremeni* (1995); *Novyi gorod* (1995); *Po obe storony imeni* (1996); *Korotkie pis'ma* (2000); *Vostochnyi kaleidoskop* (2001); *Kontinent*, 1990, 65; *Feniks*, 1995; *Postskriptum*, 1995, 1; *Znamia*, 1996, 4; 1998, 7; 1999, 1; 2000, 8, 2001, 4 & 2001, 11; *Novy mir*, 2001, 3 & 2002, 4; *In the Grip of Strange Thoughts*

274. Kerchina, Larisa (1962, Ufa) –- *Arion*, 1996, 2; *Antologiya rus. verlibra*

275. Khatkina, Natalya (1956, Donetsk) – *Lekarstvo ot liubvi* (1999); *Ptichka dozhila* (2000); *Arion*, 2001, 2; *Antologiya rus. verlibra; Strofy veka*

276. Khairutda, Yuliya – *Arion*, 2001, 3

277. Khmel', Olga (Kiev) – *Antologiya rus. verlibra*

278. Khodynskaya, Liudmila – *GF*, 1993, 18; *Indeks-2*

279. Khoziaeva, N. —*Lit. gazeta*, 14-20.3.2001

280. Khrolova, Irina (1956, Mariupol'/Moscow)' – *Esli mozhesh – voskresni* (1996); *Rus. poeziya. XX vek*

281. Khrushch, Nina (1947, Gur'evsk) – *Svet obruchal'nyi; Nash sovremennik*, 2002, 3

282. Khrustaleva, Elena (Vologda) – *Territoriya melochei* (2001)

283. *Khvostova, Olga (1965, Kyrgystan/Krasnodarskii krai) – *Pamir; Arion; Znamia*, 1994, 11 & 2002, 2

284. Khusainovich, Aidar – *Nostal'giya*, 03 (1991)

285. Kil'chevskaya, Galina (1953, Moscow) – *Kol'tso* (1989); *Rus. poeziya. XX vek*

286. Khvostova, Anastasiya (1972) – *Kontinent*, 1989, 59

287. * Kil'dibekova, Mariya (1976, Moscow) – *Arion*, 2001, 1; Internet

288. Kireenko, Olga – *Kontinent*, 1990, 62

289. Kirponos, Evgeniya – *Den' poezii*, 2000

290. Kisina, Yuliya – *Mitin zhurnal*, 19

291. Klimova, Galina (1947, Moscow) – *Antologiya rus. verlibra*

292. Klinushkina, Svetlana (1967, Moscow) – *Moskva; Almanakh Poeziya;*

Antologiya rus. verlibra; Kontinenet, 1992, 71

293. Kliment'eva, Anna – *Arion,* 2002, 1
294. Kniazeva, Marina (Moscow) – *Antologiya rus. verlibra*
295. Kochina, Natalya (1976, Moscow) – *Antologiya rus. verlibra*
296. Kogan, Nadezhda (1949) – *Den' poezii,* 2000
297. Kolesnikova, Elena – *Den' poezii,* 2000
298. Kolotvina, Marina (1963. Novokuznetsk) – *Antologiya rus. verlibra*
299. Kol'tsova, Olga (1957, Moscow) – *Strofy veka*
300. Kondakova, Nadezhda (1949, Orenburg/Moscow) – *Miraculous Day* (1975); *I Love – Therefore I'm Right* (1989); *Lit. gazeta,* 9.6.93; *Novyi mir,* 1994, 10; *Novaya volna; Third Wave; Strofy veka; Crossing Centuries*
301. Konopleva, Natalya (Moscow) – *Ostanovis', nezrimyi povodyr'* (1990); *Antologiya rus. verlibra*
302. Konstantinova, Liudmila (1959, Donetsk) – *Antologiya rus. verlibra*
303. Konstantinova, Nina (Kostroma) – *Ot pervogo litsa; Novaya volna; Antologiya rus. verlibra*
304. Kopasova, Lidiya – *Den' poezii,* 2000
305. Korkiya, Viktoriya (1948, Moscow) – *Svobodnoe vremia* – (1988); *Dvoinaya raduga; Rus. poeziya. XX vek*
306. Korkina, Alla (Kishenev) – *Nash sovremennik,* 2000, 6
307. Koroleva, Nina (1933, Moscow/SPb.) – *Medlennoe chtenie* (1993); *Lit. gazeta,* 13.2.91; *Zvezda,* 1997, 10 & 2001, 8; *Neva,* 2001, 2; *Strofy veka*
308. Korsakova, Mariya – *Drp,* 2000, 5
309. *Kossman, Nina (1959, Moscow/New York) – *Pereboi* (1990); *Po pravuiu ruku sna* (1996)
310. Kosmolinskaya, Vera – *Den' poezii,* 2000
311. Kostina, Tatyana (Leningrad/Izrael/London) – *Ostrova; Kontinent,* 1986, 50
312. Kostyleva, Elena (1980) – recom. by D Kuzmin, Internet
313. Koti, Tatyana – *Den' poezii,* 2000
314. Kotliar, El'mira (1925, Kazan'/Moscow)' – *Vetka* (1958); *Svet-gorod; Akvareli; V ruki tvoi; Novyi mir,* 1992, 12; 1995, 1; 1997, 4 & 9; 1998, 5; 1999, 7; *Antologiya rus. verlibra; Den' poezii,* 2000
315. Kotliarevskaya, Ekaterina – *Urok* (2002)
316. Kotova, Anna – *Arion,* 1996, 4
317. Kotova, Tatyana – *Rus. mysl',* 29.7.1988
318. Kotova, Irina (Voronezh) – *Den' poezii,* 2000
319. Kotovich, Tatyana (SPb) – *Ostrova; Kontinent,* 1986, 48
320. Kotovkaya, Raisa (Stavropol') – *Den' poezii,* 2000
321. *Kovaleva, Irina (1964, Moscow) – *V proshedshem vremeni* (2002); *Rus. poeziya. XX vek*
322. Kovaleva, Svetlana – *Den' poezii,* 2000
323. Kozhevnikova, Natalya – *Oktiabr',* 1998, 12
324. Kozhina, Vera – *Nash sovremennik,* 2002, 3

325. Kozyreva, Aleksandra (1953) – *Den' poezii*, 2000

326. Krasnova, Nina (1950, Riazan'/Moscow)'– *Razbeg* (1979); *Takie krasnye tsvety* (1984); *Poteriannoe kol'tso* (1986); *Plach po rekam* (1989); *Istoki*, 1999, 6; *Antologiya rus. verlibra*; *Den' poezii*, 2000; *Vremia i my*, 2000, 148; *Rus. poeziya. XX vek*

327. Kravets, Tamara – *Istoki*, 1999, 6

328.. Kresikova, Iza – *Istoki*, 1999, 6 & 2000, 8

329. Krestova, Valeriya – *Arion*, 1998, 2

330. Kriukova, Elena (1956, Nizhnii Novgorod) – *Volga*, 1990, 6; *Lit. gazeta* 11.12.91; *Poryv*; *Novyi mir*, 1993, 1; *Znamia*, 1998, 12; *Strofy veka*

331. Krupskaya, Dina – *Arion*, 1994, 4

332. Kruteeva, Yuliya (1966, Ekaterinburg) – *Sovr. ural'skaya poeziya*

333. *Krylova, Ella (1967, Moscow/SPb.) – *Znamia*, 1991; *Proshchanie s Peterburgom* (1993); *Apokrif* (1998); *Sozertsatel'* (1999); *Spasi i sokhrani* (2000); *Sineva* (2001); *Pchela na levkoe. Izbrannoe* (2001); *Arion*, 1997, 1 & 1998, 4; *Zvezda*, 1996, 8 & 2001, 9; *Znamia*, 1999, 1; *Strofy veka*; *Den' poezii*, 2000

334. Krylova, Zoya – *Istoki*, 1999, 6

335. Kuchkina, Olga (Moscow) – *Arion*, 1995, 2 & 3, 1997, 2 & 1999, 3; *Novyi mir*, 1995, 12; *Zvezda*, 1996 12; *Znamia* 1998, 11; 1999, 10 & 2000, 9; *Oktiabr"* 1999, 3;

336. *Kudimova, Marina (1953, Tambov/Moscow) – *Perechen' prichin* (1982); *Chut' chto* (1987); *Oblast'* (1989); *Arys'-pole* (1990); *Druzhba narodov*, 1998, 12; *Znamia* 1989, 8 & 1999, 2; *Molodaya poeziya* 89; *Novaya volna*

337. Kudina, Tatyana (1964, Moscow) – *Almanakh Poeziia*; *Antologiya rus. verlibra*

338. Kudriakova, Natalya – *Kontinent*, 1992, 71

339. Kudriasheva, Larisa —*Drp.*, 2000, 5

340. Kulakova, Marina (1962, Nizhnii Novgorod) – *Neva*, *Yunost'*, *Novyi mir*; *Antologiya rus. verlibra*

341. Kulesh, Darya – *Arion*, 2002, 1

342. Kulieva, Elizaveta (1973, Moscow) – *Den' poezii*, 2000

343. *Kulishova, Inna (1969, Tbilisi) – *Na okraine slova* (2000)

344. *Kunina, Yuliya (1966, Moscow) – *Kairos* (1991); *Stikhi* (1992); *Diurer pered zerkalom*; *Kontinent*, 1992, 70; *Arion*, 1996, 4; *Strofy veka*, *Poberezh'e*; *Crossing Centuries*; *Vavilon*, 2001, 8

345. Kutyeva, Anna – *Den' poezii*, L. 89

346. Kuralova, Svetlana (1959, Kemerovo) – *Druzhba narodov*, 2001, 10

347. Kurillo, Irina (1940-93) – *Istoki*, 2000, 8

348. Kuvshinnikova, Elena – *Drp*, 2000, 5

349. Kuzmina, Natalya – *Arion*, 1994, 4 & 6, 1998, 4

350. Kuznets, Olga (1975, Stupino) – *Nash sovremennik*, 2000, 3

351. Kuznetsova, Olga (1975, Arkhangel'sk) – *Stikhi* (1995); *Daugava*, 1994, 3; *Znamia*, 1995, 4; *Novyi mir*, 1995, 7; *Arion*, 1995, 2

352. Kuznetsova, Inga – *Arion*, 1998, 3

353. Kuznetsova, Anna – *Arion*, 2001, 2

354. Kuznetsova, Svetlana (1934, Irkutsk – 1988, Moscow) – *Protaliny* (1962); *Svetlana* (1982); *Sobolinaya tropa* (1983); *Stikhotvoreniya* (1986); *Vtoroe gadanie Svetlany* (1989); *Izbrannoe* (1990); *Novaya volna; Strofy veka; Dvoinaya raduga; Rus. poeziya. XX vek*

355. Kuzovleva, Tatyana (1939, Moscow) – *Rossiya. Bereza. Rosa* (1965); *Vereteno* (1982); *Chas zhavoronka* (1986); *Novaya volna; The Poetry of Perestroika; Rus. poeziya. XX vek*

356. Landre, Liudmila – *Istoki*, 2000, 7

357. Lankovskaya, Natalya – *Den' poezii*, L. 89

358. Lapshina, Tatyana – *Den' poezii*, L. 89

359. Latysheva, Lina – *Molodaya poeziya 89*

360. *Lavut, Evgeniya (1972, Moscow) – GF, 1993, 8;Poems about Gleb the Good Gentleman-Landowner, about King David, Foma and Erema, Luther and others* (1994); *Amur i dr.* (2001)

361. Lazortseva, Inessa – *I vsiakie*

362. *Lazutkina, Elena (1975, Krasnodar / Moscow) – *Arion*, 1995, 1 & 1997, 4; *Znamia*, 1999, 3 & 2001, 4

363. L'dova, Liubov'– *Molodaya poeziya 89*

364. Lebedeva, Ekaterina – *Arion*, 1999, 2; 2000, 1 & 2001, 4

365. Lebedeva, Nadezhda – *Istoki*, 2000, 8; *Drp.*, 2000, 5

366.. Leont'eva, Svetlana (Sverdlovsk) – *Nash sovremennik*, 2000, 10

367. Leshcheva, Nadezhda – *Molodaya poeziya*, 89

368. Lesnaya, Irina —*Istoki*, 1999, 6

369. Levinzon, Rina (1949, Moscow) – *Lirika* (1977); *Sneg v Ierusalime* (1980); *Tretya volna*, 1984, 17; *Gorst' vetra* (1983); 22, 1986, 47; *Kontinent*, 1984, 41; 1987, 56; *Pervyi dom . . . poslednii dom . . .* (1991); *Strofy veka*

370. Levitan, Alla (Moscow / California) – *Almanakh poezii*, 4, 1997

371. Liaskovskaya, Natalya (1958, Ukraine / Moscow) – *Okno v vishnevyi sad* (1986); *Svetaet* (1991); *Molodaya poeziya 89; Rus. poeziya. XX vek; Nash sovremennik*, 2000, 8 & 2002, 3

372. Libertseva, Liudmila – *Drp*, 2000, 5

373. Libova, Irina (1976-1999, Moscow / Boston) – *Almanakh poezii*, 7, 2000

374. Limanova, Natalya – *GF*, 1992, 1; *Novaya lit. gazeta*, 1994, 8; *Arion*, 1995, 3

375. Lin'kova, Liudmila – *Molodaya poeziya 89*

376. Lin'kova, Vera (1954, Kazakhstan) – *Videniya v gorode nishchikh* (1993)

377. Lipnitskaya, Alla (1949, Sumsk) – *My tol'ko putniki s toboi* (1992); *Antologiya rus. verlibra*

378. *Lisnianskaya, Inna (1928, Baku / Moscow) – *Eto bylo so mnoiu* (1957); *Vernost'* (1958); *Ne prosto – liubov'* (1963); *Iz pervykh ruk* (1966);

Vinogradnyi svet (1978); *'Stikhi'* (Metropol', 1979); *Dozhdi i zerkala* (1983); *Na opushke sna* (1984); *Vozdushnyi plast* (1990); *Stupeni.* Nakhodka otdykhayushchego (1990); *Stikhotvoreniya* (1991); *Posle vsego* (1994); *Odinokii dar* (1995); *Veter pokoya* (1998); *Muzyka i bereg* (2000); *Metropol'*, 1979; *Kontinent*, 1983, 38; 1986, 47 & 1990, 64; *Arion*, 1998, 1; 1999, 2, 2000, 1; *Znamia*, 1987, 9; 1994, 7; 2001, 1 & 9; *Oktiabr'*, 1990, 9; *Zvezda*, 2001, 3; *Novyi mir*, 1992, 10; 1993, 12 & 2002, 1; *Den' poezii*, 2000; *Novaya volna; Twentieth-Century Russian Poetry; In the Grip of Strange Thoughts; Rus. Women Writers*

379. *Litvak, Sveta (1959, Moscow) – *Raznotsvetnye prokazniki* (1992); *Pesni uchenika* (1994); *Kontinent*, 1986, 47; *Znamia*, 1987, 9; 1990, 12; 2001,10 & 2001, 9; *Arion*, 1998, 1 & 4; 2000, 2; 2001, 1 & 3; *Samizdat veka*, 1997; *Crossing Centuries; Antologiia rus. palindroma*

380. Logvinova, Anna – *Arion*, 2000, 4

381. Lokshina, Nina – *Rodstvo vremen* (1992)

382. Lorents, Inessa – *Den' russkoi poezii*, 2000, 5

383. Loseva, Natalya (Tver') – *Steklianye zonty* (2000)

384. Lovina-Lovich, Ekaterina – *Arion*, 1998, 3

385. Lukanina, Mariya – *Istoki*, 1999, 6 & 2000, 7

386. Lukina, Tatyana (SPb./Munchen) – *Den' poezii*, 2000

387. Lukomskaya, Liudmila (Khar'kov/California) – *Almanakh poezii*, 4, 1997

388. Lukyanova, Irina (1969, Novosibirsk/Moscow) – *Radost' moya* (1998); *Rus. poeziya. XX vek*

389. Lur'e, Liudmila (New York) – *Moi sentiabr'* (1999); *Almanakh poezii*, 7, 2000

390. Lutokhina, Marina – *Istoki*, 1999, 6

391. Lutkova, Lida – *Podchinenie liubvi* (1995)

392. Makarova, Tatyana (1940-74, Moscow) – *Strofy veka*

393. Makhova, Mariya – *GF*, 1992, 17

394. Makovetskaya, Nina – *Den' poezii*, 2000

395. Maksimova, Mariya (Moscow) – *GF*, 1992, 1; *Poluostrov* (1997); *Crossing Centuries*

396. Maksimova, Svetlana (1958. Khar'kov/Moscow) – *Vol'nomu volia* (1988); *Rozhdennye sfinksom* (1988); *Molodaya poeziya 89*; *Oktiabr'*, 1998, 3; *Rus. poeziya. XX vek*

397. Maksimenko, Tatyana – *Strofy veka*

398. Malakhieva-Mirovich, Varvara – *Monastyrskoe* (1994)

399. Malakova, Stella – *Den' poezii*, 2000

400. Mal'mi, Valentina (1949, Moscow) – *Rus. poeziya. XX vek*

401. Mal'tseva, Nadezhda (1945, Moscow) – *Strofy veka*; *Rus. poeziya. XX vek*

402. Mal'tseva, Alina – *Drp*, 2000, 5

403. Mamaenko, Anna (Krasnosar) – *Den' poezii*, 2000

404. Markgraf, Nina (1954, Altai/Moscow) – *Tsar'-serdtse* (1989); *Molodaya poeziya* 89; *Rus. poeziya. XX vek*

405. Markova, Rimma – *Den' poezii*, L. 89

406. Markova, Olga – *Arion*, 1996, 3

407. Markova, Vera – *Arion*, 1994, 3

408. Martishina, Natalya (1967) – *Zolotoe kolechko* (2000); *Den' poezii*, 2000

409. Martova, Zosia – *Kontinent*, 1987, 52

410. Martova, Olga – *Strofy veka*; *Den' poezii*, 2000

411. *Martynova, Olga (1962, Krasnoyarsk/Leningrad/Frankfurt) – *Sumasshedshii kuznechik* (1993); *Chetyre vremeni nochi* (1998); *Brief an die Zypressen* (2001); *Nezamechennaya zemlia* (1991); *Kamera khraneniya*, 1989, 1 & 1994, 4; *Crossing Centuries*; *Avrora*; *Kontinent*; *Sumerki*; 22; *Zerkalo zagadok*; *Ural*; *Manuskripte*; *Akzente*; *Rus. mysl'*

412. Martynova, Tatyana – *Arion*, 2001, 4

413. Mar'yan, Marina – *Drp*, 2000, 5

414. Martova, Zosia – *Kontinent*, 1987, 52

415. Mashinskaya, Irina (1958, Moscow/New Jersey) – *Prostye vremena* (2000); *Stikhotvoreniya* (2001); *Posle epigrafa* (2002); *Arion*, 1997, 3 & 2000, 3; *Russkie poety v Amerike*; *Rus. mysl*, 2001, 1-7,11; *Strofy veka*; *Vremia i my*, 2002, 116

416. Matlina, Svetlana (Ulyanovsk) – *Nash sovremennik*, 2000, 5 & 2002, 1

417. Matveeva, Novella (1934, L./Moscow) – *Lirika* (1961); *Korablik* (1963); *Dusha veshchei* (1966); *Lastochkina shkola* (1973); *Reka* (1978); *Strana priboya* (1983); *Krolich'ya derevnia* (1984); *Khvala rabote* (1987); *Izbrannoe* (1989); *Proza v stikhakh* (1989); *Bormatukha: stikhi i poemy* (1991); *Nerastorzhimyi krug* (1991); *Menuet* (1994); *Pastusheskii dnevnik* (1998); *Melodiya dlia gitary* (1998); *Sonety* (1998); *Kasseta snov* (1998); *Znamia* 1997/98; *Rus. Poetry: Modern Period*; *Al'manakh poeziya*, 1989, 52; *Twentieth-Century Rus. Poetry*; *20th Century Rus. Poetry*; *Sovremennye rus. poety*; *Znamia*, 1998, 1, 1999, 1 & 3; 2000, 7; 2001, 6; *Arion*, 2001, 1; *Post-War Rus. Poetry*; *Rus. poeziya. XX vek*

418. Matveeva, Margarita – *Drp*, 2000, 5

419. Mazharova, Valentina – *Den' poezii*, 2000

420. Medvedeva, Natalya (1958, SPb.) – *The Blue Lagoon*, 2B; *Chelovek i priroda*, 1992, 1; *Arion*, 1999, 2

421. Mekshen, Svetlana (1941, Lipetsk) – *Priznanie*; *Zavisimost'*; *Rus. poeziya. XX vek*; *Lit. gazeta*, 6-12.3.2002

422. Mel'nik, Elena (1956, Donetskaya obl.) – *Antologiya rus. verlibra*

423. Merzliakova, Natalya – *GF*, 1992, 1

424. Mialova, Olga (1982, Orienburg/Moscow) – *Nash sovremennik*, 2000, 1

425. Mikhailichenko, Elizaveta (1963, Stavropol') —*Kontinent*, 1988, 57

426. Mikhailovskaya, Tatyana – *Solnechnoe spletenie. Kniga odnostishii* (1995)

427. Mikhalevich, Alla – *Ekho. Stikhi* (1990); *Arion*, 1999, 1 & 2001, 2

428. *Miller, Larisa (1940, Moscow) – *Bezymiannyi den'* (1977); *V ozhidanii Edipa* (1993); *Between the Cloud and the Pit* (2001); *Motiv*, 2002; *Novyi mir*, 1993, 6 & 7; 2002, 3; *Arion*, 1996, 4; 2002, 1 & 3; *Lit. gazeta* 25.10.1995 & 6-12.3..2002; *Vremia i my*, 2000, 146; *Strofy veka*; *Rus. poeziya. XX vek*

429. *Milova, Tatyana (1965, Moscow) – *Nachal'niku khora* (1998); *Petropol'*; *Yunost'*; *Novaya Yunost'*; *GF* 1993, 21; *Arion*, 1996, 4 & 1997, 4 & 1999, 2; *Druzhba narodov*, 1998, 10; *Rus. poeziya. XX vek*

430. Milovidova, Yuliya (1985) – *Istoki*, 1999, 6

431. Mineeva, Ekaterina (Cheliabinsk) – *Algoritm*, 1997, 2

432. Minevich, Anna (Minsk/Cleveland, Ohio) – *Almanach poezii*, 4, 1997

433. Mirkina, Zinaida (Moscow) – *GF*, 1991, 10; *Lit. gazeta* 25.10.95, *Sovremennye rus. poety*

434. Miroshnichenko, Nadezhda (1943, M./Syktyvkar) – *Vse konchaetsia dobrom* (1984); *Sykryvkarskii variant* (1986); *Khochetsia schastya* (1988); *Zachem ne sberegli* (1989); *Nash sovremennik*, 2000, 7; *Rus. poeziya. XX vek*

435. *Mnatsakanova, Elizaveta (1922, Baku/Vienna) – *Shagi i vzdokhi. Chetyre knigi stikhov* (1982); *Beim tode zugast / U smerti v gostiakh* (1986); *Das Buch Sabeth. Kniga v piati chastiakh* (1988); *Vita breve* (1994); in *Blue Lagoon Anthology, 2A*; *Apollon 77*; *Vremia i my*, 1978, 27; *Sintaksis*, 1983, 11; *Mitin zhurnal*, 1992, 45/46; *Kommentarii*, 1995, 6; *Segodnia* 1996. 31.5

436. Moiseeva, Irina (1954, SPb.) – *Pozdnie peterburzhtsy*; *Drp.*, 2000, 5; *Rus. poeziya. XX vek*

437. Moliarova, Irina – *Den' poezii*, L. 89; *Drp.*, 2000, 5

438. *Morits, Yunna (1937, Kiev/Moscow) – *Razgovor o schast'e* (1957); *Mys zhelaniya* (1961); *Schastlivyi zhuk* (1969); *Loza. Kniga stikhov, 1962-1969* (1970); *Surovoi nityu* (1974); *Malinovaya koshka* (1976); *Pri svete zhizni* (1977); *Poprygat''– poigrat''* (1978); *Tretii glaz* (1980); *Izbrannoe* (1982); *Zakhodite v gosti* (1982); *Sinii ogon': Stikhi* (1985); *Domik s truboi* (1986); *Na etom berege vysokom* (1987); *Muskul vody* (1990); *V logove golosa* (1990); *Rasskazy o chudesnom* (2002); *Post-war Rus. Poetry*; *Russian Poetry: The Modern period*; *Three Russian Poets*; *Novaya volna*; *The Poetry of Perestroika*; *Contemporary Rus. Poetry*; *XXth Century Russian Poetry*; *Strofy veka*; *Rus. Women Writers*; *Sovremennye rus. poety*; *In the Grip of Strange Thoughts*; *Rus. poeziya. XX vek*

439. Morotskaya, Stella (1962, Nizhnii Novgorod) – *Metafizika svobodnogo poleta* (1993); *Vse 33 i drugie* (2001); *Arion*, 1995, 2 & 1999, 2; *Antologiya rus. verlibra*

440. Moskalenko, Irina (1961, Rostov-na-Donu) – *Antologiya rus. verlibra*

441. Moskovtseva, Elena – *Novaya volna*

442. Muliarova, Elena – *Arion*, 1996, 4 & 1999, 2
443. Murav'eva, Irina (1952, Moscow/Boston) – *Kontinent*, 1986, 49
444. Murav'eva, Mariya (1951) – *Chernaya zvezda; Den' poezii*, 2000; *Nash sovremennik*, 2000, 6
445. Muravina, Elena (1953, Los Angeles) – *Strofy veka*
446. Muromskaya, Natalya – *Oktiabr'*, 2001, 12
447. Murzina, Valentina (Kuibyshev/Moscow) – *Antologiya rus. verlibra*
448. Mussalitina, Elena – *Den' poezii*, 2000
449. Mysina, Margarita – *Den' poezii*, 2000
450. Nadler, Nora (Danilova, Sibir'/Mariupol') – *Antologiya rus. verlibra*
451. Narovchatova, Olga (1942, Moscow) – *Arion*, 1995, 2; *Ne vse . . .* (1998); *Rus. poeziya. XX vek*
452. Nasekina, Svetlana – *Soglasie*, 1994, 2
453. Nesmeyanova, Mariya – Manuscript
454. Natrukhina, Natalya – *Den' poezii*, L., 89
455. Naumova, Elena (Viatka) – *Oktiabr'*, 2001, 12
456. Nazarova, Tatyana – *Istoki*, 1999, 6
457. Nechaeva, Galina (Vologda) – *Letuchii gollandets* (2000)
458. Nechaeva, Olga – *Arion*, 2001, 1
459. Nechai, Svetlana – *GF*, 1992, 1; *Novaya lit. gazeta*, 1994, 8
460. Nechaeva, Olga – *Arion*, 2001, 1
461. *Negar, Hazan-Zadeh – *On Wings over the Horivzon: Selected Poems* (2002)
462. Negrul', Laga (Moscow) – *V chuzhom domu zabytaya svecha* (2001); *Vremia i my*, 2001, 151
463. Neiman, Liudmila (Samara) – *Antologiya rus. verlibra*
464. Nekrasova, Mariya – *Lit. gazeta* 5.9.2000
465. Nemirovskaya, Yuliya – *GF*, 31
466. Nent'eva, Nanisha'– *Oktiabr'*, 1999, 12
467. Neporent, Liudmila – *Istoki*, 1999, 6 & 2000, 8
468. Nerpina, Galina – *Arion*, 1996, 3
469. Nepritsa, Galina – *Molodaya poeziya* 89
470. Neshumova, Tatyana – *GF*, 1993, 2
471. Nevolina, Yuliya – *Lit. gazeta*, 14-20.3.2001
472. Nikishina, Natalya – *Molodaya poeziya* 89
473. Nikitina, Tamara – *Den' poezii*, L., 89; *Drp.*, 2000, 5
474. *Nikolaeva, Olesia (1955, Moscow) – *Sad chudes* (1980); *Na korable zimy* (1986); *Smokovnitsa* (1990); *Zdes'* (1990); *Rien d autre que la vie* (1991); *Amor fati* (1997); *Ispanskie pis'ma* (2000); *Arion*, 1994, 2; 1996, 3; 1998, 2, 2000, 4; *Novy mir*, 2001, 5; *Novaya volna; The Poetry of Perestroika; Strofy veka, In the Grip of Strange Thoughts; Rus. poeziya. XX vek*
475. Nikolaeva, Olga (1945, Leningrad/Riga) – *Nemerknushchii sad* (1976); *Zhivye iskry* (1980); *Vysokaya gornitsa* (1990); *Rus. poeziya. XX vek*
476. Nikolaevskaya, Elena – *Novyi mir*, 1998, 4; *Den' poezii*, 2000

477. Nikolenkova, N. – *Arion*, 1995, 1
478. Nikologorodskaya, Tatyana (1951, Moscow) – *Serebrianyi bor* (1981); *Est' muzyka* (1987); *Rus. poeziya. XX vek*
479. Nikol'skaya, Larisa – *Den' poezii*, L. 89
480. *Nikonova, Rea (Anna Tarshis) (1942, Eisk/Sverdlovsk/Germany) – *Novyi Sizif*, 1996, 8; *Arion*, 1996, 2 & 1998, 1; *Antologiya rus. monostikha*; *Crossing Centuries*
481. Nikulina, Maya (1937, Sverdlovsk) – *Strofy veka*
482. Nishchina, Rosa – *Den' poezii*, 2000
483. Nogteva, Margarita – *Den' poezii*, 2000
484. Nosova, Marina – *Novaya volna*
485. Novitskaya, Ira (1946, Moscow) – *Almanakh poeziya*; *Den' poezii*; *Antologiiya rus. monostikha*; *Antologiya rus. verlibra*
486. Novitskaya, Galina – *Den' poezii*, L., 89
487. Nutrikhina, Natalya – *Den' poezii*, L. 89
488. Odintsova, Lada – *Al'manakh poeziya*, 1989, 52; *Novaya volna*
489. Ogol'tsova, Izol'da (USA)' – *Drugie*
490. Oleinik, Tatyana – *Arion*, 1995, 4
491. Oleyash, Ella (Leningrad/Israel) – *Al'manakh poeziya*, 7, 2000
492. Orlova, Elena (1967, Moscow) – *Antologiya rus. verlibra*
493. Orlova, Marina (1960, Donetsk) – *Antologiya rus. verlibra*
494. Orlova, Natalya – *Arion*, 1994, 4; *Novyi mir*, 2000, 12; *Znamia*, 2001, 11
495. Orlova, Olga – *Novyi mir*, 2000, 12
496. Osanina, Galina – *Den' poezii*, 2000
497. Ozernaya, Marianna – *Kontinent*, 1987, 54
498. Ozerova, Irina (1934, Voronezh – 1984, Moscow) – *Strofy veka*
499. Paderina, Erta (Novosibirsk) – *Vesennie golosa* (1985); *Antologiya rus. verlibra*
500. Pakhomova, Valentina (1954, Moscow) – *Perovskie stranitsy* (1990); *Antologiya rus. verlibra*; *Arion*, 1997, 2
501. Pakhomova, Ella – *Drp.*, 2000, 5
502. Palamarchuk, Lidiya – *Den' poezii*, 2000
503. Palvanova, Zinaida — *Arion*, 2001, 3
504. Panchenko, Irena (Pskov) – *Den' poezii*, 2000
505. Papetina, Liubov (1981) – *Den' poezii*, 2000
506. Paporkova, Nadezhda – *Istoki*, 1999, 6
507. Patskaya, Elena (Moscow) – *Gor'kii dar* (1997); *Derevtse* (1998); *Lodka na meli* (2001)
508. Parchevskaya, Irina – *Zvezda*, 2001, 2 & 11
509. Parollo, Alla — *Den' poezii*, 2000
510. Pavlova, Muza (1916, Perm'/Moscow)' – *Antologiya rus. verlibra*
511. *Pavlova, Vera (1963, Moscow) – *Yunost'*, 1990; *Nebesnoe zhivotnoe* (1997); *Vtoroi yazyk* (1998); *Liniya otryva* (2000); *Chetvertyi son* (2000);

Intimnyi dnevnik otlichnitsy (2001); *Sovershennoletie* (2002); *Vezdes'* (2002); *Arion*, 1989, 4; 1995, 3; 1999, 2

512. Pavlova, Muza – *Antologiya rus. verlibra*

513. Pavlovich, Nadezhda – *Rus. mysl*, 25.5.1990

514. Pepeliaeva, Anna (Rostov-na-Donu) – *Vol'naya dusha. Stikhi* (1992); *Blagovest* (1996)

515. Peredel'skaya, Tania – *Istoki*, 1999, 5

516. Perepelitsa, Oksana – *Lit. gazeta*, May 2000

517. Perevezentseva, Natalya – *Den' poezii*, L., 89; *Zvezda*, 1998, 10

518. Perunova, Irina – *Istoki*, 1999, 5

519. Petrishcheva, Ella – *Istoki*, 2000, 8

520. *Petrova, Aleksandra (1964, SPb. / Rome) – *Nezamechennaya zemlia*, 1991; *Kontinent*, 1991, 69; *Mitin zhurnal*, 1992, 47-48, 1993, 51 & 1994, 53; *Liniya otryva* (1994); *Znamia*, 2001, 2; *Crtossing Centuries*

521. Petrova, Elina – *Arion*, 2001, 2;

522. *Petrushevskaya, Liudmila (1939, Moscow) – *Karamzin derevenskii dnevnik* (2000); *Oktiabr'*, 2002, 5

523. Pisareva, Natalya (1958, Donetsk) – *Antologiia rus. verlibra*

524. Pimenova, Marina – *Drp.*, 2000, 5

525. Pirogova, Elena – *Istoki*, 1999, 6

526. Pisareva, Natalya – *Antologiya rus. verlibra*

527. Pivovarova, Irina (1939-86, Novosibirsk) – *Strofy veka*

528. Pogozheva, Galina (1954, Moscow / Paris) – *Kontinent*, 1991, 68; *Den' poezii*, 2000

529. Poletaeva, Tatyana – *Nauka liubvi* (2000); *Znamia*, 1994, 3; *Novyi mir*, 2002, 5

530. Poliachenko, Tatyana (1960, Moscow) – *Molodaya poeziya* 89; *Kontinent*, 1991, 67

531. Poliakova, Nadezhda (SPb.) – *Den' poezii*, L. 89; *Zvezda*, 1996, 3; 2001, 7 & 12; *I vsiakie*

532. Polianskaya, Ekaterina (SPb.) – *Neva*, 2001, 1 & 10

533. Polonskaya, Anzhelika – *Istoki*, 1999, 5

534. Pokrovskaya, Svetlana (Saratov) – *Poslednii ekzempliar*, 1993, 1

535. Pokrovkaya, Yuliya – *Novyi mir*, 1993, 7

536. Ponomareva, Tamara – *Den' poezii*, 2000

537. Ponomareva-Shakhovkaya, Olga – *Istoki*, 2000, 7

538. Popova, Olga (1960, SPb.) – *Proshchanie* (1995); *In the Grip of Strange Thoughts*

539. Popova, Valentina – *Den' poezii*, 2000

540. Popova, Sofya (1953, Perm) – *Zolotaya igra* (1996); *Sovremennaya ural'skaya poeziya*

541. *Postnikova, Olga (1943, Voronezh / Moscow) – *Poryv* (1993); *Novyi mir*, 1994, 1; 1995, 6; 1997, 3 & 1998, 3; 2002, 3; *Znamia*, 1997 / 98; *Stofy veka*

542. Postnikova, Nina (SPb.) – *Priblizhenie: Stikhi* (2002)

543. Postovalova, Elena (Ekaterinburg) – *Al'manach 'Algoritm'*, 1997, 2
544. Potasheva, Olga – *Drp.*, 2000, 5
545. Prikhod'ko, Marina – *The Blue Lagoon Anthology*, 3B
546. Pronkina, Inna (1970, Moscow) – *Antologiya rus. verlibra*
547. Prozorova, Liudmila – *Istoki*, 2000, 7; *Indeks-2*
548. Pudovkina, Elena (1950, SPb.) – *Den' poezii*, L., 89; *Znamia*, 1997 / 98; *Novyi mir*, 2002, 4
549. Rabkina, Olga (1961, SPb.) – *Strofy veka*
550. Radetskaya, Tatyana (Yuzhno-Sakhalinsk) – *Antologiya rus. verlibra*
551. Ragozina, Kseniya – *Arion*, 1999, 3
552. Rakhlina, Marlena (1925, Khar'kov)' – *Dom dlia liudei*; *Mayatnik*; *Nadezhda sil'nee menia* (1990); *Rus. mysl'*, 5.06.1987; *Kontinent*, 1986, 60
553. Rakitskaya, Evelina – *Dozhdit do 30* (1993; *Den' poezii*, 2000
554. Rashkovskaya, Irina – *GF*, 1994, 5
555. Rastopchina, Natalya – *Istoki*, 1999, 6
556. *Ratushinskaya, Irina (1954, Odessa / London / Moscow) – *Stikhi, Poems, Poemes* (1984); *Ia dozhivu* (1986); *Vne limita* (1986); *No, I am not afraid* (1986); *Beyond limit* (1987); *Stikhi* (1988); *Pencil Letter* (1988); *Poemes* (1989); *Dance with a Shadow* (1992); *Stikhi* (1993); *Wind of the Journey* (2000); *Grani*, 1985, 137 & 1987, 143; *Kontinent*, 1985, 43; *Against Forgetting*; *Novyi mir*, 2001, 1 & 2; *In the Grip of Strange Thought*; *Rus. poeziya. XX vek*
557. Razorenova, Olga – *Istoki*, 1999, 5
558. Rebrova, Tatyana (1947, Igarka / Moscow) – *Kitezhanka* (1982); *Krovinka* (1987); *Znamia*, 2001, 12; *Dvoinaya raduga*; *Novaya volna*; *Rus. poeziya. XX vek*
559. Rebusova, Irina – Manuscript
560. Repina, Irina – *Istoki*, 2000, 8
561. *Retivova, Tatyana (1954, New York / Kiev) – on Internet, manuscripts
562. Reznik, Raisa (S.-Francisco) – *Almanakh poezii*, 7, 2000
563. Riabinina, Natalya (1941, Stalingrad / Moscow) – *Zhivaya dusha* (1985); *Moroznoe pole* (1989); *Rus. poeziya. XX vek*
564. Rizdvenko, Tatyana (1969, Moscow) – *Yunost'*; *Znamia*; *Oktiabr'*, 2002, 2; *Arion*; *Rus. poeziya. XX vek*
565. Pomaniuk, Anna – *Znamia*, 2001, 11
566. Rodchenkova, Elena (SPb.) – *Drp.*, 2000, 5; *Nash sovremennik*, 2000, 6; *Oktiabr'*, 2002, 2; *Dlia slovaria, dlia bukvaria* (2002)
567. Rodionova, Olga – *Istoki*, 2000, 7
568. Romaniuk, Anna – *Znamia*, 2001, 11
569. Romanova, Raisa (1943, Tatariya / Moscow) – *Podorozhnik* (1976); *Pod utrennim luchom* (1979); *Po sledu Chelubeya* (1991); *Liubi vo imia* (1997); *T'ma zolotaya* (1998); *Novaya volna*; *Rus. poeziya. XX vek*; *Den' poezii*, 2000
570. Romasheva, Olia (1985) – *Den' poezii*, 2000
571. Rostova, Antonina (1954, Poltava / Moscow) – *Orel – reshka* (1991);

Rus. poeziya. XX vek

572. Rovner, Marina – *Arion*, 1996, 4
573. Rozenfeld, Svetlana – *Den' poezii*, L., 89; *Strofy veka*; *Neva*, 2001, 7
574. Rozhanskaya, Olga (Moscow) – *Kontinent*, 1990, 62; *Stikhi po-russki* (1993)
575. Rozhkova, Natalya (1963, Moscow) – *Zvonkie zvezdy* (1992); *Derevo tseli* (1994); *Molodaya poeziya* 89; *Arion*, 1995, 1; *Rus. poeziya. XX vek*; *Lit. gazeta*, 6-12.3.2002
576. Rudenko, Mariya (1965, Moscow) – *Almanakh Poeziya*; *Antologiya rus. verlibra*
577. Rumarchuk, Larisa (1935, Ufa/Moscow) – *Dom* (1966); *Ya rodilas' v kholodnom mesiatse* (1967); *Osenne kupan'e* (1983); *Antologiya rus. verlibra*; *Den' poezii*, 2000; *Rus. poeziya. XX vek*
578. Rychkova, Ol'ga – *Arion*, 1999, 1; *Lit. gazeta*, 6-12.3.2002
579. Sablina, Elena – *Arion*, 1999, 3
580. Saenko, Irina (1978, Pavlovsk) – *Nash sovremennik*, 2000, 12
581. Safarova, Tatyana —*Rus. mysl'*, 21.9.1990
582. Safronova, Elena (Riazan') – *Den' poezii*, 2000
583. Sanina, Inna (Belorussia/California) – *Tsvety vremeni* (1984); *Smysl* (1995); *Almanakh poezii*, 4, 1997 & 7, 2000
584. Sanina, Margarita – *Antologiya rus. monostikha*
585. Saran, Elena – *Molodaya poeziya* 89
586. Sarancha, Nina – *GF*, 1994, 4
587. Savel'eva, Tat'yana'– *Drp.*, 2000, 5
588. Savinskaya, Luiza – *Den' poezii*, 2000
589. Sazonova, Mariya – *Skazki, istorii, pritchi* (1996)
590. *Sedakova, Ol'ga (1949, Moscow) – *Vrata, okna, arki* (1986); *Kitaiskoe puteshestvie, Stely i nadpisi, Starye pesni* (1990); *Stikhi* (1994); *The Silk of Time* (1994); *The Wild Rose* (1998); *Stikhi* (2001); *Puteshestvie volkhvov. Izbrannoe* (2001); *Volga*, 1984, 6; 1991, 10 & 12; 1992, 7; *Druzhba narodov*, 1988, 10 & 1992, 9; 1993, 11; *Vestnik novoi literatury*, 1990, 2; *Laterna Magica*; *Novyi mir*, 1990, 5; *Znamia* 1991, 6; 1992, 8; *The Poetry of Perestroika*; *Third Wave*; *Contemporary Rus. Poetry*; *An Anthology of Russian Women Writing*; *Crossing Centuries, Rus. Women Writers*; *In the Grip of Strange Thoughts*
591. Sedykh, Svetlana – *Molodaya poeziya*–89
592. Selezneva, Tamara – *Istoki*, 1999, 5; *Den' poezii*, 2000
593. Sel'vinskaya, Tatyana (Moscow) – *Posviashchenie* (1989); *Antologiya rus. verlibra*
594. Semenova, Yuliya (1975, Riga/Moscow) – *Stikhi* (1995); *Arion*, 1997, 2
595. Semenova, Irina (1949, Orel) – *Polei nebroskie tsvety* (1984); *Zvezdy v burane* (1984); *Molodaya poeziya* 89; *Rus. poeziya. XX vek*
596. Senkevich, Valentina (1926, Kiev/USA) – *Ogni* (1973); *Nastuplenie*

dnia (1978); *Tsvetenie trav* (1985); *Zdes' ia zhivu* (1988); *Rus. poeziya. XX vek*

597. Sergeeva, Galina – *GF*, 1992, 13

598. Sergeeva, Irina – *Istoki*, 1999, 5

599. Sergeeva, Irena (SPb.) – *Den' poezii*, L. 89; *Istoki*, 1999, 5; *Drp*, 2000, 5; *Den' poezii*, 2000

600. Shalaginova, Liudmila – *Istoki*, 1999, 5

601. Shamborant, Olga – *Poems*

602. Sharapova, Alla (1949, Moscow) – *Arion*, 1994, 1; *Novyi mir*, 1995, 1; *Strofy veka*

603. Sharnina, Liubov – *Istoki*, 2000, 8

604. *Shats, Evelina (Odessa / Milan) —*Variazioni sul nero* (1992); *Poezia per Armanda* (1997); *Ieroglif beskonechnosti* (1999); *Hotel Londonskaya* (1999, 2001); *Pivnoi larek* (2001); *Semeinaya khronika goroda Mykina* (2002); *Mytinskii zamok* (2002)

605. Shchapova, Elena – *Ekho*, 1979, 2-3 & 1980, 1; *Istoki*, 1999, 5

606. Shchepot'eva, Elena – *Istoki*, 1999, 5

607. *Shcherbina, Tatyana (1954, Moscow) – *Lebedinaya pesnia* (1981); *Tsvetenie reshetki* (1981); *Novyi Panteon* (1983); *Natiurmort s prevrashcheniyami* (1985); *Nol' Nol'* (1987 / 1991); *Prostranstvo* (1988); *Poryv; Parmi les Alphabets* (1992); *L'ame deroutee; Zhizn' bez* (1997); *Dialogi s angelom* (1999); *Kniga o pliuse i minuse...* (2001); *Molodaya poeziya 89; Third Wave; Strofy veka; In the Grip of Strange Thoughts; Crossing Centuries; Teatr; Yunost'; Zolotoi vek; Strelets; Mitin zhurnal; Domovoi; Ogonek*

608. Shchipakhina, Liudmila (Sverdlovsk / Moscow) – *Neva*, 2002, 3

609. Shegal', Raisa – *Molodaya poeziya, 89*

610. Shekhanova, Tatyana (1952, Moscow) – *Molodye golosa* (1981); *Den' poezii*, 2000; *Rus. poeziya. XX vek*

611. Shemelina, Tatyana (Kemerovo) – *Antologiya rus. verlibra*

612. Shemetovskaya, Lidiya – *Istoki*, 1999, 6

613. Shemiakina, Ekaterina (1993, Ekaterinburg) – *Ural*, 2000, 9

614. Shevchenko, Ekaterina – *Novyi mir*, 1995, 7; *Arion*, 1997, 2

615. Sheveleva, Ekaterina – *Izbrannoe* (1979); *Koster na snegu* (1985); *Lit. gazeta*, 20.03.1999; *Dvoinaya raduga; The Poetry of Perestroika; Strofy veka*

616. Shevtsova, Nina – *Molodaya poeziya–89*

617. Shidlovskaya, Alla – *Arion*, 1998, 4; *Den' poezii*, 2000

618. Shikina, Liudmila (1934, Bashkiriya) – *Rovesnitsa* (1966); *Ispytanie* (1970); *Slepye kovyli* (1973); *Vsemu nachalo chelovek* (1977); *Chas solntsa* (1982); *Blagodarenie* (1983); *Ptitsy belye* (1986); *Izbrannoe* (1989); *Rus. poeziya. XX vek*

619. Shilova, Svetlana – *Strofy veka*

620. Shmyglovskaya, Yuliya – *Drp*, 2000, 5

621. Shneiderman, Asya – *Poeziya bezmolviya; Arion*, 1996, 2; *Oboznachit' molchanie slovom* (1998)

622. Shpak, Galina (Novosibirsk) – *Stikhotvoreniya* (2000)

623. Shumakova, Irina – *Istoki*, 2000, 8
624. Shumiakovskaya, Yaroslava – *Den' poezii*, 2000
625. Shuvalova, Elena – *Istoki*, 2000, 7
626. *Shvarts, Elena (1948, SPb.) – *Tantsuyushchii David* (1985); *Stikhi* (1987); *Trudy i dni Lavinii iz ordena obrezaniya serdtsa* (1987); *Storony sveta* (1989); *Stikhi* (1990); *Lotsiya nochi: Kniga poem* (1993); *Paradise* (1993); *Pesnia ptitsy na dne morskom* (1995); *Mundus imaginalis* (1996); *Zapadno-vostochnyi veter* (1997); *Opredelenie v durnuiu pogodu* (1997); *Solo na raskalennoi trube* (1998); *Stikhotvoreniya i poemy* (1999); *Dikopis' poslednego vremeni* (2000); *Krug*; *Ekho*, 1980, 1; *Strelets*; *Kovcheg*; *Muleta*; *Gnozis*; *Glagol*; *Grani*; *Den' poezii*, L. 89; *Ekho*, 1978, 1 & 1979, 2; *Rodnik*; *Raduga*; *Avrora*; *Neva*; *Znamia*, 1992, 12 & 2001, 8; *Zvezda*, 1992, 5-6; 1997, 6 & 2001, 1; *Vestnik russkoi literatury*, 1990, 2; 1993, 5 & 1994, 8; *Kamera khraneniya*, 1994, 4; *Arion*, 1995, 1; *Novyi mir*, 2000, 7; *Sovremennye rus. poety*; *Child of Europe*; *The Poetry of Perestroika*; *Twentieth-Century Russian Poetry*; *Contemporary Rus. Poetry*; *The Third Wave*; *Anthology of Women Writing*; *Strofy veka*; *Russian Women Writers*; *In the Grip of Strange Thoughts*; *Crossing Centuries*
627. Sidorova, Natalya (1947, Moscow) – *Vysokaya roshcha* (1984); *Koren' slova* (1985); *Mirokolitsa* (1987); *Rus. poeziya. XX vek*
628. Simakina, Svetlana (1962, Novosibirsk) – *Vestnik RKhD*, 2001, 182
629. Simina, Ekaterina – *Istoki*, 1999, 6
630. Simonova, Ekaterina (1977, Nizhnii Tagil) – *Ural*, 2000, 9
631. Sinel'nikova, Rina (1916, SPB. / Moscow) – *Almanakh poezii*, 4, 1997
632. Sizova, Zhanna (1969, Moscow / Irkutsk / SPb.) – *Izhitsy* (1998); *Arion*, 1999, 4
633. Skliarova, Tatyana – *Nash sovremennik*, 2000, 6
634. Skorodumova, Yuliyia (1964, Moscow) – *Otkuda prikhodit mysh* (1993); *Chtivo dlia pal'tsev* (1993); *Evrodil*; *Sochinil sebe litso* (1997); *GF*, 1994, 7; *Crossing Centuries*; *Rus. poeziya. XX vek*
635. Slepaya, Irina (1963, Kaluga) – *Ogonek*; *Yunost'*; *Antologiya rus. verlibra*
636. Slepakova, Nonna (1936, SPb.) – *Dp.*, L 89; *Slepota otchuzhdeniya* (1998); *Samizdat veka*, 1997; *Strofy veka*
637. Slutskina, Polina – *Arion*, 1998, 4
638. Smagina, Evgeniya – *Novyi mir*, 2001, 2
639. Smertina, Tatyana (1948, Podmoskovye) – *Yagodinochka* (1976); *Selo Sorvizhi* (1982); *Marya – zazhgi smega* (1982); *Deva Lyanitsa*; *Novaya volna*; *Den' poezii*, 2000; *Rus. poeziya. XX vek*
640. Smirnova, Nina – *Istoki*, 1999, 6
641. Smirnova, Natalya – *Arion*, 1996, 3
642. Smirnova, Marianna – *Znamia*, 1997 / 98
643. Smolovskaya, Elena – *Arion*, 1998, 2
644. Smorodinova, Elena – *Istoki*, 1999, 6

645. Sokolova, Elizaveta – *Arion*, 1994, 3
646. Sokolova, Olga – *Aprel'skie kapli* (1992)
647. Sokolova, Tatyana (Krasnodar) – *Nash sovremennik*, 2002, 3
648. Sokolovskaya, Natalya (1956, SPb.) – *Priroda sveta* (1988); *Nezapechatannye pis'ma* (1988); *Rus. poeziya. XX vek*
649. Solomonova, Liubov (1977, Rzhev) – *Nash sovremennik*, 2000, 12; *Arion*, 2002, 1
650. Solov'eva, Irina (Ivanovo)' – *Muzykoi podniat' do tishiny* (1998)
651. Solozhenkina, Svetlana – *Den' poezii*, 2000
652. Sominskaya, Lina (California) – *Almanakh poezii*, 4, 1997 & 7, 2000
653. Sorokina, Arina – *Istoki*, 1999, 6
654. Sorokina, Olga (Moscow) – *Nash sovremennik*, 2000, 6
655. Spak, Galina (Novosibirsk) – *Stikhotvoreniya* (2000)
656. Spelaya, Irina – *Antologiya rus. verlibra*
657. Spolitak, Katiusha (1990, Yakutiya) – *Istoki*, 1998, 5
658. Stanovaya, Lidiya (Rzhevsk) – *Nash sovremennik*, 2002, 3
659. Starostenko, Svetlana – *Molodaya poeziya*–89
660. Starostina, Tatyana (Samara) – *Nash sovremennik*, 2000, 8
661. Stasenko, Tatyana – *Istoki*, 1999, 6
662. Stegnii, Natalya (Moscow) – *Antologiya rus. verlibra*
663. Stel'makh, Natalya – *Den' poezii*, 2000
664. *Stepanova, Mariya (1972, Moscow) – *Yunost'*, 1988, 3; *Znamia*, 1993, 3 & 2000, 6; *Zerkalo*; *Urbi*; *Vavilon*; *Pesni severnykh yuzhan* (2001); *O bliznetsakh* (2001); *Tut-svet* (2001); *Stikhi* (2001)
665. Stepanova, Marina – *Istoki*, 1999, 6
666. Stiuart, Elizaveta (Novosibirsk) – *Den' poezii*, 2000
667. Stozhkova, Nina – *Molodaya poeziya* 89
668. Strakhova, Tamara (Leninsk-Kuznetskii) – *Antologiya rus. verlibra*
669. Stroilo, Alla – *Den' poezii*, 89; *Strofy veka*
670. Struchkova, Nina (1955, Tambov / Moscow) – *Mgnoveniya svetlye* (1987); *Zhizn' beskonechnaya* (1990); *Antologiya rus. verlibra*; *Den' poezii*, 2000; *Rus. poeziya. XX vek*
671. Strukova, Mariya (1976, Moscow) – *Solntse voiny*; *Nash sovremennik*, 2000, 1 & 11
672. Suetenko, Larisa – *Den' poezii*, 2000
673. Suglobova, Irina (1958, Tambov / Moscow) – *I grekh moi predo mnoi est' vynu* (1997); *Rus. poeziya. XX vek*
674. *Sukhovey, Darya (1977, SPb.) – *Avtom* (1997); *Katalog sluchainykh zapisei* (2001); *Vavilon*, 1999, 6; 2000, 7; 2001, 8
675. *Sul'chinskaya, Olga (1966, Moscow) – *Stikhotvoreniya* (2000); *Arion*, 1997, 2; 1999, 3 & 2002, 1; *Znamia*, 1998, 12 & 2001, 3; *Novyi mir*, 1999, 8 & 2000, 11
676. Suntsova, Elena – *Kniga stikhov* (2000)
677. Suslova, Olga (Yakutiya) – *Istoki*, 1999, 5

678. Svetogorskaya, Liubov (NY) – *Drugie*
679. Svitneva, Evgeniya – *Arion*, 1997, 3
680. Syrova, Margarita (Kostroma) – *Antologiya rus. verlibra*
681. Syrneva, Svetlana (1957, Kirov) – *Nochnoi gruzovik* (1989); *Sto stikhotvorenii* (1994); *Rus. poeziya. XX vek*
682. Syryshcheva, Tatyana (Moscow) – *Beresklet* (1965); *Zelenye rukova; Minuty stanut vekom; Skazhu nechto; Antologiya rus. verlibra; Rus. poeziya. XX vek*
683. Tabachnikova, Olga (1967, Ukraine/London) – *MPT*, 17, 2001
684. Taiganova, Tatyana (Cheliabinsk) – *Musornyi veter* (1997); *Pishcha bogov* (1999)
685. Talalaeva, Galina – *Den' poezii*, 2000
686. Taneeva, Elena – *Istoki*, 2000, 8; *Den' poezii*, 2000
687. Tarakanova, Larisa (1947, Zakarpat'e/Moscow) – *Ptitsa voobrazheniya* (1971); 681. *Ditia moe* (1977); *Eto – ya* (1983); *Tret'e oko* (1987); *Novaya volna; Rus. poeziya. XX vek*
688. Tarasova, Mariya – *Arion*, 1999, 2
689. Tatarinova, Olga (1939, Moscow) – *Den' poezii*, 2000
690. Te, Vita (1971, Ekaterinburg) – *Antologiya rus. verlibra*
691. Telegina, Valentina (Perm') – *Nash sovremennik*, 2000, 8
692. Temershina, Olesia (Yakutiya) – *Istoki*, 1999, 5
693. Temkina, Marina (1948, NY) – *Blue Lagoon Anthology, 2B; Kontinent*, 1987, 51 & 1988, 56; *Strofy veka; Novyi zhurnal*, 1995, 196
694. Ter-Akopian, Alla(Moscow) —*Antologiya rus. verlibra; I vsiakie*
695. Terebinova, Tatyana (1950, Samara) – *Antologiya rus. verlibra*
696. Tereshchenko, Dina – *Den' poezii*, 2000
697. Tifbenkel', Yana – *Istoki*, 1999, 5
698. Tikhomirova, Larisa – *Oktiabr'*, 2001, 11
699. Timoshenkova, Lidiya – *Istoki*, 1999, 6
700. Tinovskaya, Elena (Ekaterinburg) – *Znamia*, 2001, 9
701. Titova, Tatyana (Nizhnii Tagil) – *Nesovremennye zapiski*, 1997, 4
702. Titova, Liudmila (1974) – *Den' poezii*, 2000
703. *Tkhorzhevskaya, Vitalina (1971, Sverdlovsk/Ekaterinburg) – *Ptichya pamiat'* (1991); *Puteshestvie v obratnuiu storonu* (1994); *Tret'e puteshestvie* (1996); *Smirennyi gnev* (1997); *Ural*, 2001, 10; *Sovremennaya ural'skaya poeziya; Crossing Centuries; Nesovremennye zapiski*
704. Tokun, Larisa – *Istoki*, 1999, 5; *Den' poezii*
705. Tolokonnikova, Tatyana (Simbirsk) – *Drp*, 2000, 5
706. Trofimova, Masha (1989) – *Istoki*, 1999, 5
707. Trushina, Katerina – *Istoki*, 2000, 8
708. Tsareva, Valentina – *Drp*, 2000, 5
709. Tsar'kova, Tatyana – *Gorod prostoliudinov* (1993)
710. Tsukernik, Marianna – *Arion*, 1998, 2
711. Tumanova, Marina – *Den' poezii*, 2000

712. Tyshkovskaya, Lesia (1969, Kiev) – *GF*, 1991, 15; *Antologiya rus. verlibra*

713. Udal'tsova, Elina (Smolensk) – *Den' poezii*, 2000

714. Ufimtseva, Galina – *Drp.*, 2000, 5

715. Ukhanova, Marina – *Crossing Centuries*

716. Ukhova, Elena – *Den' poezii*, L. 89

717. Ulybasheva, Marina (Kaluga) – *Hash sovremennik*, 2000, 6

718. Unskova, Kari (1940, SPb) – *Arion*, 1994, 1; *Antologiya rus. verlibra*

719. *Ushakova, Elena (Nevzgliadova,1945, SPb.) – *Nochnoe solntse* (1991); *Metel'* (2000); *Zvuk i smysl*; *Novyi mir*, 1992, 1; 1993, 6; 1999, 3 & 2001, 11; *Arion*, 1996, 1 & 1999, 4; *Znamia*; *Zvezda, Neva, Sintaksis*; *Strofy veka*

720. Urakova, Olga – *Vavilon*

721. Uvarova, Liudmila – *Den' poezii*, 2000

722. Uvarova, Tatyana – *Den' poezii*, 2000

723. Vanetsova, Olga – *GF*, 1992, 21

724. Vankhonen, Natalya (Moscow) – *Zima imperii* (1998); *Arion*, 1996, 2; *Strelets*, 1997, 1; *Neva*, 2001, 1

725. Vardenga, Mariya – *GF*, 1991, 3

726. Vasil'eva, Larisa (1935, Khar'kov / Moscow) – *L'nianaya Luna* (1966); *Ognevitsa* (1969); *Lebeda* (1970); *Russkie imena* (1980); *Izbrannye proizvedeniya* (1989); *Strannoe svoistvo* (1991); *The Poetry of Perestroika*; *Strofy veka*; *Rus. poeziya. XX vek*

727. Vasil'kova, Irina (1949, Moscow) – *Poverkh lesov i vod* (2001); *Molodye poety Moskvy*; *Derzost'*; *Tverskoi bul'var*, 25 (1987); *Den' poezii*, 1989; *Rus. poeziya. XX vek*

728. Vatutina, Mariya – *Arion*, 2001, 1; *Novyi mir*, 2001, 3; *Znamia*, 2001, 10

729. Veksler, Asia – *Den' poezii*, L. 89

730. Velikhova, Zoya – *Arion*, 1997, 4

731. Venediktova, Liubov – *Drp*, 2000, 5

732. Veretennikova, Yuliya (1976, Kirov) – *Nash sovremennik*, 2000, 8

733. Vermisheva, Seda (1932, Tbilisi / Erevan) – *Solntse stoit vysoko* (1971); *Mertsayushchii punktir* (1974); *Listya* (1982); *Naskal'nyi ornament* (1988); *Nagor'e* (1990); *Antologiya rus. verlibra*

734. Vernikova, Bella – *Priamoe rodstvo* (1993)

735. Veselova, Tatyana (1952, Gor'ky / Moscow) – *Dvadtsat' let* (1978); *Rozhdenie pesni* (1979); *Rus. poeziya. XX vek*

736. Veselovskaya, Nadezhda – *Den' poezii*, 2000

737. Vetrova, Evgeniya (1945, Kiev) – *Antologiya rus. verlibra*

738. Vetrova, Viktoriya – *Lit. gazeta*, 6-12.3.2002

739. Vezhina, Diana (SPb.) – *Vremia zhit'* (1995); *Gorod, kotorogo net* (2000); *Neva*, 2001, 7

740. Viazminitova, Liudmila – *GF*, 1993, 6; *Arion*, 1998, 3

741. Vigurina, Liudmila – *O mnogom i ob odnom* (1994)
742. Viner, Yuliya – 22, 1986, 46
743. Vinogradova, Liliya (Milan) – *Latinskii kvartal*
744. Vinogradova, Nina (Khar'kov)' – *Arion*, 1995, 4 & 1999, 3; *Znamia*, 1998, 10
745. Vinogradova, Tatyana – *Arion*, 1998, 1; *Istoki*, 2000, 8
746. Virta, Marina – *Al'manakh poeziya*, 1989, 52
747. Vishnevskaya, Svetlana – *Den' poezii*, L. 89
748. Vitukhnovskaya, Alina – *Lit.gazeta*, 4.10.95; *Novyi mir*, 1996, 2 & 5; *Den' literatury*, 2001, 13
749. Vladimirova, Liya – 22, nos. 6, 10, 20, 28, 37; *Kontinent*, 1983, 37; *Laterna Magica*; *Rus. mysl'*, 1.2.91
750. *Vlasova, Ekaterina (1976, Cheliabinsk) – *Malen'kii Vishnu* (1998); *Ural'skaya nov'*; *Nesovremennye zapiski*
751. Volchenko, Viktoriya – *GF*, 1992, 17
752. Volkonskaya, Vera (Moscow) – *Antologiya rus. verlibra*
753. Volkova, Liudmila – *Den' poezii*, 2000
754. Volodimirova, Larisa – *Den' poezii*, L. 89
755. Volodina, Tamara – *Mitin zhurnal*, no. 29
756. Voloshina, Liudmila (1937, Ordzhonikidze) – *Almanakh Poeziya*; *Antologiya rus. verlibra*
757. *Vol'tskaya, Tatyana (SPb.) – *Dve krovi* (1989); *Svitki* (1990); *Strela* (1994); *Ten'* (1998); *Novyi mir*, 1995, 12; 1998, 11 & 2001, 5; *Znamia*, 1994, 12; 1996, 1; 1998, 3 & 8; 2001, 2; *Oktiabr'*, 1996, 2; *Grani*, 1996, 182; *Arion*, 1997, 3; *Zolotoi vek*, 1999, 13; *Zvezda*, 1995, 5; 1996, 2; 1997, 2; 1998, 5; 1999, 5; 2000, 3 & 2001, 3; *Feniks*, 1998; 2000, 6 & 2001, 3; *Druzhba narodov*, 1992, 8; 1994, 2; 1996, 1 & 2000, 1; *Slavia*, 1999, 3; *Poesia* (Milan), 2001, 146
758. Vorob'eva, Evgeniya – *Arion*, 2000, 2
759. Voronova, Yuliya – *Istoki*, 1999, 6
760. Voronova, Nadezhda – *Drp.*, 2000, 5
761. Voronovskaya, Isanna (1955, Rostovskaya obl.) – *Almanakh Poeziya*; *Antologiya rus. verlibra*
762. Voskresenskaya, Mariya – *Al'manakh Poeziya*, 1989, 52; *I vsiakie*
763. Voznesenskaya, Yuliya (1940, Leningrad / Munich) – *Grani*, 1978, 108 & 1979, 111-12; *Tret'ia volna*, 1979, 6; *Vestnik*, 1979, 128; *Mariia*, 1981, 1; *The Blue Lagoon Anthology*, 5B
764. Vrubel', Tatyana – *Istoki*, 1999, 5
765. Yagodintseva, Nina (1962, Cheliabinsk) – *Amarkllis* (1999); *Na vysote meteli* (2000); *Ural'skaya nov'*, 2000, 8; *Sovremennaya ural'skaya poeziya*
766. Yakovleva, Alena – *Istoki*, 2000, 8
767. Yakunina, Galina (Vladivostok) – *Den' poezii*, 2000
768. Yanikova, Miryam – 22, 1985, 45
769. Yarbusova, Francheska (1942, Alma-Ata / Moscow) – *Antologiya rus. verlibra*

770. Yarkova, Margarita – *Drp.*, 2000, 5
771. Yavorskaya, Nora – *Den' poezii*, L., 1989
772. Yudina, Nadezhda – *Drp.*, 2000, 5
773. Yusupova, Liliya (Gorno-Altaisk) – *Kachaetsia mayatnik* (1999)
774. Zadorozhnaya, Tatyana (California) – *Almanakh poezii*, 7, 2000
775. Zagotova, Svetlana (1956, Donetsk) – *S mirom po moriu* (1999); *Antologiya rus.verlibra*; *Oktiabr'*, 1999, 8
776. Zagraevskaya, Inna (1933, Moscow) – *Stikhi i poemy* (2001)
777. Zaitseva, Liudmila (Krasnodar)–*Ostrov. Kniga stikhotvorenii* (2001)
778. Zakharevich, Natalya – *Kontinent*,1988, 58
779. Zakharova, Antonina – *Istoki*, 1995, 5 & 2000, 8
780. Zalata, Alla (Tolyatti) – *Gorod, Den' poezii*, 2000; *Nash sovremennik*, 2000, 6
781. Zalogina, Olga (SPb.) – *Stikhi* (1994); *Pesnia ognia* (1997)
782. Zaripova, N.V. (Rzhev) – *Sbornik stikhov* (1995); *Sbornik stikhov rzhevskikh poetov* (2000)
783. Zavel'skaya, Darya'– *GF*, 1991, 14
784. Zelenina, Galina (1979, Moscow) – *Vavilon*; *'Zh'* (2000); *Vremia "Ch"*; *Solnechnoe spletenie*, 2001, 18 / 19
785. Zelenova, Tatyana – *Khoziaika platinovykh gor* (2001)
786. Zhegis, Valentina – *Den' poezii*, 2000
787. Zhdanova, Varvara (Podolsk)–*Den' poezii*, 2000; *Nash sovremennik*, 2002, 3
788. Zhirmunskaya, Tamara (1936, Moscow) – *Raion moei liubvi* (1962); *Konets sezona*; *Novyi mir*, 1996, 8; *Istoki*, 1999, 5, *Strofy veka*; *Rus. poeziya. XX vek*
789. Zhmailo, Tatyana (Vologda) – *Sol'-minor* (1999)
790. Zhukova, Vera – *Den' russkoi poezii*, 2000, 5
791. Zinger, Gali-Dana (Leningrad / Jerusalem) – *Sbornik* (1992); *Adel-Kil'ka. Iz* (1993); *Solnechnoe spletenie*, 2001, 18 / 19
792. Zinov'eva, Liubov – *GF*, – 1993, 11
793. Zlobina (1936, Moscow) – *Cheremukha*; *Vesny*; *Rus. poeziya. XX vek*
794. Znamenskaya, Irina (1951, SPb.) – *Poryv*; *Den' poezii* (L., 1989); *Zerkala*; *Petropol', al'manakh, II* (SPb., 1990); *Molodaya poeziya 89*; *Glaz vopiiushchego* (1997); *Pozdnie peterburzhtsy*; *I vsiakie*; *Strofy veka*
795. Zolotkova, Yuliya (1969, Arkhangel'sk) – *Ural*, 2000, 9
796. Zonberg, Olga (Moscow) – *Kniga priznanii* (1997); *Stikhi* (1997); *Arion*, 1998, 2 & 1999, 1
797. *Zubova, Liudmila (1946, SPb.) – *The New Review*, 1994, no. 195; manuscripts.
798. Zubova, Ekaterina – *Istoki*, 1999, 6
799. Zueva, Elena – *Dusha prostranstva* (1990)
800. Zyrianova, Zhanna (1939-1994, Novosibirsk) – *Granitsa snegov* (1981; *Nezvanoe* (1992); *Rus. poeziya. XX vek*

Biographies

Poets

Bella Akhmadulina was born in Moscow in 1937. She is of partly Tatar origin. She came to prominence as one of the 'New Wave' poets of the so-called Thaw period, after Stalin's death, being at one time married to Yevtushenko. Her first collection appeared in 1962. She was later criticised as being "too intimate" and was expelled from the Writers' Union. Akhmadulina was awarded the State Prize for Literature in 1989. She lives in Moscow.

Liana Alaverdova was born in Baku, Azerbaijan. She graduated in history from Azerbaijan University and worked at the Institute of Philosophy and Law of the Azerbaijan Academy of Sciences. Her poems, translations from English and Azerbaijani into Russian, essays, and articles have been published in Azerbaijan, Israel and in the USA to which she emigrated in 1993. She received the Korchak Award in Azerbaijan in 1991 for her cycle of poems about Yanosh Korchak, teacher and humanist who was killed in Poland in the Second World War. Alaverdova is also the author of two plays. She lives in Brooklyn and works as a Librarian at Queens Public Library.

Vera Anserova (pseud. for Natalya Tishchenko) was born in 1958, in Donetsk. She graduated from the Medical College in Donetsk and lives and works in Makeevka, Donetsk region.

Mariya Avvakumova was born in 1943, in Arkhangelsk region. A graduate of Kazan University's Department of Journalism, she has worked as a journalist in Uzbekistan and Tatarstan. She has also taken part in geological expeditions in Baikal and Kamchatka. Her poetry collections include: *Severnye reki* (*Northern rivers*), 1982 and *Iz glubin* (*From the depths*) in 1990. Avvakumova lives in Moscow. Her poems have appeared in *Novy mir* (e.g. 'Baltic Meditations') and in a number of anthologies.

Polina Barskova was born in 1976 in Leningrad. Since 1998 she has been a graduate student at Berkeley, University of California. Barskova has published several collections of poetry, her first at the age of fifteen: *Christmas* (1991). Another four collections of poetry followed, the last two being *Evradei and Orfika* and *Arias*. Barskova writes: "I wrote poetry only in Russian and I write a lot. I study and relate to the world around me in English and carry in my head smatterings of Latin and Greek, French and Czech. I am seriously interested in film. At this time, on my desk is lying a book by Bakhtin, probably the main hero of my future (EBZh [God permitting] – as Tolstoy said) dissertation."

Tatyana Bek was born in Moscow, in 1949, into the family of the celebrated writer, Aleksandr Bek. She graduated from Moscow State University, from the Department of Journalism, and has worked as a bibliographer and editor. At present she teaches a poetry seminar, at The Gorky Literary Institute in Moscow. Bek is a contributor to *Voprosy literatury* and *Obshchaya gazeta*. She has received prizes awarded by the journals *Znamia* and *Zvezda* and the All-Russian Golden Gong Award. She is the author of six collections of poetry.

Larisa Berezovchuk was born in 1948 in Kiev. She is a graduate of the historical department of the Kiev Conservatory and completed graduate studies at the Leningrad Institute of Theatre, Music and Cinematography. She has taught in the Kiev Theatrical Institute and has been writing poetry since 1990. After Chernobyl, she moved to St Petersburg, where she still lives. She is also the author of a number of articles on Aleksandr Gornon (see Internet).

Marina Boroditskaya was born in Moscow, in 1965. She graduated from the Moscow Institute of Foreign Languages. She works as a guide, translator and teacher of English. She has published in magazines since 1978. She is better known as a translator of English (and French) poetry, including Donne, Burns, Chesterton and Kipling. She is the author of many books for children and her own first poetry collection was published in 1994. The second appeared in 2002. She works for Radio Russia and lives in Moscow.

Ekaterina Boyarskikh was born in 1976. She lives in Irkutsk. She is a graduate of the philological department of Irkutsk University, specialising in the history of the Russian language. She is a winner of the national Debyut Prize for 2000 for her text "Echo of women". Her work is hitherto unpublished.

Vera Chizhevskaya was born in 1946, in Belorussia. She lives in Obninsk, where she works as a journalist. She has published a collection of poetry, *Chekanka* (1990).

Svetlana Chulkova was born in 1958, in Moscow. She is a graduate of the Moscow Pedagogical Institute of Foreign Languages. Chulkova's poetry has appeared in a number of Russian periodicals, such as *Istoki* and *Poezya*.

Svetlana Den'gina was born in 1968 in Kuibyshev (now Samara). She graduated from Kuibyshev University. She lives in Samara.

Regina Derieva was born in 1949 in Odessa. She has lived in Karaganda and in 1991 emigrated to Israel. She now lives in Sweden. Her poetry ahs been translated into German, Bulgarian, Ukrainian and English. She has published three collections of poetry in Russian and one in English *The Inland Sea* (1999) from which the present selection has been taken. Brodsky wrote of her poetry: "You, Regina, are indeed a great poet. For the poem "Mne ne tam khorosho" ("I don't feel at home where I am"), yours only by name and by craft. The real author is poetry itself. It is nearer to you than your pen is to paper. I have seen nothing like it either in Russian or in English poetry . . ."

Marina Dolia (b. 1951, Kiev) writes of herself: "Her family is a genetic product of Kiev at the beginning of the twentieth century. She absorbed a puritan stoicism and humility in the face of the inevitable. Her wisdom, such as it is, is simply what has survived from the old generation. As for poetry, she was first inspired by the ballads of Vasily Zhukovsky. Her first mentor, so to speak, was Innokenty Annensky. Born at the beginning of the 50's she was automatically marginalised. She graduated from Kiev University's Department of Mathematical Linguistics and was interested in cybernetics as well as theatre. Brodsky's poetry became for her a model for overcoming the fear of being. Her distinguishing features are that she is an eternal student, a good friend to her friends, and capable of total empathy."

Irina Ermakova was born in 1951, in Crimea. She graduated from the Moscow Institute of Transport Engineers, specializing in bridges and tunnels. For twelve years she worked as a designer, since when she has held various positions. At present she is freelancing as a literary editor, translator, and adapting stories for radio etc. Her first publication was in *Za Rodinu!* in 1987. She has published in *Literaturnaya gazeta, Arion, Oktiabr, Druzhba narodov* etc and is the author of three collections of poetry: *Provintsiya* [Provinces] (1991); *Vinogradnik* [Vineyard] (1994); *Steklyannyi sharik* [Glass sphere] (1998).

Galina Ermoshina was born in the Saratov region, in 1962. She is a graduate of the Kuibyshev Institute of Culture and works as a librarian. She lives in Samara. Ermoshina has published many collections of poetry and was awarded a prize at the Moscow Prose-Poetry Festival in 1999. She translates contemporary American poetry.

Zoya Ezrokhi was born in 1946 in Leningrad and graduated from the Technological Institute. She has written poetry from the age of four. Her poetry, especially on the subject of cats, has appeared in many magazines and anthologies. Her most important collection, *Just in Case*, was published in 2002.

Elena Fanailova was born in 1962, in the Voronezh district. She practised as a doctor and taught at Voronezh University. She is the author of three poetry collections, and of a "Theatrical Novel" with Aleksandr Anashevich. She was awarded the Andrei Bely Prize in 1999. Fanailova is the Moscow correspondent of Radio Liberty.

Nina Gabrielian was born in 1953, and lives in Moscow. She is a graduate of the Moscow Institute of Foreign Languages. She writes prose and criticism, as well as poetry. She also translates contemporary poetry of the East. From 1994-7, Gabrielian was chief editor of the feminist journal, *Preobrazhenie* (Transformation). From 1996-8, she was an editor of *Vestnik Zhenshchina i kultura* (Bulletin of Woman and Culture). She now directs an education programme for women, The Independent Women's Forum.

Mariya Galina was born in 1958 in Tver. Her childhood and adolescence was spent in Odessa. She is by training a biologist. Her first publication was in *Yunost*, in 1991. In 2000-1 she was a regular columnist ('Poetry Non-Stop") for "Literaturnaia gazeta". Dmitry Kuzmin write: "Marina Galina's poetry is distinguished by its range, from Church Slavonic to the terminology of science, with an intermixture of Yiddish and Ukrainian. She recreates the unique and virtually lost social dialect of the Russian-Jewish intelligentsia of Ukraine, the only example of this in modern Russian poetry."

Anna Glazova was born in Dubna, Moscow region, in 1973. She was educated at the Moscow Architetural Institute and the Berlin Technische Universität, as well as the University of Illinois, Chicago and Northwestern University, Chicago, where she is a doctoral student in comparative literary studies. Her work is to be found on various websites and she has participated in the Franz Kafka scholarly project and the online journals *Speaking in Tongues* and *Text.only*.

Natalya Gorbanevskaya was born in Moscow in 1936. Expelled from Moscow University, she graduated from the philological department of Leningrad University. She was arrested in 1968 for protesting against the Soviet-led invasion of Czechoslovakia. The circumstances of Gorbanevskaya's life in the Soviet Union is described in the article by

Kublanovsky printed here. She now lives in Paris and works for the paper *Russkaya Mysl'*, for which she regularly writes on topical themes. She also regularly publishes poetry collections. A selection of her early work, translated by Daniel Weissbort, was published by Carcanet in 1972. Typecast as a "political poet", Gorbanevskaya's is, in fact, one of the most distinct voices of contemporary Russian poetry, combining the folk-inspired modernism of Tsvetayeva with the narrative clarity of Akhmatova.

Nina Gorlanova was born in a village in the Perm district. She is a graduate of Perm State University and the author of two books of prose. Her work has appeared in several journals, including *Daugava, Avrora, Oktiabr, Ural*. She lives in Perm.

Lydiya Grigoryeva was born in 1945, in the village of Lysy, in Voroshilov region of Ukraine. She is a graduate of Kazan University and has worked as a schoolteacher and journalist. Grigoryeva lived for many years in Moscow, and now lives in London with her husband, the poet and translator Ravil Bukharayev. She has published numerous collections of poetry and has been nominated for the 2002 Booker Prize for her poetic text, 'The Russian Wife of an English Gentleman'.

Faina Grimberg was born in 1951. She is a playwright and graphic artist, as well as poet. By training she is a philologist and Slavist. She has published a collection of poetry, *Green Weaver* and more recently *Stikhi o Chechne* (Poems about Chechnya).

Elena Ignatova was born in Leningrad. She writes prose as well as poetry. Her poetry appeared in *samizdat* and from 1975 in Russian publications abroad. In 1976 a book was published in Paris and another in Leningrad, in 1989. In 1992 *Nebesnoe zarevo* (Celestial glow) was published in Jerusalem. Ignatova's poetry has appeared widely in Russian and foreign periodicals and is represented in several anthologies of twentieth-century Russian poetry. In 1997 *Zapiski o Peterburge* (Notes on Petersburg), on the history of the city from the eighteenth to twentieth centuries, was published in St Petersburg.

Nina Iskrenko was a leading underground poet in Moscow until her untimely death from cancer in 1995. Her performances of her work and her participation in various artistic "happenings" made her a central figure in the alternative culture of late Soviet and early post-Soviet Russia. Her poems are distinguished by a bold mix of themes, from the political and prosaic to the frankly sexual, and of tone, from the audacity of informal conversation to philosophical strivings after the sublime.

Her early 'Hymn to Polystylistics' stands as a manifesto of this self-conscious amalgamation. Iskrenko carefully divided her work into volumes, which have continued to appear since her death.

Olga Ivanova was born in Moscow in 1965, and is a graduate of the Gorky Literary Institute. Her first publication was in *Novy Mir* in 1988. She has also published in *Kontinent* and other periodicals. She has occasionally published under the pseudonym Polina Ivanova.

Svetlana Ivanova was born in Leningrad in 1965, and is a graduate of the Art School and the Gorky Literary Institute in Moscow. She is an artist and critic, as well as a poet. She has published three collections of poetry and has appeared in many periodicals, especially *Zvezda* and *Arion*. She has also edited an anthology of Russian émigré poetry (*Russian Atlantis*). Ivanova lives in Moscow.

Ina Kabysh was born in Moscow, in 1963. She studied at the Pedagogical Institute and worked as a school teacher. Her poetry has appeared in *Znamya*, *Druzhba narodov*, and *Novy mir*. Her first individual collection was published in 1994.

Katia Kapovich was born in Kishinev, in 1960. She lives and teaches in Boston. Her first book *Day and Night of the Angel* was published in Israel in 1992, and the poems here, written in the 90's come from that book. She also writes fluently in English.

Svetlana Kekova was born, in 1951, in Sakhalin. She lives in Saratov. Trained as philologist. Among her influences is the early poetry of Nikolay Zabolotsky. Kekova teaches in the Pedagogical Institute and has been widely published in all leading journals.

The well-known poet Vladimir Gandelsman writes (*Ogonek*, No. 7, 1997): "Kekova's interest in Zabolotsky's work is no accident. This has less to do with a similarity of poetic means, than with an existential tendency to return to the first principles. For Kekova the task is so urgent that the traditional formula, i.e. to look at life through a prism – will not do. The poet stubbornly looks THE OTHER WAY, trying not to surrender to the optimistic illusions of real life, which – the author is convinced – conceals the mystery." Kekova is not a modish poet. Her serious and even solemn relationship to her own life contrasts sharply with that daring which, in epidemic proportions, characterises the work of so many contemporary versifiers."

Olga Khvostova was born in 1965 in Maili-Sai Sai, Oshsk region. She used to live in Dushanbe. Khvostova is trained as a teacher of Russian language and literature and has published poetry in a Dushanbe periodical and also in London. In 1990, she emigrated to Gulkevichi, in the Krasnodarsk region. She works wherever she can.

Mariya Kildibekova was born in Moscow in 1976. Her poetry has been published in a number of magazines, including *Arion*. A graduate of the Moscow Literary Institute, she lived for several years in Yemen and Libya. She has worked as a journalist.

Nina Kossman, born in Moscow in 1959, emigrated in 1973, and lives in New York. A bilingual Russian-American poet, she has published two books of poetry in Russian, *Pereboi* (Moscow, 1990) and *Po pravuyu ruku sna* (Philadelphia, 1996), and a collection of short stories about her Moscow childhood, *Behind the Border* (New York, 1994). Her work has been translated into several languages. Her fiction won a UNESCO/PEN Short Story Award in 1995. She has translated two books of Marina Tsvetaeva's poetry and is the editor of *Gods and Mortals: Modern Poems on Classical Themes* (OUP, 2001). Two plays have been produced in New York City.

Irina Kovaleva, trained as a philologist, is Professor in the Department of Classics, Moscow State University. She has published over seventy articles on Ancient and Modern Greek Literature, and Russian Literature, as well as translations from ancient and modern languages (Seferis, Elytis into Russian; Brodsky and Sedakova into Greek). She has written commentaries on works of Classical authors published in Russian, including editing Joseph Brodsky's *Kentavry. Antichnye siuzhety* (Centaurs. Classical subjects; St Petersburg, 2001). A collection of her own poems, *V proshedshem vremeni*, was published in Moscow in 2002.

Ella Krylova was born in 1967, in Moscow. Her first publication was in *Znamia* in 1991. She has published widely in *Druzhba narodov, Zvezda, Yunost* and in Russian periodicals in France and the USA. She has published six collections of poetry. Since 1993, she has been living in St Petersburg.

Marina Kudimova was born in Tambov, in 1953. She graduated from Tambov Pedagogical Institute. She was influenced by Tsvetaeva and was published in *Novy mir* and *Znamya* after Glasnost. Kudimova is the author of three poetry collections. She lives outside Moscow.

Inna Kulishova was born in 1969, in Tbilisi. She graduated from Tbilisi University. Her doctorate, on Joseph Brodsky, was completed in 1998. Brodsky had a high regard for Kulishova's poetry, which she has been writing since the age of six. She has published one collection of poetry.

Yuliya Kunina was born in 1966 in Moscow. She is a graduate of the philological department of Moscow State University. Her first book was published in 1991. In addition to scholarly articles, she has published translations of seventeenth-century English poetry. Her own poetry has appeared in many journals and anthologies. The poets to whom she feels closest are Khodasevich and Derzhavin. She is working on a doctorate on translation theory at New York University.

Evgeniya Lavut was born in 1972 in Moscow and graduated in Romance and Germanic Languages, Moscow State University. Her first published book, in 1994, was entitled *Gleb the Good Gentleman Landowner, about King David, Foma and Erema, Luther and Others.*

Elena Lazutkina was born in 1975, in Eisk, Krasnodar region. She studied in the St Petersburg Institute of Film and Television. She lives in Moscow and hands out flyers in the street about foreign-language teaching.

Inna Lisnianskaya was born in Baku, in 1928. Her first publication was in 1948 and her first collection of poetry appeared in 1957. In 1960 Lisnianskaya moved to Moscow; several more books were published. After her participation in the *Metropol* almanach, in 1979, her books were published only abroad (France and USA). In recent years she has published several more collections and appears regularly in all the leading Russian literary periodicals. Lisnianskaya is married to the poet Semen Lipkin.

Sveta Litvak was born in 1959 in Kovrov. She is a graduate of the Ivanovo Art Institute. In Moscow she has worked in the Soviet Army Theatre as a scene-painter. Her work has appeared in a number of exhibitions of young artists and in 1999 she had a one-man show. She is a member of the Moscow Writers Union. In 1996, with Nikolay Baitov, she founded a literary club for the performance of poetry. Litvak has published two collections: *Raznotsvetnye prokazniki* [Motley mischievous children] (1992) and *Pesni Uchenika* [Songs of a pupil] (1994), as well as a prose book, *My Journey to the East* (1998). She is a regular contributor to *Znamia* and *Arion*.

Olga Martynova was born in 1962, in Siberia. She grew up in Leningrad and graduated from the Leningrad Pedagogical Institute. Since 1991 she has lived in Germany with her husband, the poet and playwright O Yurev. She has published two poetry collections in Russian and one in

German and has written numerous critical essays and reviews for the German press. In 2000 she was awarded the Hubert Burda Prize.

Larisa Miller was born in 1940. She is a graduate of the Moscow Institute of Foreign Languages. Her first collection appeared in 1977, but her poetry has been in print since the mid-Sixties. She has published eight books of prose and poetry. Miller lives in Moscow.

Tatyana Milova was born in the Moscow region in 1965, and graduated in journalism from Moscow State University. She has worked as an editor, night watchman and boiler-man. Her first publication was in 1989. Her work has appeared in *Petropol*, *Yunost* and *Arion*. She has also published a volume of poetry.

Elizaveta Mnatsakanova was born in 1922 in Baku. She studied at Moscow University (philology) and at the Moscow Conservatory (piano and music theory) and subsequently earned a living writing articles and books on music. Her first literary-artistic texts date from the late 1940s. In 1975 she emigrated to Vienna, where she now lives. Soon after her arrival in Vienna she adopted the pen-name Netzkowa. Her poetic works are characterized by rich paranomasia and quasi-musical forms involving repetition and development of word and phrase kernels. Memory and death are prominent themes in her poetry.

Yunna Morits was born in Kiev, in 1937, and was evacuated from there at the time of the German invasion in 1941. She graduated from the Gorky Institute of Literature in Moscow, in 1961. Her first collection appeared in Kiev, in 1957. In 1956 she had participated in an Arctic expedition, which profoundly affected her. Besides many collections of poetry, Morits has published several books of verse for children and translated a good deal, including a volume of poems by the Jewish poet Moisei Teif. After Glasnost' she began to publish short prose works as well, including memoirs. She attended the International Writing Program at the University of Iowa and has read at Poetry International in London. Morits lives in Moscow, where she continues regularly to publish groups of poems and to draw, sometimes using a technique developed by herself employing cigarette stubs. She was recently awarded the Triumf Prize.

Negar (Negar Hasan-Zadeh) was born in 1975 in Baku. She graduated in philology from Baku University and is fluent in four languages: Russian, Azeri, Turkish, and English. In 2000, in Baku, she published her first book of poetry in Russian, which includes poems from her teenage years and early twenties. In 2001 she became the youngest member of the

Azerbaijan Union of Writers. Since 2000 Negar has made her home in London. Her first book, in England, *On Wings Over The Horizon*, was translated by Richard McKane (Caspian Publishing). In 2001, this volume was awarded the Azerbaijan Academy's National Public Prize.

Olesia Nikolaeva was born in 1955, in Moscow. She started writing poetry at the age of seven, prose at the age of sixteen, and began to publish at the same age. She is a graduate of Moscow's Gorky Literary Institute where she teaches a course in the history of Russian religious thought. Her first collection, *The Garden of Miracles* (1980), was followed by several collections of poetry and prose. She has been widely published especially in *Arion*, *Znamia* and *Novy mir* and has participated in a number of international festivals. In 1998, she was awarded the Töpffer Prize.

Rea Nikonova (Anna Tarshis) was born in 1942, in Eisk and grew up in Sverdlovsk, where she studied music, returning to Eisk in 1975, and from there emigrating to Germany in 1998. She and her husband, Sergei Sigei produced the multimedia samizdat journal *Transponans* (36 issues from 1979 to 1987). Perhaps the premier avant-garde poet of Russia, she has invented and writes in an enormous variety of forms and styles, ranging from gesture poems and elaborately gridded texts to short lyrics and *zaum*. She has compiled a multi-volumed *System* which attempts to survey and exemplify all possible kinds of poetry.

Vera Pavlova was born in 1963, in Moscow. She graduated from the Schnittke College of Music and the Gnesin Academy, specialising in the History of Music. Up to the age of 18 she studied to become a composer. She also worked as a guide in the Shaliapin Museum and published essays on music. For about ten years she sang in a church choir. She began writing poetry at the age of twenty, after the birth of her first daughter, publishing from the age of twenty-four when she was pregnant with her second. The first selection of her poetry appeared in the journal *Yunost*. Her first collection appeared in 1997, followed by no fewer than five other collections, the last containing 800 poems, written over a period of eighteen years. Pavlova's celebrity dates from the appearance in the paper *Sevodnia* of no fewer than 72 poems (with a postscript by Boris Kuzminsky), which gave rise to the rumour that she was a literary hoax. Her poetry was published in many papers and most of the major journals. Pavlova also directs "Zodiak", a literary workshop for children.

Aleksandra Petrova writes: My biography is short for the moment: two books, two land changes, two daughters. I studied in Tartu and for me it is important.

Liudmila Petrushevskaya was born in 1938 and attended Moscow University. She worked as a journalist, 1961-70, and has also worked as a radio reporter, teacher, editor, and translator (from Polish). She came to prominence during the Gorbachev years when her uncompromising depictions of the seamier side of life began to be published. She was shortlisted for the Russian Booker Prize for her dark family saga, *The Time: Night*, 1992. Best known of course for her starkly realistic prose and drama, Petrushevskaya is also well known in the world of cinema. She took to poetry comparatively late. Her 'Karamzin: Village Diary', which also shows her preoccupation with monologue, self-absorption, isolation, appeared in *Novy mir*, in 1994 and a full version was published in St Petersburg in 2000.

Olga Postnikova was born in 1943 in Evdakovo, Voronezh region. She lives in Moscow and is a graduate of the Moscow Institute of Chemical Technology. She has worked as a restorer of old buildings and churches. She is the grand-daughter of a Russian priest who perished in the camps. Postnikova has been published in many magazines and anthologies including *Novy mir* and *Znamia*. A collection of poetry, *Stikhi*, appeared in 1993.

Irina Ratushinskaya was born in Odessa in 1954. She graduated from Odessa University and taught at the Odessa Pedagogical Institute. In 1976, Ratushinskaya was arrested for dissident activity and sentenced to seven years in a strict-regime prison. A collection of poems was published in 1984 by International PEN, with an Introduction by Joseph Brodsky. This helped to focus attention on her case. She was released in 1986 and left for England, where her poetry was published by Bloodaxe. She returned to Russia in 2001. Her poetry has been translated into every European language and she has published many collections of poetry and prose, including a chronicle of her prison ordeal. Ratushinskaya has won many international awards.

Tatyana Retivova was born in New York in 1954, studied poetry with Richard Hugio at the University of Montana, and then with Joseph Brodsky at the University of Michigan. She writes poetry in both English and Russian and has been living in Ukraine for over seven years.

Olga Sedakova was born in Moscow, in 1949. She first appeared in print at the age of eleven. Sedakova is a polyglot translator (Eliot, Pound, Hardy, Claudel, Rilke, Petrarch, Horace and Dante) and a celebrated essayist. In the late 80s her poetry appeared in unofficial journals in Moscow and Leningrad. She is perhaps the leading confessional Christian poet writing in Russian today, but some critics complain that her work shows little interest in the feminist literary tradition. Sedakova enjoys the distinction of having been the only Russian Poet-in-Residence at a British University (Keele). She is the first and, so far, only poet to receive the Vatican Prize for Literature, awarded in 1999.

Evelina Shats was born in Odessa and has lived and worked in Italy for many years. She writes poems in Italian and Russian. An artist and performer, essayist, journalist and critic, theatre director etc, she has published widely in Italy, Russia and elsewhere. She has been a regular contributor to *Corriere della Sera*, as well as to TV and radio shows. Shats is Vice-president of the international Consortium for Art Masterpieces (strategies and new technologies for culture) in Moscow. She has exhibited object-books, limited editions, visual poems and conceptual works.

Tatiana Shcherbina was born in Moscow in 1954. She is a graduate of Moscow State University. Five collections appeared in *samizdat*, as well as a novel. In 1989 she represented alternative ("second") literature at the Poetry International in Rotterdam, where she met Joseph Brodsky and Derek Walcott. Brodsky encouraged Walcott to translate Shcherbina's poem 'About Limits', which is published here for the first time, together with the drafts. In 1989, Shcherbina's poems began to be published in the official Soviet press. She worked for Radio Liberty in Munich in 1991 and from 1992-97 lived in Paris, working for Radio Liberty. Shcherbina speaks fluent French, writes poems in French and Russian and has translated a number of French poets into Russian. In 1994 she was awarded a scholarship by the French Ministry of Culture. Her own poetry has been widely translated. She returned to Russia in 1997 and now lives in Moscow, in 2001 becoming deputy editor of the journal *Vestnik Evropy* (European messenger).

Elena Shvarts has long been acknowledged as one of the most interesting poets in contemporary Russia, and after several decades of publication, she continues to impress her readers with her ever-changing work. She is a prolific, compelling poet who mixes the skepticism of post-modern sensibilities with the haunted primitivism of ancient Slavic folk belief. Her work emerged from the Petersburg artistic underground of late Soviet Russia, and she continues to explore its themes of marginalization, poverty, and commitment to authentic, dangerous utterance. The poems translated here by Stephanie Sandler are among her most recent, and they pay tribute to and memorialize her mother, Dina Shvarts, who died in 1998.

Mariya Stepanova was born in Moscow in 1972 and has written poetry from early youth. Her first publication was in *Yunost* in 1988. Stepanova has also appeared in *Znamya*. She has published three collections of poetry. She was shortlisted for the Andrei Bely Prize last year.

Darya Sukhovei was born in 1977 in Leningrad and graduated from St Petersburg University. She is a poet and the Literary Curator of the Internet project "The St Petersburg Literary Guide", with information about literary life in St Petersburg. Sukhovei is the author of two poetry collections.

Olga Sulchinskaya was born in 1966 in Moscow. She graduated from Moscow State University and has published poems in *Arion*, *Znamya* and *Novy mir* as well as a chapbook of poems.

Vitalina Tkhorzhevskaya was born in Sverdlovsk in 1971. Her first poems appeared in samizdat and in the journal *Ural*. Since then she has published three collections of poetry, most recently *Smirennyi gnev* (Meek wrath, Moscow, 1997). She lives and works in Ekaterinburg.

Elena Ushakova was born in 1945 in Leningrad. She graduated from Leningrad University. Ushakova is a philologist, critic, essayist, as well as poet. Her main field of studies is the theory of poetic speech and she has written numerous articles and a book on the subject. She has published two collections of poetry and was awarded the Severnaya Palmira Prize in 1999.

Ekaterina Vlasova was born in 1976 in Zlatoust. She has published poetry in *Uralskaya nov* and *Nesovremennye zapiski*. A collection appeared in 1998. She now lives in Chelyabinsk.

Tatyana Voltskaya was born in Leningrad and graduated from the Krupskaya Institute of Culture. For a short while she worked in the Institute's library, afterwards as a guide in the Pushkin Museum in Pushkino. Poet, member of the St Petersburg Union of Writers, author of three collections, as well as critical essays, which have appeared in leading journals: *Znamia*, *Novy mir*, *Oktiabr*, *Druzhba narodov*, *Zvezda*, and *Neva*. Her poetry has been translated into English, Italian, Dutch, Swedish and Finnish.

Voltskaya began working as a journalist in 1987-88 on Petersburg (at that time still Leningrad) Radio, with programmes on early twentieth-century Russian philosophers, journals, contemporary writers and poets. She is a member of the St Petersburg Union of Journalists and since 1992, has been a correspondent for the Petersburg paper *Nevskoe vremia*; she has also contributed to *Novaya gazeta*, published in Petersburg, the BBC in London (a religious journal *Voskresenie*); in Moscow articles have appeared, mainly, in *Literaturnaya gazeta*, *Vremia i my* and the journal *Znamia*; in Paris, in *Russkaya mysl*. Since 2000 she has been a correspondent of the Svoboda radio station (Radio Liberty).

The focus of her articles and interviews has been culture: religion, as well as literature and art. But she has also written on more public themes, in particular such subjects as anti-Semitism, racism, the imperial mentality, war, military problems, democracy and free speech.

As regards her principal interest, poetry, hard as it may be to define one's own creative position (for this it is better to approach from outside), nevertheless, she would probably associate herself with the Petersburg school of poetry. As Akhmatova once said of her own poetic generation, that it sprang from the "The Cypress casket" (having in mind a collection of poems by Innokenty Annesky), so Voltskaya can say, that her contemporaries were all children of the Silver Age of Russian culture. In her development such poets as Mikhail Kuzmin, Aleksandr Blok, Nikolai Zabolotsky were of the utmost importance. Mandelstam and Brodsky were permanent features of this poetic landscape.

This succession is no accident – in itself it distinguishes between writing and postmodernism, culture, unifying and eliminating stylistic and linguistic strata. The Petersburg school seems to Voltskaya a kind of island, threatened but not yet overwhelmed by the waves of post-modernism.

Furthermore, it seems to her that one should write not so as to demonstrate craftsmanship, which has just attained great heights, but – however jejune this may sound – because one's a powerful spiritual and emotional impulse demands it. Without this, as she sees it, art simply ceases to exist.

Liudmila Zubova was born in 1946 and graduated from Leningrad University where she is now a professor, teaching the history of the Russian language. She wrote most of her poetry in the 60s and 80s. At present she is researching contemporary poetics and has published two major studies on Marina Tsvetaeva.

Translators

Christopher Arkell is the chief shareholder in *The London Magazine*. He also owns *The London Miscellany* and writes occasional pieces on current affairs for *The European Journal*. He has published translations, done in collaboration with Eugene Dubnov, of other Russian poets, including Pushkin.

Kevin Carey is a poet and translator. He was born in 1952 in Ohio. He was educated at Williams College, Massachusetts, and at Georgetown University, Washington. For some years he has been member of the US diplomatic corps. For the last ten years he has worked for the Church in Jerusalem.

Jenefer Coates teaches literary translation at Middlesex University and also works as translator, writer and editor. Until recently she coedited *In Other Words*, the journal of the Translators Association. She is writing a book on Vladimir Nabokov and translation.

Maura Dooley has edited *Making for Planet Alice: new Women Poets* (1997). *The Honey Gatherers: A Book of Love Poems* is due from Bloodaxe in 2003. *How Novelists Work* (2000) was published by Seren. Her latest collection, *Sound Barrier, Poems 1982-2002* was published by Bloodaxe this year and draws on several collections, two of which were Poetry Book Society Recommendations and one of which was short-listed for the TS Eliot prize.

Terence Dooley has published original work in many magazines and journals, most recently *The Swansea Review* and *Smiths Knoll*. He translates widely from Spanish, Italian and French and has just completed a verse translation of Paul Valery's *Le Jeune Parque*.

Yuri Drobyshev was born in Leningrad and graduated from the Naval Engineering Academy. He emigrated to Britain in 1978. He has contributed to the anthology *The Poetry of Perestroika* (Iron Press, 1989), as well as to the Ratushinskaya collection, *Pencil Letter* (Bloodaxe, 1988) and, with Carol Rumens, to *Evgeny Rein, Selected Poems* (Bloodaxe, 2001).

Ruth Fainlight's twelfth collection of poems, *Burning Wire*, has just been published. The title poem of her last book, *Sugar-Paper Blue* (shortlisted for the 1998 Whitbread Poetry Award) is based on a visit to Leningrad in 1965 and the shock of discovering that the footsteps she could hear in the flat above were those of Anna Ahkmatova. Collections of her poems have been published in Portuguese, French and Spanish translation, and she has published translations from the same languages.

Elaine Feinstein is a poet and novelist. In 1980, she was made a Fellow of the Royal Society of Literature. In 1990, she received a Cholmondeley Award for Poetry, and was given an Honorary DLit from the University of Leicester. Her versions of the great Russian poet Marina Tsvetaeva have remained in print since 1970. Her most recent books of poems are *Daylight* (Carcanet, 1997), a Poetry Book Society Recommendation; and *Gold* (Carcanet, 2000). Her fourteenth novel, *Dark Inheritance* (Women's Press), was published in 2001, and her biography of *Ted Hughes: The Life of a Poet* (Weidenfeld and Nicholson) in the same year. Her *Collected Poems and Translations*, a Poetry Book Society Special Commendation, was published in 2002.

Roy Fisher was born in 1930 in Handsworth, Birmingham. Poet and jazz piano-player, he has worked as a school and college teacher. He retired as Senior Lecturer in American Studies from Keele University in 1982. He is now a freelance writer and lives in Derbyshire. Roy Fisher is the author of several collections of poetry, including *Poems, 1955-1987* (OUP), and *The Dow Low Drop: New and Selected Poems* (Bloodaxe, 1996).

Peter France, who recently retired from a chair in French at Edinburgh University, has translated *An Anthology of Chuvash Poetry* (1991) and collections of poems by Gennady Aygi, Joseph Brodsky, Vladimir Mayakovsky and (with Jon Stallworthy) Aleksandr Blok and Boris Pasternak. He is the author of *Poets of Modern Russia* (1982) and the editor of the *Oxford Guide to Literature in English Translation* (2000).

Gerald Janecek was born in New York, in 1945. He is Professor of Russian at the University of Kentucky. He specializes in avant-garde Russian poetry and has written on and translated Andrei Bely, Russian Futurist poetry, and contemporary Russian poetry. He is the author of *The Look of Russian Poetry* (1984), *ZAUM: The Transrational Poetry of Russian Futurism* (1996), *Sight & Sound Entwined: Studies of the New Russian Poetry* (2000), and a number of articles on these subjects.

Catriona Kelly is Reader in Russian at Oxford, and Tutorial Fellow at New College. She has a large number of publications about Russian literature and cultural history, including, most recently, *Russian Literature: A Very Short Introduction* (OUP). Published translations include work by various Russian poets and prose writers in her anthologies, *Utopias: Russian Modernist Texts 1905-1940* (Penguin), and *An Anthology of Russian Women's Writing, 1777-1992* (OUP), and also novels by Leonid Borodin and by Sergei Kaledin (Harvill), poems by Elena Shvarts (in *Paradise*, Bloodaxe Books) and by Olga Sedakova (in *The Silk of Time*, Keele University Press).

Angela Livingstone is Emeritus Professor of Russian at Esssex University and has written widely on Russian literature, translating Boris Pasternak, Marina Tsvetayeva (*The Rat-Catcher*, Bloodaxe) and, with Robert Chandler, Andrei Platonov (Harvill).

Christopher Mattison received his MFA in Translation from the University of Iowa. He is currently the Managing Editor of Zephyr Press and the Co-Director of Adventures in Poetry, in Boston.

James McGavran recently finished undergraduate studies at Kenyon College in Gambier, Ohio, where he majored in modern languages and literatures. He will begin graduate school in Slavic literatures at Princeton University in fall 2002. He intends to focus on contemporary Russian poetry and translation.

Max Nemtsov writes: Well, there's not much to say. I'm 39, born in Vladivostok, currently live in Moscow, a freelance translator/editor, am responsible for the Speaking In Tongues web publication (http://spintongues.msk.ru/).

Robert Reid is Reader in Modern Languages (Russian) at Keele University. He has written and edited many books and articles on Romanticism and is co-editor of *Essays in Poetics*, the journal of the British Neo-formalist Circle, to which he has also regularly contributed translations of modern Russian poetry. He has translated Russian poetry for various other collections and anthologies, including work by Brodsky, Prigov and Sedakova.

Carol Rumens has published eleven collections of poetry, a novel, short stories and literary journalism, and has edited several anthologies. With Yuri Drobyshev she has contributed translations from the Russian to several publications, including *Evgeny Rein, Selected Poems* and *After Pushkin* (Carcanet, 1999). Recent poetry books include *Best China Sky* (Bloodaxe, 1995) and *Holding Pattern* (Blackstaff, 1998). Based in Belfast for some years, she has held several residencies and currently teaches at the University of Bangor, North Wales.

Stephanie Sandler is a scholar of modern Russian poetry and of the Pushkin period, with a special interest in women's writing. Her publications include *Distant Pleasures: Alexander Pushkin and the Writing of Exile* and several edited collections, *Sexuality and the Body in Russian Culture* (with Jane T Costlow and Judith Vowles) and *Rereading Russian Poetry* among them. She is Professor of Slavic Languages and Literatures at Harvard University.

Jason Schneiderman was educated at the University of Maryland, New York University and The Herzen Institute (St Petersburg, Russia). His poems have appeared in *The Penguin Book of The Sonnet, Columbia,* and other places. His essays have appeared in *Frigate* and he teaches creative writing at Hofstra (Hempstead, New York). He lives in New York City.

Steven Seymour is a freelance simultaneous interpreter of Russian, currently living in New York.

Dennis Silk (1928-1998) was born in London and from 1955 lived in Jerusalem. His collections of poetry include: *Punished Land, Hold Fast, Catwalk and Overpass* (Penguin / Viking) and *William the Wonder-Kid,* plays, puppet plays and theatre writings (Sheep Meadow Press).

Lydia Stone is a first generation American, who makes her living as a technical translator from Russian and devotes a large portion of her spare time to translating poetry. She is the editor of the *SlavFile,* newsletter of the Slavic Language Division of the American Translators Association. In 2000 Cornerstone Press in Chicago published a book of poems by Irina Ratushinksaya *Wind of the Journey,* translated by Lydia Stone.

Daniel Weissbort edits *MPT,* writes poetry, and translates it occasionally, especially if it is in Russian. He has co-edited a *Historical Reader in Translation Studies* which will be published by OUP and is working on a book on Ted Hughes and translation (also for Oxford). His *Letters to Ted* (Poems) and *From Russian with Love* (a translational memoir of Joseph Brodsky) will both be published by Anvil Press in autumn 2002.

Three Russian Poets

Translated by Stephen Capus

Stephen Capus *studied Russian literature at the Universities of Birmingham and London. He has published poems and translations in various magazines, including* Acumen *and* Thumbscrew. *He currently works as an administrator at University College London.*

Anna Akhmatova (1889-1966)

Mayakovsky in 1913

I never knew you in the days of your glory,
Your turbulent dawn is all I know;
But perhaps I'm qualified to tell the story
At last of that day from long ago.
The lines of your powerful verse were filled with
Strange new voices we'd never heard . . .
And your youthful hands were never still as
You raised up a terrible scaffold in words.
Whatever you touched was no longer the same as
The thing it had been before that time,
All that you censured and covered in shame was
Condemned to death in your thunderous lines.
So often alone and disaffected,
You impatiently tried to speed up fate,
For already you freely, gladly accepted
That soon you must go and take part in the great
Struggle. And as you read an answer
Of rumbling dissent could be heard all round
And the angry rain eyed you askance as
You debated at length with the outraged town.
And now a name, unknown, obscure,
Was flashing around the stuffy hall,
And all through the land today it endures,
Reverberates still like a warrior's call.

Vladimir Mayakovsky (1893-1930)

To Comrade Nette – The Steamship and the Man*

I had cause to shudder – it wasn't a spectre.
Into port, gleaming in the molten light,
Entered Comrade 'Theodore Nette'.
Yes, it was him alright.
I knew him from the lifebelt-glasses he was wearing,
Just like in the old days. Nette, how are you?
I'm so glad you're still with us, alive and sharing
In the smoky confusion of cables and cargoes.
Come closer – if it's not too shallow for you here
After steaming from Batum through the open seas.
Nette, d'you recall how in your previous career
As a man you once drank tea on a train with me?
The others were all snoring like dormice but you
Stayed awake and talked about Romka Jakobson
And poetry all night – yet your eyes stayed glued
To the diplomatic bags – till finally round dawn
You nodded off to sleep with your hand still clamped
So tightly round your gun you must have had cramp
In your finger . . . You're welcome to come and have a go,
If you've got the nerve! At the time did you dream the
Moment would arrive in a year or so
When we'd meet again – and that you'd be a steamer?
The moon glows like a conflagration.
And now it's declined, dividing the flood.
As though you trail behind you from that confrontation
On the train a heroic stream of blood.
Communism from books is never quite real.
'Any kind of nonsense can find support
In books.' But the act which you performed reveals
The essence and soul of communist thought.
We live, united by a common conviction;
For its sake we'll endure all manner of affliction:
To live in a unified world, made happier
By the absence of divisions like Russia and Latvia.
Blood, not water, flows through our veins.
Marching through a storm of bullets, we try
To ensure that one day we'll be born again
In steamships, in words – in things that never die.

*

I'd like to live, careering through the years.
And yet I can think of nothing better
Than to face my death without regrets or fears
The way it was faced by Comrade Nette.

* At readings, Mayakovsky often introduced this poem with the folloiwng
anecdote: 'Nette was one of our diplomatic couriers . . . I knew Comrade Nette
well . . . In Rostov I heard the newspaper-vendors shouting in the street: "Attack
on Soviet couriers Nette and Makhmastl." I was stunned. This was my first
meeting with Nette after his death. Soon the initial grief abated. I found myself in
Odessa. I boarded a steamship for Yalta. As our ship was leaving harbour, it was
met by another, bearing the name, written in golden letters gleaming in the sun:
"Theodore Nette". This was my second meeting with Nette; but by now he was
no longer a man, but a steamship.'

Marina Tsvetaeva (1892-1941)

The Poet

The poet acquires his speech from afar.
Speech carries the poet beyond the stars.

The obliquities of parables and portents – those
Are the way of the poet . . . Between *yes* and *no*
Leaping headlong from the dizzy top
Of a tower, he still contrives to stop
And make a detour . . . Because the poet travels

The way of comets. Causality unravelled,
Its links dispersed – that's the law which guides
The poet's eclipses. Look up at the sky
And despair, astronomer! For the poet's path
Can't be plotted by the curve of a graph.

He's the one no granite Bastille can hold,
The one whose tracks have always gone cold.
He defies the laws of number and weight,
He's the train for which everyone is always late.

He asks the questions even Kant doesn't know
The answer to . . .

Because the poet goes
The way of comets, he doesn't warm,
He burns, he doesn't nurture – he's violence and storm.
Poet, the trajectory of your fiery path
Can't be plotted by the curve of a graph!

Editor's Note: These translations by Stephen Capus appeared in *MPT* 18
in a seriously mangled form, the wrong proofs having been returned to
the printer. We apologise for our mistake and are glad to have this
opportunity to print the poems as they should be.

The Prince George Galitzine Memorial Library St Petersburg

Max Hayward, translator of Pasternak and Solzhenitsyn, was described on his death by his collaborator Patricia Blake, as having 'acted as custodian of Russian literature in the West, until such a time as it can be restored to Russia'. That time arrived far sooner than either of them could have dared to hope in the form of The Prince George Galitzine Memorial Library which opened in St Petersburg in October 1994.

The Galitzine Library is home to several thousand volumes of tamizdat writing and historical biographies never previously seen in Russia before. Through hosting talks, lectures, readings and seminars, mainly on the theme of 'Russia abroad', the Library has established itself as an important cultural centre in the city of St Petersburg.

Prince George Galitzine, an expert on Russian history and art, led cultural tours to Russia throughout the Soviet years. After his death in 1992, he was remembered at a conference at the Smithsonian Institute by James Billington, the Librarian of Congress, with these words: 'We all owe a debt to George Galitzine, for keeping the cultural doors open to Russia – he paved the way for us.' His widow, Jean, and daughter, Katya, created the memorial library as a fitting tribute to a man whose love of Russia was passed on to his family.

The Library is housed at 46 Fontanka, a beautiful mansion that formerly belonged to the family of Prince George's mother. It has a recently renovated reading room with an up-to-date reference section, and the use of the former ballroom as a 'lecture hall'. One grateful reader wrote a thank you to the library, saying it had 'books one never knew existed, and others one had heard of and never hoped to hold in one's hands.'

Guest speakers at The Galitzine Library have included Orlando Figes, Suzanne Massey, Professor Efim Etkind, as well as local authors and historians. Over the years, universities throughout the British Isles have donated books, as have many collectors and authors, such as Professor Anthony Cross, Isaiah Berlin, Asa Briggs, Kyril (Fitzlyon) Zinovieff, Colin Thubron, Robert Massie, the Bodleian Library, the School of Slavonic Studies and Trinity College, Dublin.

Funded entirely by The Galitzine-St Petersburg Trust, a London based charity (No. 1015036), our aim is to inform, instruct and inspire. We continually need help in raising money and new interest in this project. Our annual outgoings are minimal, but in order to continue funding our running costs, events, and the purchase of books, many of which are rare and valuable, we do need donations however small.

◆ ◆ ◆

"Every blade of grass makes a meadow"

The Galitzine Library is open to everyone, if you are in St Petersburg, please pay us a visit!

The Prince George Galitzine Memorial Library
46, Fontanka Embankment
St Petersburg 191025
Russia
Tel/Fax: +7 812 311 1333
kontakt@attglobal.net

Should you wish to help The Prince George Galitzine Memorial Library, please make your donation payable to:
The Galitzine-St Petersburg Trust
c/o Wedlake Bell, 16 Bedford Street, London WC2E 9HF
Registered with the Charities Commission No. 1015036

MENARD PRESS   8 The Oaks • Woodside Avenue
London N12 8AR
Tel/Fax 020 8446 5571

Then and Now

W. D. JACKSON

2002, 144pp, £7.99, ISBN 1 874320 04 7
Published in association with MPT Books

Begun in the North of England in 1981, *Then and Now* constitutes the first – self-contained – instalment of an extended work-in-progress on the subject of history and individual freedom. Consisting of translations, quotations and notes as well as original poetry, the sequence proceeds by adopting and adapting personal, cultural, political and (not least) literary history in the step-by-step creation of a Borgesian 'imaginary identity' – or mind's-eye view – or (to adopt/adapt an idea of Joseph Brodsky's) a *moving picture* of both viewer *and* view . . . Alternatively, the reader is free to conduct his or her side of the dialogue which the author believes any book – unless it is to remain a lifeless object – inevitably is, by approaching the individual poems and translations separately.

W. D. JACKSON was born in Toxteth, Liverpool, in 1947 and grew up on Merseyside. He attended Wirral Grammar School and St Catherine's College, Oxford, where he read English. After abandoning a B.Litt. thesis on Tennyson's prosody, he went to live first in Italy, then in Munich, where he has mainly remained (with his German wife, and son and daughter) since 1973, apart from frequent visits to England – where *Then and Now* takes place. Except for a couple of years at the University of Passau he has for the most part earned his living by freelance work in management training and in-house journalism.

ALSO PUBLISHED IN 2002
THE CYCLOPS: poems, translations of Homer and Theocritus, and an essay by **FRED BEAKE**
96 pp, £6.99, ISBN 1 874320 38 1

For a complete catalogue of Menard Press books, please write to Menard Press at the above address or e-mail: menardpress@hotmail.com

Back issues still available

MPT *(New Series) No.1* – Bonnefoy + others

MPT *No.2* – Franz Baermann Steiner (bi-lingual number featuring a single poet translated and introduced by Michael Hamburger)

MPT *No.4* – Second Jerusalem International Poets Festival

MPT *No.5* – Galician-Portuguese Troubadour Poetry + others

MPT *No.6* – Brazil + others

MPT *No.7* – Welsh poetry

MPT *No.8* – Special French issue (+ some others)

MPT *No.9* – The Philippines + Far East + others

MPT *No.10* – Russian Poetry

MPT *No.11* – Peru, Russia + others

MPT *No.12* – Dutch and Flemish Poets

MPT *No.13* – Greece + others

MPT *No.14* – Palestinian and Israeli Poetry + A Tribute to Ted Hughes

MPT *No.15* – Contemporary Italian Poets + A Pushkin Portfolio

MPT *No.16* – German and French poetry

MPT *No.17* – Mother Tongues: Non English-Language Poetry in England – Revised edition

MPT *No.18* – European Voices